D0761108

*the*
# CANADIAN SUBMARINE
## Service in Review

# *the* CANADIAN SUBMARINE
## Service in Review

J. DAVID PERKINS

**Vanwell Publishing Limited**
St. Catharines, Ontario

Vanwell Publishing acknowledges the financial support of the Government of Canada through the Book Publishing Industry Development Program for our publishing activities.

Design: Linda Moroz-Irvine

Vanwell Publishing Limited
1 Northrup Crescent
P.O. Box 2131
St. Catharines, Ontario  L2R 7S2

Printed in Canada

Canadian Cataloguing in Publication Data

Perkins, J. David, 1937-.
        The Canadian submarine service in review

Includes bibliographical references and index.
ISBN 1-55125-031-4

1. Submarines (Ships) – Canada – History.  2. Submarines (Ships) – Great Britain – History.  3. Submarines (Ships) – United States – History.  4. Canada.  Royal Canadian Navy – Submarine forces.  I. Title.

V859.C3P477 2000        359.9'33'0971        C00-9300344-8

# CONTENTS

This book is dedicated to all Canadians who serve in submarines.
It has been my privilege to serve in their company.

## A SUBMARINERS' PRAYER

*O Father hear our prayer to Thee*
*From your humble servants, beneath the sea.*
*In the depths of oceans as oft we stray,*
*So far from night, so far from day.*
*We would ask your guiding light to glow*
*To make our journey safe below.*
*Please oft times grant us patient minds,*
*Then ere the darkness won't us blind.*
*We seek thy protection from the deep*
*And grant us peace when ere we sleep.*
*Of our homes and loved ones far away,*
*We ask your care for them each day*
*Until we surface once again*
*To drink the air and feel the rain.*
*We ask your guiding hand to show*
*A safe progression, sure and slow.*
*Dear Lord, please hear our prayer to Thee,*
*From your humble servants, beneath the sea.*

*Amen*

# PREFACE

THE SUBMARINE is a weapon of war. There can be no denying this nor should one attempt to glamourize that end. However, there exists an undeniable fascination with the machine itself that has little to do with its sinister purpose, and it is this that makes submarines attractive to so many. As well, Canada's submarines are manned by Canadian sailors who conduct themselves professionally and with great courage on behalf of their nation and navy, and their story deserves to be told. This account is about the machines and those who sail in them and particularly about Canada's involvement with submarines and submariners.

The Canadian submarine community has always had a strong connection with the Royal Navy in operating submarines, and to both Britain and the United States in its types of submarines. Nevertheless, the spiritual roots of Canadian submariners undeniably lie in England. Although those roots sometimes become obscured by nationalistic sentiment, any honest description of Canadian submarines must be told from that perspective. However, it must be emphasized that there is a very dedicated, truly Canadian submarine community and hence, a distinct Canadian way of being a submariner and of running a submarine service.

When I was serving in submarines, and afterwards, I sometimes found myself debating with my shipmates about who did what, where, when, how and to whom? It was often a heated discussion based mostly on uncertain personal recollections and a few assorted facts, and very often, no one really knew the answers. This made me determined to one day provide the details of our collective experience in such a way that all could have access to the information.

In this account, I've tried to set down the facts about our Submarine Service as they are recorded in official documents and reputable histories. It is my hope that these pages will give future debaters enough information to put the discussion into perspective. For the rest of the submarine fraternity, it will serve as a framework on which to hang their own part of this fascinating story. For interested observers I sincerely hope it will provide them with a compass to keep them on course in a sometimes obscure and troubled sea.

My own generation was born in the shadow of the First World War, grew up in the midst of the Second World War and the Korean conflict, and matured in the Cold War era. The conditions, terms and concepts used in this book were a familiar part of our consciousness. However, I appreciate that post-war generations may not be familiar with these things. Indeed, what was common forty or fifty, or even just ten years ago, has largely been replaced by new terms, abbreviations and acronyms. Some of the terminology used in the recent Gulf War was completely alien to me, and I spent a lifetime in the navy, so what must it be like for someone who is interested in events that transpired eighty years ago but has not been exposed to military ways? I hope the glossary at the back of this book will help to explain the old terminology and that the following will provide some insight into what a submarine is.

I had a long and happy association with submarines and submariners and am grateful for the opportunity to provide this record for the enjoyment of all like-minded individuals.

J. David Perkins, CD
ex-Chief Petty Officer and Canadian submariner
Boutilier's Point, Nova Scotia
2000

# NOTES

## MEASUREMENTS

Both imperial and metric measurements are used in the text. Where a particular method was the one in common use for the subject, it has been used as the primary notation. Where explanation is considered necessary, the nearest equivalent value in the other method has been included in parentheses, e. g. "Many British submarines carried a 3-inch (76mm) gun while the 8.8cm (3.46-inch) weapon was mounted on many German U-boats." Where no possibility of confusion would arise, metric notation is used.

For convenience, when discussing displacement the ton and the tonne are usually not distinguished. To all practical intents and purposes, they are the same and very often the source reference did not make the distinction.

Both the twelve-hour and the twenty-four-hour time notation methods have been used as appropriate to the historical period and the subject.

## COMMISSIONING CONVENTION

In the Royal Navy it is customary for submarines to be commissioned as "(His) Her Majesty's Submarine." In writing this is normally abbreviated as HMS/M in order to distinguish between ships and submarines. However, in the Canadian Armed Forces submarines are commissioned as "(His) Her Majesty's Canadian Ship."

# ACKNOWLEDGEMENTS

IN WRITING this book I have had the good fortune to receive the freely given help and encouragement of friends and shipmates, submarine enthusiasts and interested acquaintances on both sides of the Atlantic and all across Canada. I would like to take this opportunity to thank my many supporters and to make note of those whose participation was particularly helpful.

Where would a story like this one be without the accounts of the actual participants? How can I ever thank Lieutenant Commander "Freddy" H. Sherwood, DSC*, RCNVR (Ret'd), Lieutenant Commander Keith Forbes, DSC, RCNVR (Ret'd) and Lieutenant Jack Cross, RCNVR, (Ret'd) for their invaluable personal accounts. I am also indebted to wartime submariners Rupert Harrison who was in HMS *Spiteful*'s crew , "Fog" Elliott, Ernie Potts, Frank Deadman and other crew members of the boats at Digby, NS, as well as the late Paul Roosjen, former crew member of the Dutch submarine *O-15*, for their personal accounts, photographs, memorabilia and words of encouragement.

I would also like to express my thanks to the Director, Commander J. J. Tall, OBE, RN, (Ret'd), and his predecessor, Commander Richard Compton-Hall, MBE, RN, (Ret'd), and the staff at the Royal Navy Submarine Museum, who have always been supportive, helpful and encouraging. In particular, the late Gus Britton, submariner extraordinaire, staunch supporter and veritable font of submarine knowledge. He is sorely missed. I also want to thank my longtime friend and collaborator Brian Head whose knowledge of World War One British submarine lore is unsurpassed. I am particularly grateful for the help given by Commander W. T. J. Fox, RN (Ret'd), the first Commander, Sixth Submarine Squadron, who did so much to ensure the accuracy of my account of that subject.

On the home front, I want to extend my appreciation to the Commander of Maritime Forces Atlantic, Rear Admiral D. E. "Dusty" Miller and his staff members, Captain(N) P. Webster, and Commander R. Davidson for their invaluable co-operation and assistance with the *Victoria* class submarine issues. I also want to thank the Director and staff at the NDHQ Directorate of History and Heritage and its predecessor organization the Directorate of History, who have always done their best to accommodate my requests for information. Thanks too to friend and one-time shipmate Commander Peter T. Haydon, CAF (Ret'd), who was kind enough to allow me access to his research into the history of the Cold War era. I also want to thank Commander Stephen Jenner, RN, (Ret'd), another Commander of the Sixth, for his contribution and support. My gratitude is also extended to the Director, Maritime Command Museum, Marilyn Gurney, who was so helpful with finding many of the photographs with which to illustrate my account.

I especially want to thank my fellow submariners, past and present, who have always been willing contributors and honest critics. Their faith in my efforts is my greatest reward.

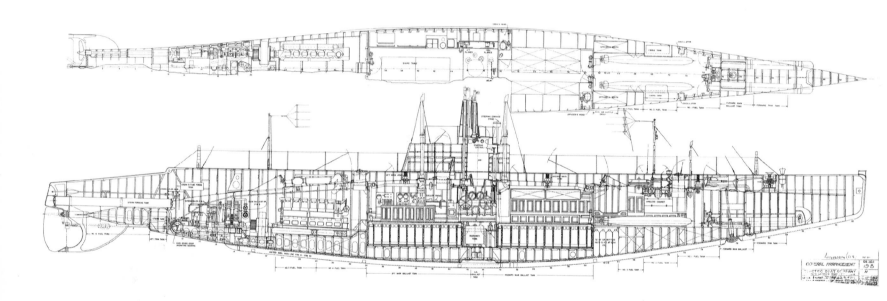

(DND)

# BEGINNINGS

ATTEMPTS have been made since the seventeenth century to construct submersible self-propelled craft for military purposes. The War of 1812 and the American Civil War half a century later witnessed the first actual attempts to use submersible warships but lacking an adequate method of propulsion and suitable weapons these endeavours met with failure. Nevertheless, the concept held promise and as long as the technical problems could be surmounted the inventors kept trying. It was not until the late nineteenth century that the materials, methods and technical expertise needed to build practical submarines became available.

At the same time other inventors were producing novel weapons. These included the pneumatic gun—which worked like an air-operated mortar and lobbed a large bomb onto the deck of the target—and the self-propelled mine, or torpedo. The idea of an invisible delivery system allied to one of these weapons was an attractive military proposition. The French, Russian, Turkish and American navies were all interested in submersibles for coastal defence and fostered development by sponsoring design competitions and providing funding for research and development. These incentives gave the inventors and their backers the encouragement and support they needed for serious investigation.

Producing a watertight craft and making it submerge and surface reliably was difficult enough, but finding a way to propel it for any distance both on and below the surface took a great deal of trial and error. Many forms of propulsion were tried—hand-crank, pedal power, steam engines, gasoline engines and the electric battery–electric motor combination. All achieved varying degrees of success, but none offered significant seagoing potential. Lacking a means of long-range propulsion the submarine seemed destined for no more than a harbour defence role.

## A Successful Design

It was not until the Irish American inventor, John Philip Holland, combined the electric battery, electric motor, an internal combustion engine and a torpedo tube all in one hull that the progenitor of the modern submarine was brought into existence. Not only could Holland's boat propel itself under water using the electric battery to drive the electric propulsion motor, and on the surface using the gasoline engine, but it could even charge its own battery using the gasoline engine to drive the electric motor as a generator.[1] There were other inventors and other concepts to be sure; some of them quite promising, but Holland's design was by far the most successful and most widely adopted of them all.

This submarine was Holland's ninth in a series begun in 1875. The vessel was built at Nixon's Crescent Shipyard, Elizabethport, New Jersey, and was the third attempt in an ongoing effort by the J. P. Holland Torpedo Boat Company to win a submarine-building contract from the USN. Originally designed to carry a pair of pneumatic dynamite guns she was reduced to only one but was also fitted with a torpedo tube for launching standard Whitehead torpedoes, a weapon that seemed to hold more promise than

1 In theory, any electric motor can also be used as a generator. When a motor is turned by an external source, the coils of the armature spinning inside the magnetic fields set up by the stator generate a current which is picked up by the brushes and sent to the battery. Conversely, when electric current from the battery is supplied to the coils of the armature through the brushes and commutator, the magnetic fields created in the armature oppose those of the stator, creating torque and causing the free-moving armature to spin. In the case of submarines, the motor-generator theory has been well proven.

# PART 1
# INTRODUCTION

*A Primer for Twentieth-Century Undersea Warfare*

**HM Submarine No. 1 (RNSM)**

the inaccurate gun. She was named *Holland VI*, made her first dive on St. Patrick's Day, 1898, and was demonstrated to USN officials on 27 March. On 11 April 1900, after many bureaucratic trials and tribulations, *Holland VI* was bought by the USN for $150,000. Four months later, on 25 August 1900, the USN concluded a contract with the Holland Torpedo Boat Company for a further six submarines. On 13 October 1900, *Holland VI* was formally commissioned in the USN[2] as the USS *Holland.*

The potential of the submersible torpedo boat was not lost on the British Admiralty. At the same time as *Holland VI* was running its trials, their Lordships decided that the Royal Navy should acquire some submarine boats, even if only for evaluation purposes. The very idea of owning submarines was politically unpopular in England, but in light of developments taking place in the French, Russian and American navies the Admiralty could not afford to ignore them.

Alternatives were considered and rejected. The only other working submarine was French, and it was in trouble. In any case, dealing with France was entirely out of the question. The Holland boat was the most successful model available and the British authorities recognized an opportunity when they saw one. When the American company was approached, they indicated they would prefer to deal through Messrs Vickers, Sons and Maxim, one of Britain's top shipbuilders. Vickers had close ties with the American company and had already been involved in at least one pioneer submarine-building venture of their own.[3] The Admiralty had no objections to this arrangement and was pleased to be able to save the time and costs involved in research and development.

The American company and Vickers entered into an agreement whereby the British shipbuilder would construct five Holland boats under licence in their shipyard at Barrow-in-Furness which they would sell to the Admiralty. An improved design, known as Type 7, or Holland Design No. 10, the same as had been selected by the USN,[4] was the one actually used. HM Submarine *No. 1* was launched on 2 February 1901, the date that now marks the official birthday of the Royal Navy submarine service.

It is said that Holland conceived the idea of his submarine as a cheap and effective means by which Irish nationalists could attack the Royal Navy. It seems ironic today to realize that the first class of Royal Navy submarines were designed by, and named after, a man who was dedicated to the destruction of that very navy. By the time his company made the deal with Britain, Holland's strong Irish-nationalist tendencies had been mellowed somewhat by time and the experience of living in America.

Although universally called submarines nowadays, these vessels were originally described as "submarine torpedo boats," hence the term *boat* by which they have been known in the submarine fraternity ever since. Neither surface ship nor true submarine,[5] they were very much a seagoing compromise. Every effort to improve performance in one element seemed to detract from their ability to cope with the other. Streamlining for underwater efficiency resulted in poor sea-keeping performance on the surface; large upper deck surfaces and gun mountings—desirable on the surface—made them slow to submerge and detracted from underwater speed and control. The struggle between surface and dived performance persisted until the widespread adoption of the snorkel during the late 1940s, which gave the underwater domain a definite edge.

## DEVELOPMENT

While the Holland Design No. 10 submarine was the first in the RN, subsequent development was made independently of the American vessel. The Holland designs were heavily encumbered by patents, which prevented the use of many essential features except under licence and the payment of fees to the Holland Torpedo Boat Company and its successor, the Electric Boat Company. Even as the first Holland boats were under construction, Vickers engineers and draughtsmen were set to work on their own design. The Vickers *A* class submarine, although based on the Holland boat concepts, was entirely new, lending credence to the claim that the *A* class, not the Holland boat, was the true precursor of British submarine development.

2 The USN celebrates the birthday of their Submarine Service on 1 April (1900).
3 Vickers has built over 320 submarines for 16 navies since launching *Nordenfelt* 1 in 1886.
4 Five boats of this design were also delivered to the Japanese navy and one to the Netherlands.
5 A true submarine is a vessel that can remain totally submerged for the duration of its mission.

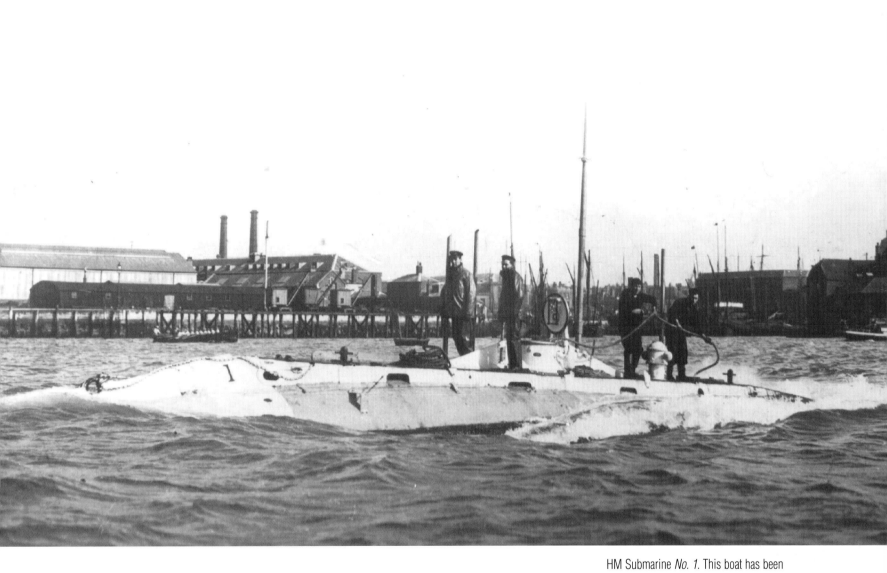

HM Submarine *No. 1*. This boat has been fitted with an early fixed periscope. (Royal Navy Submarine Museum [RNSM])

The USN, on the other hand, used a succession of J. P. Holland and Electric Boat Company patented designs to build up its submarine forces. The products of J. P. Holland's biggest competitor, Simon Lake, were also tried but on a lesser scale. When the USN undertook designing its own submarines, they incorporated the best of both the Electric Boat and the Lake features, while the former company became the principal submarine builder for the USN.

## IDENTIFICATION

When someone looks at a submarine one of the first things they often ask is "Which one is it?" Identifying the vessel is the first step in finding out about it. Submarines, like surface ships, are organized into groups, or classes, the members of which are all built to the same basic design. In the Admiralty scheme, these classes are identified by a letter of the alphabet. The RN has gone through the alphabet twice in the past century and has already started on the third time around. The third series of A class submarines is currently under construction. Traditionally I, Q, Y and Z are not used while X and W are reserved for experimental boats. The letter U was avoided in the first instance, because of the U-boats in World War One, but was used subsequently.

For accounting and identification purposes, every shipbuilder assigns a unique job number to each hull under construction in the yard, but these numbers are usually forgotten almost as soon as the vessel leaves the shipbuilder's hands. An Admiralty committee determines the names and numbers by which naval vessels are known from that point onwards. The very first British submarines were simply given numbers beginning with the numeral one, as in Holland class *No. 1*.

The second class of British submarines, the first to be wholly designed and built in Britain, started the alphanumeric sequence becoming the original *A* class. Numbers, beginning at one for each class and preceded by the class letter, were assigned according to the order in which the boats were laid down. To distinguish individual boats, these numbers were painted on the outside of the hull, usually on the bows or both sides of the conning tower. These are the pennant numbers. Different, and sometimes confusing, numbering schemes were tried prior to the First World War, but by 1914 all boats were known by their alphanumeric identity.

In 1926 the Admiralty decided to give submarines names, following the pattern set for destroyers. In this system, the vessel's name began with the class letter, such as *Odin* and *Porpoise,* which were *O* and *P* class boats respectively. During this period, named submarines displayed two large identification letters on the sides of the conning tower. These letters were derived from their names, e.g. PD for *Pandora* and PX for *Phoenix* etc.

During the Second World War, all submarines under British command were allocated alphanumeric pennant numbers which were painted on the sides of the conning tower. These were usually prefixed by the letters N or P while the minelayers bore the letter M. Existing boats that already had pennant numbers kept their original numbers, but the class letter was replaced with the N or P. The pennant numbers assigned to new construction had no connection to the peacetime system, although the new numbers were still allocated according to class. The *U* and *V* classes were numbered from P31; the *S* class from P211 and the *T* class from P311 while lend-lease boats on loan from the USN received numbers from P511. Submarines under construction for foreign countries and taken over by Britain were given numbers from P611. In late 1942, the prime minister restored the 1926 policy of providing names for all submarines. For the rest of the war names were discreetly displayed on the conning towers while the pennant numbers were painted in large characters of a contrasting colour.

A few years after the war, the pennant numbers, although still allocated, were suppressed and only names were displayed. In the mid 1950s, a NATO numbering scheme was adopted and all British boats were allocated pennant numbers preceded by the letter S. In 1961, the submarine fleet was renumbered to accommodate the numbering of post-war construction from S 01 upwards. During the early 1970s, a new policy of having no visible identity at all was adopted. The *S* numbers though still allocated, are not "worn." When in harbour, portable nameboards, the ship's badge and bell are displayed on the fin.

Since 1926, submarine classes have been identified by the name of the lead ship in the class; e.g., the last RN conventional class was the *U* class, which was known publicly as the *Upholder* class after the first boat. However, it was still popular to identify submarines by the class letter, particularly the wartime classes. Describing famous submarines as belonging to the *Swordfish, Tarpon* or *Unity* classes would elicit puzzled frowns from most, but a mention of *S, T* and *U* class boats will bring instant recognition. Oddly, the *A* class of 1945 was never referred to by a boat's name. Although *Amphion* was the lead ship, they were universally referred to as A-boats. The post-war *Porpoise* and *Oberon* classes were known as well by name as by class letter.

In the USN, submarine hulls are numbered in a single continuous series, designated SS. This system appears to have been imposed retroactively during the 1920s. The numbering begins with USS *Holland,* which in the historical records became *SS1.*

Submarines *SS2* through *SS8* were the first submarines to be built for the USN. These were all given names and called the *Adder* class after the lead ship, *SS3.* In 1911 they were renamed as the *A* class taking the numbers *A1* through *A8* while the USS *Holland* became *A1.* The USN, like the RN, chose to identify succeeding classes by letters of the alphabet. From *SS9* through *SS162,* individual USN submarines were not named but were identified by their alphanumeric class designator, e.g. *SS23* was F class submarine number 3, or simply *F3,* much like the British boats.

The USN abandoned the alphanumeric system after the *V* class of 1924. Beginning in 1935 with *SS172, Porpoise,* and her nine sisters, classes were named after the lead ship. From then until the late 1950s all USN boats received the names of fish.

At various times between the wars either the SS hull number or the alphanumeric class identification was displayed on the tower or the bows or on both. At other times, the hull number was displayed preceded by a single letter S, but usually just the number appeared. Some specialized types were numbered in separate ST (training), SC (cruiser), SF (fleet) and SM (minelaying) series. Some of these specialist types were later renumbered in the standard SS series. During the Second World War, it was USN practice to not display any external identity on operational boats and even names were removed.

Following the Second World War, new designation variations were adopted, including SSK (hunter-killer), AGSS (guided missile carriers), SSN (nuclear-powered submarine), SSBN (nuclear-powered ballistic missile submarine), etc., but only the hull numbers were displayed. During the Cold War, all external identity was again suppressed. Currently, operational USN submarines are unmarked. In harbour, the usual decorated gangway screen, portable nameboards and the ship's badge are displayed.

With the advent in 1958 of SSBN598, USS *George Washington,* names of famous American presidents and personalities were introduced and since then, the names of American states and those of major cities have been extensively used as well.

Throughout the history of submarine construction for the German navy, the authorities adopted a practical approach and issued blocks of numbers with the different contracts. These numbers were assigned to the individual submarines as they were laid down. They were used both for accounting and identification and remained with each boat until it was destroyed or disposed of. Consequently, the numbers are not necessarily sequential by class, or group, either numerically or by date. When determining the antecedents of a particular German submarine the researcher must consult the contract records.

The U-boat pennant numbers were always prefixed with the letter U although there was some variation. During the First World War a second letter was used to denote a submarine of a type other than the standard U-boat. An A was added to denote the large cruiser-type UA-boat armed with torpedoes and heavy guns. The B distinguished the small torpedo-armed coastal UB-boats while the C was used for the notorious UC-boat coastal minelayers. The large, long-range U-boats fitted with torpedo tubes, minelaying gear and heavy guns, were known as the UE-type. Other than a small class of supply submarines, these specialized types were not perpetuated in the Second World War and all Third Reich German submarine pennant numbers were prefixed with the letter U only.

Submarines belonging to unified Germany and the former Federal German Republic, are built using the traditional U-boat number allocation, but do not display these numbers. Although identified by the U-number, they display standard NATO-style numbers prefixed by the letter S in a series that began in 1965 with submarine *U1* which bears the pennant number S180. This submarine is the third *U1* to be commissioned in the German navy.

Occasionally, submarines of different nations bearing the same class identity served together. The first instance of this was during the First World War when British and Italian *H* class boats were working together in the Mediterranean. In these instances, the foreign boats had their country initial added to their usual numbers; e.g. the Italian *H3* became *IH3*. The same thing happened when British and American *L* class boats operated together from Bantry Bay in Ireland. The American boats became *AL* class submarines. During the Second World War the Germans used a similar system for Axis and captured submarines. In their system, Italian boats under German command became UIT, which can be loosely translated as meaning U-boat Italian, and captured Dutch boats were UD, U-boat Dutch.

Until recently, Canada loosely followed the naming convention of the country of origin. The so-called *CC* class boats of the First World War and the renamed *CH* class acquired in 1919, were typical American-built Holland-type submarines. They generally followed the established alphanumeric pattern except for the addition of the letter C for Canadian. The two ex-USN fleet boats of the 1960s adhered to the American convention for the class when they were given fish names (*Grilse*, a young salmon, and *Rainbow*, for the rainbow trout) and RCN pennant numbers. The *O* class were named in the traditional way using the names of Canadian First Nations beginning with the class letter while the RCN numbering sequence established with the submarine *Grilse* was continued. However, by the time the Vickers Type 2400 submarines[6] were acquired in 1998 a new ship naming policy had been established whereby all warships are named after Canadian communities. Consequently, these boats have been named after secondary Canadian ports, which, the government maintains, will bring them into closer contact with the Canadian public. The numbering of these boats follows the established pattern for Canadian submarines except that they are being numbered in a new 800 series; i.e. HMCS *Victoria* is S876, carrying on from *Rainbow*, which was S75.

---

6   Four submarines originally built for the RN as the *Upholder* class which are coming into service with the Canadian navy as the *Victoria* class.

WHEN submariners refer to the boat they are serving in as "a stinking, black, upholstered sewer pipe," their colourful, if somewhat perverse, description is entirely apt. The hull of a submarine certainly resembles a piece of steel tubing. Certain areas of the interior are provided with upholstery, and some of the tanks do indeed contain all kinds of waste matter, which sometimes gives off a distinctly unpleasant odour. Most of the time there is a great deal of moisture present and for the past thirty years, the exterior has been painted black. How else would they describe it?

### THE HULL

Essentially, a submarine consists of a steel cylinder strengthened by ribs, or frames, that is capped at both ends by strong bulkheads to make it watertight and pressure resistant. This is the pressure hull and everything essential to the operation of the boat will be found inside it except for the propeller shafts, propellers, control surfaces, masts and periscopes.

As was usual in the shipbuilding industry of the day, the early submarines were riveted together. Some German submarine builders used welding in a limited way from a very early date, but this was exceptional. Welding produces a much stronger structure, but until the techniques were perfected and its use became widespread, it was not an economical proposition and riveting remained the method of choice. Welding was introduced into British shipbuilding very gradually beginning in the late 1920s, but was not employed for pressure hull construction until the Second World War. Since then, all submarines have been of welded construction.

The first successful hulls came in a variety of shapes, some cylindrical, others spindle-shaped. In these boats the hull was generally made up of concentric rings aligned on a common centre line. Most of these shapes were inherently unstable. As the vessels became larger and underwater stability better understood, submarine designers adopted a long, straight cylindrical shape with a slight taper forward to provide for fine lines at the bows. The stern varied in shape, but usually featured a nearly straight run along the top and a sharp sweep upwards from the keel to provide a space for the propellers, rudder and after control surfaces under an overhanging stern. The internal diameter was sufficient to allow a single deck where needed. This configuration lent itself reasonably well to both surfaced and submerged operations. Although it was realized at an early date that the teardrop was the most efficient underwater shape, it was not well suited to surface operation and, with a few notable exceptions, remained experimental for almost five decades.

As modern submarines remain submerged most of the time, the long, lean hull that catered to surface operation has evolved into a shorter, broader shape ideally suited to submerged operations. The pressure hulls of most of today's submarines are parallel-sided cylinders capped at both ends by hemispherical dome bulkheads. The diameter of the hull is sufficient to permit several internal decks and the hull is extended by using free-flooding external structures to produce what can best be described as an oversized torpedo shape.

It was never intended that the early submarines should dive to any great depth. Pressure hull strength was not a matter of particular concern other than going deep enough for invisibility when attacking and passing safely beneath surface vessels. The typical J. P. Holland designs were theoretically built to reach 100 feet (30.4 m) in safety, although the

HMS Holland *No. 1*, ca 1905. The tall checkered pole is the original pivoting periscope.

construction methods of the day tended to produce a structure much stronger than planned.

As hulls became longer, internal bulkheads were introduced, both to add strength and to facilitate damage control. As hull size increased, so it became necessary to go deeper for safety. By 1912, 200 feet (60.8 m) was the calculated normal maximum diving depth for American designs. In Britain, a 100-foot operating depth and a 200-foot maximum depth was considered adequate until the experiences of the First World War dictated otherwise. In order to escape the effects of anti-submarine weapons, and to dive below defensive nets and minefields, submarine captains were being forced to take their boats deeper and deeper. During the war, British submariners asked for a 200-foot minimum operating depth. Actual testing of hulls and fittings previously rated for 100 feet demonstrated that they were strong enough for twice that depth, which was something the submariners had already found out for themselves. By the end of the First World War, submarines were being built for a normal operating depth of between 200 and 250 feet (76.2 m).

By the beginning of the Second World War most British classes were built for a depth of 300 feet (91.4 m) and were provided with a 100-foot safety margin. At that time British designers were not so much building hulls that would go deeper, but rather hulls that would better resist the effects of depth charges. This was achieved mostly through the use of tougher steel and improved building methods. Undoubtedly, submariners appreciated the ability to go deeper as much as the stoutness of the hull and fittings. During the Second World War, continued improvements in the quality of steel and the widespread adoption of welding added considerably to hull strength and the last British wartime class boasted a normal diving depth of 500 feet (457.2 m).

With a somewhat different range of wartime experiences behind them, German designers set their sights on an operating depth of 150 m (472 feet) and this became the standard for the majority of U-boats used in the Second World War. Most of the American boats built during the Second World War had a modest operating depth of 350 feet (106.68 m).

Advances in the oceanographic sciences, particularly during the Second World War and on into the Cold War era, brought about a new understanding of the nature of the ocean depths and the behaviour of sound under water. Submariners had already discovered how to use such naturally occurring features as sea water density layers and temperature variations to advantage. However, they lacked the means to accurately predict or evaluate these occurrences. The oceanographers and acoustics scientists studied these phenomena and applied their results to all aspects of anti-submarine warfare. The behaviour of sound in water and the effect that depth and water temperature have on sound qualities have since become critically important subjects for both the submarine and the submarine hunter.

One outcome of these investigations was an appreciation of the phenomenon known as cavitation. Simply put, cavitation is caused when an object moving through the water causes pressure to build up around it creating tiny pockets of vacuum. Nature abhors a vacuum, and when these tiny spaces implode a shock wave, or noise, is created. Cavitation is typically caused by propellers but can also be generated by irregular angular shapes passing through the water at speed. It was found that the deeper the cavitation-causing object is, the less it cavitates. The deeper, the quieter.

After the Second World War, designers and steel makers collaborated to take the boats as deep as possible in order to meet the demands for stealth and speed that characterized submarine operations during the Cold War. Any self-respecting conventional submarine from the 1980s onwards has an operating limit in excess of 245 m (800 feet). Nuclear-powered submarines are capable of depths in excess of 300 m (1,000 feet). Some submarines with hulls built of special, expensive alloys, can attain extreme depths.

The measurement of a submarine's depth was a peculiar thing. Today, depth is universally measured at the keel; i.e. the depth gauge shows the depth of the bottom of the keel relative to the surface. This is known as keel depth. In the Holland boats, and in British submarines up until the mid 1950s, depth was measured at the waterline and the gauges showed zero feet when on the surface. It therefore became a watchkeeping officer's first concern to learn how much hull there was below datum so he could avoid running the boat aground on the surface or unexpectedly hitting the bottom when dived. The other critical measurement was the depth at which a fully extended periscope would break the surface. This was periscope depth, which is what the captain would order when he wanted to have a look at what was going on around the boat "up top."

## INSIDE THE PRESSURE HULL

For the uninitiated, identifying a particular location inside a submarine can be challenging. There are numerous compartments and nowadays several decks and there are very few, if any, obvious signposts. Nevertheless, every nook and cranny must be identified in detail. In any ship there are several common elements that are used as a means for determining a specific location. The most basic reference points are the bow (front) and stern (rear), the two sides—port (left) and starboard (right)—and the decks (floors) and deckheads (ceilings). As well, there are the transverse watertight bulkheads, which are walls that divide the hull into watertight sections, and, most importantly, the frames.

Submarines, like surface warships, are divided into compartments and spaces. A compartment is a large enclosed area of the vessel that can be completely isolated. This includes control of doorways, ventilation ducting, piping, electrical power and any other systems that enter that area, all of which can be isolated from either inside or outside the compartment. Major compartments are bounded by watertight bulkheads and except in very large ships, these usually extend from the keel to the underside of the upper deck and may include several deck levels. Each deck level within that major compartment may also be considered as a compartment. This subdivision allows for degrees of response to damage. When there is a fire or penetration damage, the most seriously affected compartment, or compartments, can be completely shut down to isolate the damage and prevent the spread of fire and smoke or flooding. Services passing through the affected area can be re-routed using portable equipment or alternative systems can be opened up to supply areas isolated by the damage.

Traditionally some compartments are often referred to as rooms, engine room, control room and torpedo room being names typically applied to submarine compartments. Conversely, the (torpedo) tube space would be, by definition, a compartment, while a relatively small enclosure like the gyro room is just that, a partitioned-off space having a door. The terminology evolved with the ships and common terms have been carried over by usage even when overtaken by the architecture.

Spaces are enclosures created by subdividing the area within the compartments. This is done for a variety of reasons—to provide privacy for living areas, to segregate noisy machinery or to provide an enclosure in which to place electronic equipment that has special ventilation requirements. The door to a space is not usually watertight, while power cables, ventilation ducting and piping often pass through without any means of isolating them.

The major structural difference between a surface warship and a submarine is the pressure hull. Because the submarine submerges, the pressure hull encompasses the whole of the exterior shell and it is strong enough to withstand the pressure of the sea down to a predetermined depth. The watertight bulkheads in a submarine span the entire circumference of the pressure hull. These are designed to be watertight in the sense of preventing water from passing from one compartment to another, and they are also proof against sea pressure. Transverse watertight bulkheads in a submarine are usually built to withstand the same pressure as the pressure hull. Consequently, the main compartments of the submarine are both watertight and pressure proof.

In modern submarines, the decks are numbered. Beginning with the uppermost interior deck, which is 1 Deck, the decks below are numbered using whole numbers, e.g. 2 Deck is below 1 Deck and 3 Deck below 2 Deck. The upper deck, or casing, is not usually referred to by a number. In Canadian submarines, the frames are numbered continuously from forward to aft beginning at the bow and ending at the last frame in the stern. In most submarines, the frames in the extremities are beyond the pressure hull boundaries. Inside the pressure hull, the numbers are painted on the actual frames as an aid to orientation. The transverse watertight bulkheads are identified by their frame locations.

Typically, location within the submarine would be described by main compartment, deck level, space, frame number and the location relative to other important spaces and the width of the boat. For instance, No. 2 battery switchboard could be described as being, "...in the amidships compartment, on 2 Deck, port side, mid-way along the passageway outside the gyro room

HMS *B8*. The lookouts and OOW head below preparatory to diving. Note the prominent compass binnacle on the after casing and the very flimsy bridge platform. (RNSM)

between frames 44 and 47." Ordinarily, most crew members would not use frame numbers unless it was necessary to be very specific or they were referring to a bulkhead.

The interior of the pressure hull is divided into a maze of self-contained spaces each designed to meet a particular need. Most of these features are a matter of common sense. The battery cells, being large and very heavy, are placed low down in the centre of the hull and are arranged to promote stability. The cells must be kept dry and, as they emit toxic and explosive gases they are housed in fully enclosed, well-ventilated spaces. As batteries also require regular maintenance, there must be a means of access. Originally, the deck above the battery spaces was made of heavy planks that could be tightly wedged in place. As it proved difficult to keep the gases in and sea water out, the battery tanks were soon being plated over and provided with strategically located air-and watertight hatches large enough to admit a cell, or a man.

Heavy machinery items like main motors and engines are placed low down in the after part of the hull both to provide stability and to minimize the length of the shafting run. Tanks for storing heavy bulk liquids such as fuel and lubricating oil, and those holding sea water used for controlling the mass, or weight, of the boat are also located low down in the hull. With so many tanks in the bottom of the hull it was expedient to provide a continuous flat, or deck, running the width of the pressure hull at about its widest point. The space beneath this deck was partitioned for the tanks, storerooms and machinery spaces, and that above was divided up into weapons stowage, living, control and engineering spaces.

Many of the early submarines possessed little longitudinal stability, so the best place for the operator was in the centre. As the hulls grew larger, control of the boat remained centralized so that those in command could give their orders easily and be in close contact with the men actually controlling the submarine. Consequently, all important control devices were brought into close proximity with the command position. In early British boats, even the propulsion switchboards were sited in the central command position. As remote-control devices and reliable communications were developed, the need to locate the actual machinery in the control room diminished, but the centralization of control remains essential even today.

## EXTERNAL FEATURES

It was appreciated at an early date that large external structures created resistance to the free movement of the boat through the water, so these were kept to a minimum. As these structures are open to the sea and are not subjected to sea pressure, they need not be as strong as the pressure hull. They are either solid, like the shafting and propellers, or of relatively light construction. Though not structurally necessary, a keel was added to give the boat something to sit on in dock or on the seabed, and as a place in which to stow the solid ballast needed to stabilize the hull. A small casing was provided along the top of the hull to give a working area for seamanlike activities. This raised deck provides a place for mounting bollards and fairleads while berthing lines and other deck tackle are stowed inside the casing. Supports for the rudder, hydroplanes and propeller shafting were also fixed to the pressure hull and these fittings became more elaborate as submarines grew larger. Usually these appendages were arranged much as they are on a ship. Lately, however, the configuration of the stern has become more streamlined and has evolved into an arrangement that resembles the afterbody of a torpedo, very similar to J. P. Holland's original configuration.

In modern submarines, where large, free-flooding external structures are part of the design, these are carefully blended in with the pressure hull to provide hydrodynamic streamlining. In the Canadian *Victoria* class (Vickers Shipbuilding and Engineering Limited's Type 2400 design) submarines of 1989, a little over a quarter of the external length of the submarine is made up of free-flooding structures, including the entire bow and stern. These contain important tanks and provide a place in which to house submersible equipment such as sonar arrays, compressed air bottles, anchors and cables, the long barrels of the torpedo tubes as well as the shafting, rudder and hydroplanes and their supports.

There were no periscopes in the very early submarines. To provide for navigating, or conning, the boat while dived, an extended hatch coaming with thick glass windows, or ports, spaced around the upper perimeter was fitted amidships. This was the conning tower, and the conning officer could look out the ports while standing on the main deck. The boat was run either trimmed down in what was termed the awash condition, with just enough buoyancy to keep the viewing ports above water, or was forced up by the propeller and control surfaces so the captain could have a look around. After an accidental collision between a dived submarine and a surface ship in which the boat sank because of a damaged tower hatch, the tower was extended so that the conning officer could stand upright inside it and an additional hatch was provided at the bottom. The tower hatches became known as the upper and lower conning tower lids.[7] A helm, magnetic compass or gyrocompass repeater, and a means of transmitting propulsion orders to the main-motor switchboard were provided inside the extended tower from a very early date

Periscopes made an appearance in time to be installed in HM Submarine *No.1* when built. The invention of a British naval engineer and a German optics manufacturer, the first models were pivoted at the base and lay flat on the hull when lowered. Before diving, they had to be manually rigged in the upright position and supported with wire stays. One peculiarity of these was that the optics displayed the object being viewed as being upright when looking ahead, pointing downwards and upwards on opposite beams and upside down when looking astern. However, within a short time, a constant horizontal image was achieved.

A retractable periscope was available for installation in the British *A* class. To allow the submarine to remain at a safe depth, these periscopes had to be quite long relative to their diameter. To support the somewhat delicate tubes, they were provided with rigid external tubular supports called "standards" or "shears." When the periscope was retracted, the exterior portion of the tube and its vulnerable lens was completely withdrawn into the standard. In many American and German submarines, two of these were often combined into a common housing for ease of construction and strength. Typically, a short periscope was fitted in the roof of the conning tower for use when running near the surface in the shut down, or awash, condition. Another much longer type was installed for use when dived. This was operated from the central command position, or control room, inside the boat proper. For the time being, the conning tower viewing ports were retained as early periscope optics left a lot to be desired.

In British practice, the first periscope standard used the front of the newly extended conning tower for support. When a second periscope was added, its standard was fitted to the back of the tower. This arrangement became a feature of British boats for a while, although the standards were soon moved away from the tower.

In German submarines and in later American boats, the conning tower evolved into a very elaborate attack and command centre. Prior to this development, the tower had been used to supply air to the engines when on the surface. When the tower was used as a command centre, this practice became unacceptable. German and American builders solved the air-supply problem by providing an induction system with intakes high in the bridge structure to bring air into the engine room without turning the tower and control room into a wind tunnel. The British, preferring to keep the attack centre activities in the control room, continued to use the tower as the main air intake as well as a means of access to the bridge. In some later classes, designed for use in the Far East, they built a captain's cabin and other amenities into the tower structure, and in these boats a bridge induction system was included.

Steaming on the surface in rough weather was a problem in the early submarines because as long as the engines were running, the low conning towers shipped a great deal of water through the open hatches. To mitigate this, many classes were provided with an extended ventilator that could be rigged as a temporary air intake so that the upper lid could be shut. Some water still came down the ventilator, but it was nothing like the amount that poured down the tower.

In the British Holland class boats, a helm was installed on top of the hull for navigating on the surface. It was connected to the steering gear inside the boat by rod gearing. Steering on the surface was done by eye. As the gyrocompass was still a convenience of the future, the early submarines relied on a magnetic compass. This was mounted inside a bronze, water-

---

7  HMS *A1* was lost after being rammed by the SS *Berwick Castle* while exercising in the Solent, 18 March 1904. The efficacy of the new hatch was tested two years later when *A9* was rammed by the SS *Coath* off Plymouth. The boat survived with only a flooded tower.

HMS *B8* in the awash condition, showing the periscope, the top of the conning tower and the viewing ports. (RNSM)

The Electric Boat Company combined binnacle and helm, as used in the *H* class. The "spider ring" is the electric helm while the forward ring is the magnetic compass face. Port and starboard main motor order switches are between the two. The whole apparatus is sealed with a pressure tight lid. (Author's collection)

tight binnacle bolted on top of the hull to keep it as far away from strong magnetic influences—such as batteries and electric motors—as possible. A reflector tube and mirrors were used to reflect the compass image to the helmsman's position inside the pressure hull.

In succeeding classes with improved seagoing ability, a navigation platform, or bridge, was built around the strong point formed by the tower and the periscope standards. The surface helm and magnetic compass were moved from the hull to the bridge. The watertight compass housing was modified so that the face of the compass could be viewed by the helmsman on the bridge as well as in the tower and at the central command steering position. When the gyrocompass was introduced in submarines around 1912, the magnetic compass was retained, usually in the form of a portable small craft compass, as a backup for the gyro. In the RN, this was affectionately referred to as "Faithful Freddy."

Initially, when on the surface, orders were simply shouted down the open tower, but as the boats became larger, this proved unreliable. A metal tube, or voice-pipe, was soon provided for communicating with the interior of the boat. A shut-off cock was fitted at the top and bottom of the voicepipe to maintain watertight integrity. To protect bridge watchkeeping personnel from the wind and spray a portable canvas screen was erected around the bridge platform. During World War One this gradually evolved into a substantial steel-framed, sheet-metal-clad, free-flooding enclosure. The whole assembly was simply referred to as the conning

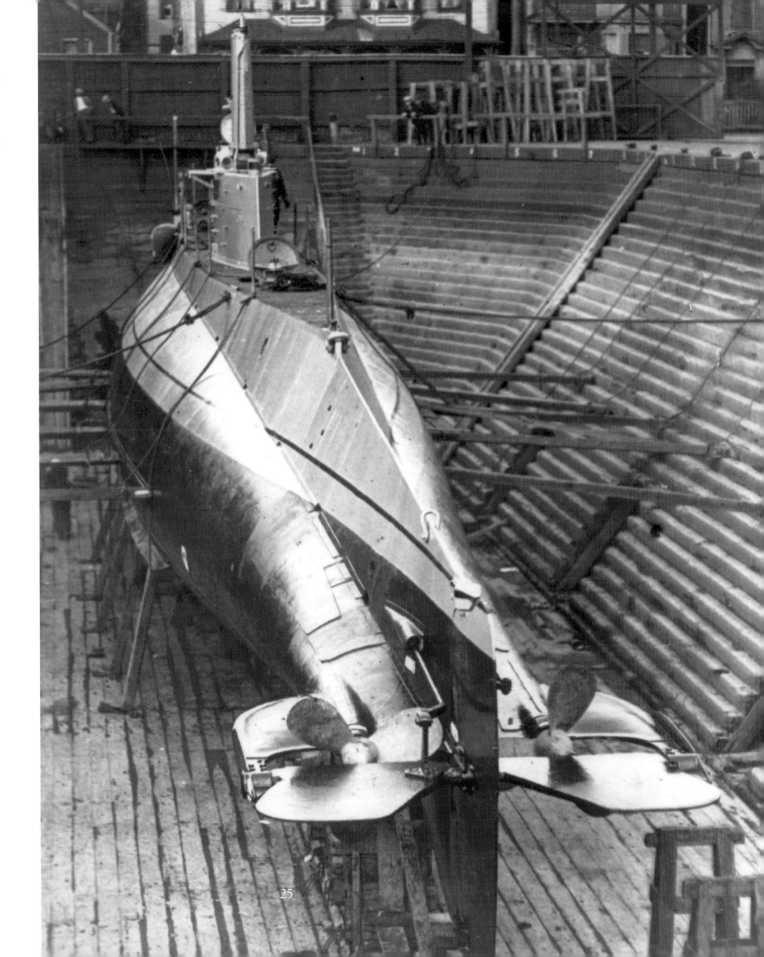

An excellent stern view of an *H* class submarine, possibly *H13*, *H16-20*, prior to transfer to Chile, at the Boston Navy Yard, summer 1917. (Author's collection)

tower. At first the viewing ports in the conning tower itself were kept clear, but as periscope optics improved and the bridges were built higher out of the water these became redundant. Viewing ports disappeared altogether after the First World War.

As the need to operate on the surface declined and hydrodynamic and acoustic streamlining became more important, the bulky bridge structure was removed and the periscopes and other mast standards were surrounded by a high, narrow, streamlined fin or sail. What had been the conning tower has become simply an extended access hatch, although it is still called the tower. In today's submarines, a small surface navigation bridge complete with instruments and electronic communications reached by a ladder from inside the fin structure, is provided in the top forward corner of the fin.

## CONTROL

The early designers had little appreciation for the dynamics of a submerged vessel. Consequently, they tended to install tanks that were often larger than necessary. Much of the time these were only partly full. When the submarine took on an angle, the liquid inside these tanks surged towards the low end, effectively shifting the centre of gravity and making the vessel very unstable. This surging of liquids is known as free surface effect and the spindle-shaped hulls were particularly susceptible.

As well, many of the early submarines used boilers for propulsion and the free surface effect of large quantities of water sloshing about inside these was considerable. The constant change in trim resulting from these factors often caused the boats to proceed through the water in porpoise fashion, almost out of control. A steep angle could overwhelm the propeller and control surfaces forcing the boat into an uncontrolled dive. To avoid this effect, most operators concentrated on getting the boats up and down on an even keel. Stubby wing-like bow and stern hydroplanes and auxiliary vertical thrusters were installed to provide more stability.

As his designs matured, J. P. Holland learned to avoid the effects of free surface water by using relatively small tanks. He was also careful to plan the contents of the tanks so that they were either empty or full when the vessel was in diving trim. Even if some of these small tanks were only partly full, the effect on longitudinal stability was negligible. Because of this, Holland was able to accept a moderate bow-up or -down angle without upsetting stability. This allowed him to utilize propeller thrust and angle to control ascent and descent while retaining control of the boat.

In Holland's design, control of buoyancy while dived was concentrated on one small tank. In *Holland VI* this was the forward trim tank. In the Design 10 submarines it was a special tank sited low down in the boat amidships at the submerged centre of gravity. The capacity of the tank provided the difference between positive and negative buoyancy when in a normal dived trim. By adjusting the quantity of water in this single tank, the boat could be brought to the awash condition or fully submerged with relative ease and on an even keel. This tank was a feature of many early submarines and was variously referred as the adjusting tank, buoyancy tank or statical diving tank.

The adjusting tank was connected to sea by a special valve and fitted with a compressed air blow to empty the tank overboard and provide buoyancy in an emergency. It was also connected to the main pumping and flooding system so that the contents could be adjusted to accommodate a less dramatic need for a temporary change in mass.

As the hulls became longer, they became unwieldy and another pair of hydroplanes, or diving rudders, was fitted forward. With two sets of planes, those aft are used to control the angle of the boat from the horizontal, while those forward are used to effect depth-changing.[8] As the submarine tends to pivot longitudinally on the stern planes, the resulting angle is always referenced to the bow, i.e. bow up or bow down. The men that operated the hydroplanes were often known as the bow and the stern ruddermen while in the RN they became the forward and after planesmen.

Originally the rudder, fore planes and after planes were all controlled using individual handwheels connected by gearing

8 Today submariners apply dive and rise to the hydroplanes. In the early classes with only after planes, or "diving rudders," they applied up rudder and down rudder.

British H-boats under construction at Vickers Canada, Montreal 1915. (Author's collection)

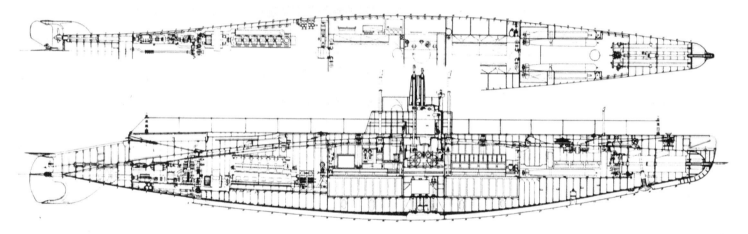

Cutaway views of the Electric Boat Co. Design 30, *H* class, *H1-H3*, 14 March 1911. (Author's collection)

to chain drives and control rodding that transmitted the movement of the handwheels to the actuating mechanism in the bow and stern. Gear-driven mechanical indicators provided the operators with an indication of the angle they were applying to the rudder or hydroplanes. To give a visual indication of the attitude of the boat, a spirit level, later replaced by a more sophisticated clinometer, was fitted fore-and-aft at the central command position along with a depth gauge. As the boats became longer, electric motors were used to power the extended runs of control rodding. When hydraulics were introduced, the rodding, gearing and electric motors were replaced by hydraulic piping that supplied the pistons that were directly

linked to the hydroplane and rudder operating mechanisms. The conventional hydroplane and helm controls were adapted to operate valves that applied hydraulic pressure to the actuating pistons. Around the same time, electrical sensors were fitted to the control surface linkages that operated electrical angle-indicators at the operating positions. These displayed the actual angle achieved by the mechanism rather than the angle applied to the handwheel, which was what was displayed with the old mechanical method.

During the 1950s, following a number of unsuccessful experiments with exotic, manually operated hydraulic valves, these controls were miniaturized, electrified and combined in a

A stern view of HMS *Thunderbolt* docked down alongside the depot ship HMS *Forth* at Saint John New Brunswick, June 1941. (DND)

single location to provide simultaneous, one-man control of depth and course keeping. Electronic inputs from the gyro, a hydrostatic pressure sensor for depth, and positional feedback signals from the control surface linkages, provided these one-man control, or OMC, units with a level of precision previously unattainable. The early OMC units also contained an electro-mechanical auto-pilot that could maintain a preset depth and course automatically.

This technology is now fully computerized and has advanced to the point where steering and depth keeping are primarily automatic requiring operator input only for course and depth changes. An OMC operator, or helmsman, is still required to be on standby to take control for such situations as entering and leaving harbour, emergency stations, action stations, when in a severe following sea, when running deep at speed or when the OMC malfunctions.

High speed has a significant impact on depth keeping as water moving over flat areas of the hull causes a planing effect. This is particularly evident when a submarine is making a hard turn, as the boat tends to heel in the direction of the turn. This heel converts some of the rudder effect into hydroplaning and the hydroplaning effect of the after planes into rudder effect. Large, flat deck surfaces, such as those found on many designs of the 1939-1945 era, and the flat sails, or fins, of modern boats can also impart a considerable hydroplaning effect. The faster the boat is moving, the more marked this becomes and it takes an experienced planesman to anticipate and offset it.

The engineers have come to the aid of the hard-pressed helmsman and the overheated electronic circuits in the OMC. Normally the port and starboard control surfaces of each set of planes are joined together by a solid link so that only one actuator is needed and the planes move in unison. With computerized depth keeping, it is now possible for the hydroplane surfaces to be independent of one another, allowing a much finer degree of control and improved stabilization. This can be applied to the conventional layout of control surfaces, and it has also given rise to some innovative arrangements. The X form of the stern of some modern classes of boat is a novel and effective adaptation of this principle. In this configuration, there are no defined rudders or hydroplanes, but the four control surfaces work together to produce a turning effect while minimizing the amount of heel experienced in sharp turns, or to effect a smooth transition to a different depth, or even to do both simultaneously.

The fact that hydroplanes protrude and, depending on design, could be entirely out of sight even when on the surface, has always meant they were vulnerable to damage. This was particularly so when going alongside and in rough weather on the surface. The after planes are sited near the propellers and are usually protected by the overhang of the stern and the hull itself. Simple steel guards at the surface waterline sufficed to protect them. However, the fore planes protrude well beyond the limits of the hull. Some navies chose to accept the inconvenience, placed them as low in the hull as possible and provided them with some form of external guard. Where the planes were above water, and especially vulnerable to wave action, it was obvious that the real answer was to retract them, or to fold them away flat against the hull or casing. Successful self-stowing, above-water fore planes were developed independently in Britain and the USA and were in use prior to the First World War. Since then, it has become normal for the fore planes to be stowable by one means or another. In modern submarines, the fore planes are effective only at low speeds and there is a need to retract them in order to streamline the front of the hull. In the *Victoria* class boats, they retract into a transverse recess in the free-flooding bow structure.

## ACCESS AND REMOVAL ROUTES

A number of hatches sited along the top centre line of the pressure hull give access to the interior of the boat. The typical hatchway consists of a short, cylindrical, vertical extension, or coaming, with a hinged watertight hatch cover on top and a ladder leading to the interior. One criteria that decides the size and construction of some hatchways is the need to periodically remove and replace machinery and battery cells. The hatches over the battery and engine compartments are positioned expressly for this purpose. Other hatches are installed specifically for escape purposes. Very often one hatch is sited to provide for the normal traffic-flow into and out of the submarine. As a general rule, only this hatch, and maybe the conning tower hatch as well, are open when alongside, while all others are shut.

The hatches for embarking torpedoes were originally rectangular sections of the hull hinged along one edge, operated by mechanical gearing and secured by portable clamps, or dogs. By the end of the First World War, the angled, circular torpedo-loading hatch located at the rear of the torpedo compartment had been adopted almost universally. Where these hatchways entered the hull in a long elliptical-shaped opening, portable strongbacks were provided that dropped in place between the gaps in the frames when the hatch was secured.

In the *Victoria* class boats, torpedoes are embarked through a circular hatch located near the top of the forward dome bulkhead, which is at the forward end of the torpedo stowage compartment. This hatch is reached from outside through a covered recess, or trough, in the casing and the torpedoes are embarked tail-first. A special band that is secured around the balance point of the torpedo is fitted with small rollers on each side that engage in side rails to guide the weapon into the compartment. Lifting fittings are provided on the top of the band to take a crane or winch pendant or the overhead hoist inside the compartment.

Removing large pieces of machinery such as engines and large electric motors from the interior of submarines has always been a problem, particularly in welded hulls. This was less so with riveted hulls when large areas of plating over the engine spaces were deliberately arranged for relatively easy disassembly. Even when German builders universally adopted welding, an area of plating overtop of the engine room was riveted for easy removal. In some classes, a section of plating over the engine room was secured using bolts. Submariners were never totally happy with this arrangement as it had a bad habit of leaking, particularly during depth charging. As cutting and welding methods and steel quality have improved, it has become an acceptable contingency to remove a portion of the hull by cutting it out, but only as a last resort. The area designated for this kind of treatment is sometimes referred to as the "hard patch." However, in the *Victoria* class boats a return has been made to a bolted-down removable hull section known as a Dutch breech. It is estimated that this feature will reduce the time required to exchange a complete diesel generator from twelve weeks to three weeks as compared to cutting out a section of the hull.

Another innovative means of accessing the engines for removal is to cut the hull into two sections at a convenient point and to draw one section away from the other. This has been done successfully by a number of navies, including Canada's, but it requires a high degree of engineering expertise for success.

## TANKS, PUMPS AND THE TRIM

In a submarine, unlike the surface ship where only positive buoyancy is normal, three kinds of buoyancy must be taken into consideration. To float on the surface, a ship or submarine must be positively buoyant; i.e. the mass of the vessel is less than that of the water it displaces. In order to submerge, the submarine must become negatively buoyant whereby the mass of the vessel is greater than that of the water it displaces. In order to keep from sinking to the bottom, which could be a very long way down, the submarine achieves a state of neutral buoyancy where the mass of the vessel is equal to that of the water it displaces. The unique feature of the submarine is that it can change its state of buoyancy at will and can adjust that condition to a very fine degree.

Various means were devised to provide for submergence and flotation. The simplest and earliest method was an internal tank, much like Holland's adjusting tank, that was flooded to provide negative buoyancy and emptied overboard for positive buoyancy. However, these tanks provided too little reserve buoyancy for good flotation, and additional tanks were soon being incorporated to give a decent safety margin. Tanks used for this purpose are referred to as main ballast tanks. In order to make the most of the limited interior space of the pressure hull, some or all of these tanks are often fitted externally along the sides and at the ends of the pressure hull. Tanks attached to the sides of the hull are called saddle tanks.

Another variation on the external main ballast tank took the form of an outer skin spaced out from the pressure hull by external framing which, for obvious reasons, is known as double-hull construction. The space between the outer skin and the hull was divided up and served admirably as main ballast tanks. External main ballast tanks are usually open to the sea at the bottom so there is no need for them to be pressure proof. All main ballast tanks are fitted with controllable openings on the top known as main vents. When these are opened the air in the tanks escapes to atmosphere. Internal main ballast tanks have special flooding arrangements controlled by large hull valves called kingston valves. In many early submarines, the inlets to all main ballast tanks were fitted with kingston valves, but it was gradually realized that this was only necessary where it was desirable to seal the tank completely.

Kingston valves can be manually operated by a quick-acting lever or in slow time by a handwheel and rodding and, since the 1920s, by power, either electrically or hydraulically. Tanks fitted with kingstons are protected by relief valves to guard against damage that could occur if the tank was inadvertently blown with the kingston in the shut position.

A variation on the main ballast tank was the auxiliary ballast tank. These were used as oversized adjusting tanks to provide for large, temporary variations in the overall mass of the boat. They were fitted with manually operated vents, compressed air blows, and hand-operated kingstons, and were usually connected to the main pumping and flooding system. Auxiliary ballast tanks were sometimes built to pressure hull standards so that they could be blown or filled at depth without fear of rupturing the tank. In submarines having only a small margin of positive buoyancy, the auxiliary ballast tanks would also be emptied when on the surface to provide maximum buoyancy. The purpose of the auxiliary ballast tank was gradually superseded by first providing a greater reserve of buoyancy in the design of the submarine, and eliminated altogether by an improved arrangement of compensating tanks and more efficient pumping systems.

In modern submarine parlance tanks are described as being hard or soft. Hard tanks are those built to pressure hull standards and can be flooded or blown at full diving depth. Soft tanks are those that are not built to withstand the pressure of full diving depth.

Ideally, when on the surface, the submarine itself is neutrally buoyant but is made positively buoyant by the air trapped inside the main ballast tanks. To dive, the main vents are opened, allowing this air to escape. The sea enters the main ballast tanks either directly through the bottom openings or through the open kingston valves. As the air is displaced the displacement decreases while the mass remains the same. At the same time, enough ballast water is admitted to the internal compensating tanks to make the boat negatively buoyant. As it loses reserve buoyancy it sinks, or dives. Once it is fully submerged, the amount of water in the internal tanks is adjusted

to achieve a state of neutral buoyancy. To surface, the main vents are shut, the kingstons opened and compressed air is blown into the ballast tanks to expel the water through the bottom openings. Filling external tanks with air increases displacement without adding weight, while expelling the water from internal tanks reduces weight for the same displacement. Both methods give the boat the required buoyancy.

As a bonus, it was soon realized that fuel oil could be carried in specially fitted external ballast tanks, and ultimately most classes carried the bulk of their fuel externally. However, in modern, deep-diving conventional submarines, a return has been made to carrying all fuel internally.

As previously mentioned, tanks are provided throughout the interior of the pressure hull for the stowage of fuel, fresh water, and other liquids as well as for sea water for adjusting the balance, or trim, and mass of the submarine. The tanks used for controlling the trim are divided into two groups—trim tanks and compensating tanks. The trim tanks are used for maintaining the longitudinal and athwartship attitude of the boat. They are normally located at the forward and after extremities and on either side amidships. The tanks are interconnected with piping commonly known as the trim line. A dedicated trim pump is used to transfer relatively small quantities of water between these tanks to adjust the balance of the boat without necessarily affecting the mass. In small submarines, the change of trim caused by even a couple of men moving from one end of the boat to the other was enough to require water to be shifted to the opposite end to restore the trim.

The compensating tanks are used to adjust the overall mass, or weight, of the boat, making it more or less buoyant. These are generally larger tanks and are used to accommodate the variations in mass caused by changes in the quantities of consumables like lubricating oil, distilled water, fresh water, gun ammunition, torpedoes and food stores. As these items are used up, water is added to the compensating tanks to keep the boat at a consistent mass.

As fuel oil is lighter than water, fuel tanks are made self-compensating by allowing sea water into the tanks to replace spent fuel. As the replacement water is somewhat heavier than the displaced fuel, water is pumped from the compensating tanks to make up the difference.

Compensating tanks are also used to make large adjustments to mass when the submarine is in waters having higher or lower density than normal or when making significant changes of depth. The higher the density of the water, the more buoyant the submarine becomes in normal trim, and the mass of the boat must be adjusted using the compensating tanks in order to dive or stay dived. In a similar way, when a submarine goes deep the hull is compressed by sea pressure with the result that it becomes relatively heavy and water must be pumped or blown out to compensate. When the boat returns to a shallower depth, the hull expands and the boat becomes lighter. Additional water must then be taken in to maintain the trim. These tanks are connected to one another and to a high-capacity pump commonly known as the ballast pump by a piping system called the main flood and drain line or more simply, the main line. Because of the importance of this system, many classes have more than one ballast pump, allowing the main line to be divided into sections. The ballast pump is also used for pumping clean bilges and to supply water pressure to the fire hose connections on the main line and to other services requiring sea water under pressure for a limited time.

Another pump and piping system is dedicated to pumping out the dirty bilges, particularly those that may be contaminated with oil. In a wartime situation a submarine could be betrayed to anti-submarine forces by the presence of oil on the surface carried there by pumping water through oil-contaminated lines. The pumping of oily bilges is always done using the dedicated system so as not to contaminate other systems that normally handle clean water only. In the past, there was the option of pumping oily bilge water into a compensating tank instead of overboard, while clean water was pumped out of another tank to compensate. In recognition of the need to prevent pollution, this procedure has now become standard, and a storage tank for oily water is provided in the design. Oil-contaminated water is landed to a treatment facility on returning to harbour.

During the First World War, some RN captains sailing in Electric Boat Company-designed submarines turned the adjusting tank into a negative buoyancy tank. Prior to sailing, the trim was set with the tank empty. While on the surface the tank was kept full. When the boat dived, the extra ballast ensured that the boat submerged as quickly as possible. When safely dived, the tank was blown to restore the submarine to a normal, near-neutrally buoyant, dived trim. The use of a tank in this way was contrary to the Admiralty's concept of the safe operation of a submarine, and, once the war was over, the use of tanks in this manner was expressly forbidden.

British submarines often found themselves having to operate in waters with considerable variations in density, even during the same voyage. This was particularly apparent when moving from the North Sea, which could be considered as normal, to the Kattegat, with a relatively high density, and the Baltic which, because it is land-locked and has a large number of rivers flowing into it has a relatively low density. It was also a problem in coastal waters where there are many river estuaries. A dived submarine could go from sea water to nearly fresh water in a matter of minutes. The auxiliary ballast tanks and ballast pumps often proved inadequate when trying to compensate for this phenomenon. During a patrol in 1916, one submarine was forced to flood a small compartment in addition to the auxiliary ballast and compensating tanks in order for it to dive in the Kattegat.

Between the wars, attempts were made to accommodate these conditions by improving the size and arrangement of auxiliary ballast tanks. To compensate for sudden changes in water density, one or two auxiliary ballast tanks were turned into quick-flooding–quick-blowing tanks. These were known as Q- (for quick-acting) tanks. Q-tanks had a number of other uses including compensating for the loss of weight experienced when firing torpedoes, effecting rapid depth changes when dived and for quick diving. The operation of the Q-tank, or tanks, was always under the direct control of the captain.

As a variation on the positive buoyancy theme, the RN fitted many submarine classes with ballast-filled sections of keel that could be detached in an emergency. Although releasing these drop keels gave immediate positive buoyancy, it was impossible to dive the boat again until the missing sections had been replaced. This practice was discontinued early in the Second World War.

## AUXILIARY SYSTEMS

The greatest challenge faced by neophyte submariners is that of learning the intimate details of the various systems that are spread throughout the submarine in a compact maze of piping, valves, gauges, pumps and control devices. To aid in

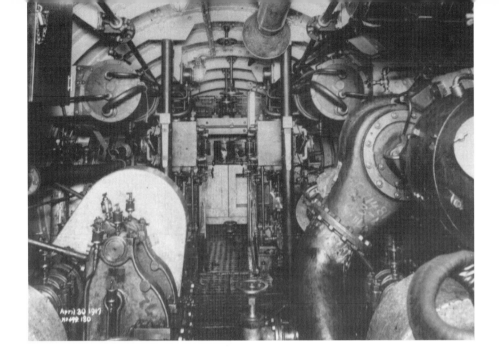

*H* class auxiliary machinery. This is the aftward continuation of the engine room. The two shaft-driven compressors can be seen furthest aft to port and starboard. The shaft-driven rotary ballast pump is on the left and the electric-motor-driven centrifugal ballast pump occupies the righthand corner. A stowage for lubricants and rags can be seen against the after bulkhead in the centre. (PAC)

quick identification, each system is assigned a distinctive colour. All pipe joints and the pipe itself for a short distance either side of the joint, are painted with the system colour. This also facilitates identification of sections of piping during re-assembly when a system is being repaired or refitted. As a further aid to identification, the handwheels on the valves in each system are distinctive, both to the eye and to the touch. All valves are coloured according to the system, and the shape of the handwheel rim also varies; some are circular, others octagonal while still others may be cloverleaf-shaped. This is useful for quick visual identification under normal circumstances and provides for identification through touch in the dark. As well, all hull valves are identified by a common feature so they can be recognized readily. In the *O* class submarines, this was a knob on the handwheel rim.

In modern submarines like the *Victoria* class, nearly all valves are operated by hydraulics controlled from a remote-control console. Relatively few valves have handwheels actually fitted and very few ever need to be operated manually in the conventional sense. Valves can be operated by hand in an emergency This involves mechanically tripping an electrical solenoid at the valve to admit hydraulic pressure to the operating mechanism or in the event of serious failure, fitting a portable handwheel and actually operating the valve by hand. The valves belonging to individual systems must still be identified as must the piping. To

this end, the valves are provided with robust, easy to read labels coded by systems and compartments while coloured bands and labelling are applied to the piping at strategic locations.

## HIGH PRESSURE AIR SYSTEM

One very important utility in all submarines is the high pressure (HP) air system. Originally provided for blowing the main ballast tanks and ejecting, or firing, torpedoes, HP air quickly came to be used for a multitude of purposes. Most services do not require full pressure and so are supplied through reducers set to supply the air at the required pressure. One useful service is that of using reduced air pressure to force the contents of a tank to another location. For example, fresh water tanks are pressurized in this way to make their contents available at taps, while the sewage tank is pressurized to blow the contents into the sea. This saves having to use electric pumps for the purpose.

HP air is supplied by compressors, and, due to the importance of this service, there are always two or more. HP air is stored in large steel bottles at pressures ranging between 138 bar in the early submarines and 276 bar (2,000 to 4,000 pounds per square inch) in modern boats. The bottles are connected by piping to form groups. In the older boats, the groups were situated throughout the interior of the submarine and were piped to group manifolds which in turn were led to a master distribution manifold in the control room.

In the *Victorias*, the HP air bottles are situated outside the pressure hull inside the main ballast tanks forward and aft. These are piped into remotely operated distribution manifolds inside the boat. The master distribution manifold is no longer necessary and its function has been replaced by an electronic control console.

HP air is distributed by means of a ring main, a pipe that runs around the inside perimeter of the boat to supply HP air wherever it is needed. In large or multi-level boats, there are very often two or more ring mains. These are normally configured as a single main to supply HP air throughout the boat. However, ring mains can be used independently, can be sectionalized and may be cross connected when necessary. In the older system, the air groups were connected to the ring main as required from the master manifold and in an emergency directly from the air groups. Nowadays the groups are directly connected to the ring main.

Grouping the air bottles provides for the contingency of a leak in the system, which could drain the entire supply very rapidly. If only one bottle group is connected to the system, or a part of the system at a time, then the loss need not be catastrophic. As soon as an air leak is discovered, the air group supplying the ring main is shut off to minimize air loss. Meanwhile, the supply to the defective component is located and shut off. After the damage has been repaired, or the faulty component isolated, the bottle group can be reconnected to the ring main and the service restored. If the damage is extensive, a whole section of the ring main can be isolated and the rest of the line supplied by bottle groups in different parts of the boat.

While some HP air groups are connected to the ring main, others are reserved for blowing main ballast. There is a separate distribution system for this purpose. In the older submarines, air for blowing main ballast was fed via the HP air distribution manifold from a dedicated bottle group to a main blowing column. This was a vertical manifold with a valve for each ballast tank. Air was piped from the valves to the individual ballast tanks through a valve in the pressure hull known as the HP tankside. These were non-return valves that allowed air under pressure to escape into the ballast tank but shut to keep sea water from entering the system when the boat was dived. Another manifold, the auxiliary blowing column, was provided

for blowing tanks other than ballast tanks. These varied considerably depending on the submarine and when it was built.

Because of its importance, HP air is always used as sparingly as possible. When surfacing, only enough HP air is blown into the ballast tanks to give the minimum necessary buoyancy. Once the boat is successfully surfaced, a low-pressure compressor is run that compresses atmospheric air to complete the filling of the ballast tanks. This compressor is known as the LP Blower and air from the blower is distributed to the ballast tanks by a separate piping system and tanksides. Heavy rolling during rough weather can cause the loss of air in external ballast tanks. During hot weather, daytime expansion can also cause the loss of an appreciable amount of air, leaving the boat with reduced buoyancy after sunset. It is standard practice to run the LP blower on the ballast tanks every evening and once per watch in very rough weather.

Other methods of topping up the ballast tanks have been used. In many designs, diesel exhaust can be directed into the tanks for the same purpose.

## HYDRAULIC SYSTEM

The use of hydraulics was first introduced into British submarines in 1913. As submarines grew in size, it became necessary to operate equipment like main vents and kingstons from the central control position without the delays that occurred when the message had to be passed by voice or telephone and the valves operated by hand. To accomplish this, a hydraulic system was installed that provided for opening and closing kingstons and other ballast-tank flooding aides simultaneously from one central position so that the boat submerged on an even keel. Within a short time, main vents were also being worked hydraulically.

By the end of the First World War, much of the machinery, such as the rudder and hydroplanes, was operated by electric motors. This was very convenient and a vast improvement over manual operation. However, the constant running of DC electric motors created heat and was a drain on the battery. Between the wars, much of the work performed by electric motors was taken over by the far more efficient hydraulic system. This includes the hoisting and lowering of periscopes and masts, control and operation of the hydroplanes and rudder, operation of the cap-

HMS *C10* passes some elegant yachts on her way alongside. Note the still prominent compass binnacle, the two periscopes, a somewhat stronger bridge structure and a larger conning tower, still with viewing ports. The emergency towing arrangement is visible forward. (RNSM)

stan and anchor winches as well as the control and operation of power-operated torpedo-loading and -lifting devices and the operation of bow and stern caps.

Electrically driven pumps supply hydraulic pressure which is stored in spring-loaded or air-loaded reservoirs usually referred to as accumulators. These hold a reserve of oil under pressure to supply the line while the pumps shut down. Normally the pumps are started and stopped automatically depending on line pressure. Hydraulic pressure is distributed throughout the boat by means of a ring main, much like the HP air system. In a similar fashion, the hydraulic system soon became widely used and consequently has become both complex and adaptable.

In British submarines, hydraulics were first installed using the patented Telemotor system that was already being used for a variety of purposes in surface ships. Until recent times, it was common to refer to the hydraulic system in British warships and submarines as the telemotor system. The term went out of vogue with the advent of nuclear-powered submarines and the general adoption of more up-to-date terminology during the late 1960s.

POWER AND PROPULSION

When dived, the conventional submarine relies on the electrical energy stored in the main battery. In the Canadian *O* class boats, this consisted of 448 lead acid cells divided equally between two battery compartments known as Nos. 1 and 2 main batteries. The whole installation weighed over 200 tons and the maximum output was 880 volts. For interest, this can be compared to the *A* class of 1903 which had 112 cells, a maximum output of 240 volts and a total weight of 49.5 tons. Physically, the cells can be divided up between any number of compartments, but electrically, they are usually connected so as to form two sections, although three, and sometimes four sections, were used in some classes.

The battery cells were stowed in tanks that were only deep enough for the cells and their associated equipment, or in compartments that were deep enough to allow the electricians to work on the battery without opening up the deck. The big difference between a battery tank and a battery compartment, is that the deck over a tank is pierced by many hatches which give access to the entire battery from above, while compartments have only one or two hatches and there is sufficient space

between the underside of the deck and the top of the battery for the maintainer to move around inside. The use of tanks or compartments depended very much on the available space. The *A* class of 1945 had one of each.

As a point of interest, even into the 1960s it was common to refer to the deck over the battery as the *boards* while opening up a battery tank for maintenance was described as "lifting, or taking up the battery boards."

Each battery section is connected to a local switchboard containing fuses and breaker switches. From the battery switchboards, power is routed via heavy cables to a main power switchboard; usually located aft in the motor room, which in turn is connected to the main motor switchboard, or switchboards.

In the O-boats, high-voltage DC power for uses other than propulsion was normally taken straight from the battery through fuses and breaker switches and distributed via the main power switchboard throughout the boat by an electrical ring main. Because this power varied in voltage depending on the state of the battery, it was known as the Variable Pressure or VP ring main. This power was used by most of the heavy-duty machinery in the boat such as the ballast pumps, compressors and hydraulic pumps.

The power requirement of the submarine, other than propulsion, is known as the *domestic*, or *hotel* load. This is supplied from a variety of sources one of which is the constant pressure, or CP, ring main which supplies 220 volts DC. This is normally supplied from DC-driven generators.

In modern submarines at least two types of alternating current, or AC, are needed as well as the DC supplied from the battery. Typically, these are a 115-volt, 400-hertz supply for the large electronic installations, and a 440-volt, 60-hertz supply for fluorescent lighting, the galley ranges, numerous domestic conveniences and commercial electric motors used throughout the boat. AC equipment takes up less space, is lighter than the equivalent DC unit and requires less power for starting and running. AC power is supplied from DC-driven AC generators.

Low-power 24 volt DC is used for a number of essential services such as critical control systems, emergency equipment circuits and emergency lighting. In the recent past this service was usually provided by electrically driven generators. In modern submarines it can also be supplied from the AC supply and is transformed into DC. To ensure its availability, the 24-volt system is backed up directly from the battery.

In the basic configuration, propulsion power was supplied to the single armature main motor, or motors, in two ways. One was with the battery sections connected in series, which was achieved by moving the main power switchboard battery grouper switch to the up position, or *group up*, which supplied the main motors with power at the maximum voltage. The other was with the two battery sections connected in parallel, or *group down*, which supplied power at half the maximum voltage.

Additional control over both the propelling power of the main motors and the generating capacity of the motor-generators was achieved through ganging two armatures on each shaft, or by mounting two motors in tandem. These refinements were introduced early in the submarine development process. By splitting the main battery, and having dual armatures, quite a number of power control permutations became possible. The actions of group up and group down soon came to include the electrical arrangement of the main motor armatures as well as the way in which the battery sections were connected. As battery, switchboard and electric motor technologies improved, so too did the efficiency of the electrical propulsion system.

With the twin armature arrangement, two other speed control ranges became possible. For very low speeds, power can be supplied in a configuration known as *shafts in series* which connects all four armatures in series to run the main motors using a very low voltage. As an alternative to running shafts in series, a very slow, or creep, speed, can be achieved by driving one, or sometimes both, shafts using a relatively small auxiliary propulsion motor or a small generator to provide low-level propulsion power.

For very high speeds, a configuration called *batteries in series* is possible which provides the maximum possible voltage to all of the armatures simultaneously.

The usual slow, half and full speeds, either ahead or astern, are available in these ranges except when the auxiliary propulsion motor is being used.

The battery is charged by means of one or more generators; each consisting of an internal combustion engine driving a generator to produce electrical current. In order to supply air to the engines, the submarine must either come to the surface and open either a hatch or the air-induction system, or come to periscope depth and extend a snorkel tube above the surface. Surfacing and opening the tower hatch, or air induction inlets, was the normal method until the adoption of the extendable *schnorkel* tube,[9] by the Germans towards the end of the Second World War. This was an important innovation as it allowed submarines to remain submerged while charging the battery. Using the German installation as their model, the *schnorkel* system was adopted universally after the war. Still called a *schnorkel* in most European navies, it is always referred to as the *snort* in the RN and is spelled and pronounced *snorkel* in the USN.

Early Holland-type submarines used gasoline engines because these were the first type of internal combustion engine commercially available. The story is told of how J. P. Holland, while making a chance visit to Madison Square Garden in New York City, witnessed the demonstration of an electric-light generator intended for remote country homes. It was a compact, self-contained unit powered by a 50-hp (37.5 kW) Otto gasoline engine. Immediately visualizing how it could be applied to the submarine, he bought the generator and installed it in *Holland VI*.

However, the early gasoline engines were inefficient and unreliable, and the fuel posed a constant danger and was relatively expensive. Early British submariners took to carrying a tame white rat or a canary on board to warn them of dangerous levels of gasoline vapour or carbon monoxide given off by the exhaust system. Gasoline vapours and carbon monoxide affected the small animals long before the crew could detect their presence.

It was appreciated at an early date that the diesel engine was reliable, more efficient, cheaper to run and repair and used much safer and cheaper fuel. However, developing a heavy oil engine for use in submarines, where weight and space were very important, took time. The diesel engine was much bulkier and heavier than a gasoline engine of the same

---

9   Patented in 1933 by Lieutenant Commander J. J. Wichers, Royal Netherlands Navy, and fitted in some Dutch boats pre-war. The German navy developed theirs from a captured Dutch submarine.

In the engine room of HMS *L23*. The twelve-cylinder Vickers diesel engines were still good for 17 knots. (Author's collection)

horsepower. The French appear to have been the first to put a diesel engine in a submarine in 1903. However, this installation was not a technical success and the French returned to steam power.

Also in 1903, Vickers installed a Hornsby-Ackroyd 500-hp (375 kW), 6-cylinder diesel in submarine *A13* and conducted an extensive series of trials. Although the engine was three tons heavier and much bulkier than the equivalent gasoline engine, it cut fuel consumption almost in half. These trials were ultimately successful and diesel engines were used in the *D* class of 1907 and in nearly all subsequent classes.

The first German submarines used paraffin-burning internal combustion engines which emitted great clouds of thick, white, smoke. Paraffin was much safer than gasoline but produced less power per cylinder. Despite their lead in diesel technology, the German engine builders encountered problems in developing a suitable lightweight diesel that met the stringent navy specifications. It took until 1910 before an acceptable diesel engine could be produced, after which it became standard in U-boats. The USN installed its first diesels in three submarines built in 1913. Interestingly, these were German-designed MAN[10] diesel engines built in the USA under licence. Similar engines were installed in Canada's first submarines. These particular engines were not a success and the USN replaced many of theirs towards the end of the First World War.

Historically, German manufacturers produced engines having the lowest fuel consumption, the lowest weight and the highest horsepower output per cylinder. The reliability and economy provided by German diesel technology contributed significantly to the success of the U-boats in both world wars.

Reversible diesel engines were tried at an early date, but these proved difficult to maintain and were slow in their reversing action. Reversing gearboxes were available but took up space and added weight and mechanical complexity where these were not wanted. As the main motors could be reversed with relative ease, it soon became the practice to propel on the main motors whenever reversing might be required. The diesels were then used to propel in the ahead direction only.

By the advent of the First World War, most submarines had twin propeller shafts with a diesel engine and a twin-armature, dual-purpose electric main motor–generator on each shaft. The shaft was sectioned using two clutches. One of these, the engine clutch, was located between the engine and the main motor. The other, the tail clutch, was fitted between the main motor and the thrust block.[11] With both clutches engaged, the entire shaft line was connected and the diesel engine drove the propellers. This was known as direct drive.

As the de-energized main motor was being rotated along with the shafting, it was soon realized that it could be utilized to generate electricity to charge the battery. Propelling and generating simultaneously was known as a *running charge*. Another possibility in this mode, where only enough power was taken from the generators to match the power being drawn from the battery by the hotel load, was known as *floating the load*. Generating while propelling imposed an additional load on the engines, causing a proportionate rise in fuel consumption.

To charge the battery without propelling, the engine clutch was engaged, the tail clutch disengaged and the diesel then drove only the electric motor as a generator to produce current. This was known as a *standing charge*. A brake, known as the *tail brake*, was provided to keep the free-wheeling propeller from spinning and causing drag on the disengaged side.

By unclutching the engine clutch, engaging the tail clutch and energizing the main motor with power from the battery, the motor drove the propeller to provide propulsion when submerged or manoeuvering on the surface.

As can be imagined, many permutations of propelling and generating were possible with this arrangement. With the appropriate engines the direct drive system could produce surface speeds of up to 22 knots (kts), although speeds between 12 and 16 kts was more usual.

In the early submarines, auxiliary machinery, such as the ballast pumps and air compressors, was mechanically driven and took power directly from the main shafting using gear trains and individual clutches. This machinery could be run whenever the shaft was rotating. To run this machinery without

---

10   Maschinenfabrik Augsburg-Nürnberg AG whose engines are still being built under licence in many countries.

11   The thrust block transmits the thrust of the propeller to the hull in order to propel the vessel and to relieve strain on the propelling machinery.

propelling, both the tail clutch and the engine clutch were disconnected and the main motor was run to power the length of shafting from which the auxiliaries took their power. Eventually, the auxiliaries were provided with individual electric drive motors making this complicated arrangement of gears and clutches unnecessary. This took up less space and permitted considerably more flexibility when siting the machinery inside the hull.

The simplest, least expensive and most efficient form of submarine propulsion is to use the main motors for propulsion at all times. In this arrangement, the diesel engines are not connected to the propeller shafts but are used only for driving generators to produce the electrical current for supplying the battery. This is known as diesel-electric drive and all modern conventional submarines are this type. In these boats, surface speed is determined by how well the diesel-generators can keep up with the demand for electric current. This generally produces around 12 kts for typical two-generator boats like the *O* class, while up to 21 kts was achieved by the big USN fleet boats of the Second World War, which had four generators.

Until recent times, maximum dived speed for most conventional submarines was in the 8 to 10 kts range. Modern conventional boats with their hydrodynamic hulls, high-capacity batteries, high-performance main motors and special propellers can achieve speeds of between 16 and 21 kts. Even when snorting, 12 to 16 kts can be maintained. As all modern conventional submarines are designed for submerged efficiency, their surface performance is not as good as their dived performance and 12 kts is typical. However, this lack of surface speed is of little consequence. These boats only need to run on the surface when entering and leaving harbour or for non-operational purposes when at sea.

In operation, all conventional submarines have the choice of running on the battery for as long as possible and then stopping, or proceeding slowly, to charge up the battery, or of preserving the battery and running on the generators or direct-drive diesels as much as possible. The former leaves the submarine in a relatively vulnerable condition for four to eight hours while the battery is charged. In the latter, the submarine is vulnerable to detection because of the noise and exhaust products from the diesel engines and from being near, or on, the surface.

During both world wars, German U-boats usually hunted on the surface, running on direct-drive diesels while preserving the battery for making submerged attacks. Even the early snorkel fitted U-boats only used the snorkel mast for near-stationary charging, as propelling at any sort of speed with the mast raised made the boat unstable. In the Pacific, American and Japanese submarines operated in much the same manner. Most USN boats used diesel-electric drive, but with up to four generators the power output could be directed to where it was most needed. When the battery was charged, the output of the generators was used to drive the main motors, so the result was much the same.

Submarines operating within a predetermined patrol area frequently remained dived during daylight and surfaced after dark to charge the battery.

## TECHNOLOGICAL PROGRESS

By comparison with modern conventional submarines, the boats of the First World War were very primitive machines. Nevertheless, for their day they were at the very forefront of the technology, as indeed were the *Victoria* class when they were commissioned during the early 1990s. As far back as 1914, almost all of the elements we consider normal in a conventional submarine of today can be identified. The safe, efficient diesel engine, near-silent electric main motors, high-capacity electrical storage battery, electrical control systems, electrically driven auxiliaries, periscopes for both navigation and attack, underwater sensors, radios, hydraulics, streamlining to reduce water resistance, torpedo tubes and self-guiding weapons were all present. By the end of the Second World War, the rest of the technological puzzle was in place, including the snorkel and sophisticated electronics.

Advanced electrical devices and electronics made an early appearance in submarines. The Electric Boat Company designs of the First World War featured portable, electric, finger-operated steering gear and electric main motor telegraphs. The hydroplanes and steering were electrically operated. Main periscopes were hoisted using electric motors and lowered by a counter-balance weight. The gyroscopic compass, essential for accurate underwater navigation, was first installed in a submarine in 1907. Radio made a very early appearance—even

Holland *No.1* was fitted for a very primitive receiver installation. The *D* and *E* classes were the first British boats to receive a full wireless radio outfit and this was authorized as early as November 1912.

The radios or wireless sets that were used in both world wars did not utilize the human voice as they do now, but transmitted and received a very rapid series of electrical pulses. These were made by closing and opening a simple hand-operated switch commonly referred to as a telegraph key. The radio-wave pulses were grouped into a universal code of short and long pulses, or dots and dashes. Called the Morse code after its inventor, Samuel F. B. Morse, this code was originally developed for the overland telegraph and was adapted for wireless telegraphy when it was brought into use. Radio operators in many navies were known as telegraphists until the latter half of the twentieth century. The use of Morse code for official purposes was universally discontinued in 1999.

The interception of the other side's wireless signals and the breaking of signal codes provided a special chapter in the history of naval warfare. So too did the science of pinpointing the location of the source of those signals. Known as Radio Direction Finding, or RDF, this science led to the development of radio navigation aids (Loran and Decca Navigator) and radar. Radar itself made an early appearance aboard British submarines in 1942, primarily as a defence against aircraft.

Signalling between submerged submarines was developed from an underwater aid to navigation system invented by Professor Reginald A. Fessenden, a Canadian-born pioneer in underwater signalling and radio. The original Fessenden underwater signalling system was devised to warn shipping of marine dangers when other audible or visible signals could not be relied on because of the weather. In its most basic form, it consisted of a bell fitted to a conventional warning buoy, but suspended underwater. Wave action caused the buoy to rock back and forth making the bell ring. Hydrophones fitted on the hulls of ships received the reverberations and converted them to electrical energy, which was used to warn the bridge of the presence of the marine hazard. The precise direction of the signal source was impossible to determine, which was why the device was always used with a marked hazard. Having been warned they were in danger, the ship's officers would be prompted to slow down if necessary, consult the charts to locate the danger and warn the lookouts.

In the submarine installation, which was introduced in the USN as early as 1909, an externally mounted bell with a remotely controlled clapper was provided for sending the signal, while a pair of hydrophones were installed in the bows for receiving and to provide at least a rudimentary determination of direction. A later refinement of the system used Fessenden oscillators in place of the bell. These were electrically operated devices capable of both transmitting and receiving sound waves. Fessenden oscillators were fitted aboard many submarines of the First World War for exchanging messages through the water using Morse code. Eventually the equipment was adapted for the detection of the propeller and machinery noises made by other vessels long before hydrophones were being used by ships for the detection of submarines. This equipment was a forerunner of the very sophisticated sonars and underwater communications equipment used by modern ships and submarines.

## WEAPONS

### TORPEDOES

The primary weapon of the conventional submarine is the torpedo. Typically, the torpedo is launched from a horizontal tube, the breech end of which extends into the interior of the submarine. The torpedo tube has a hinged, watertight door on each end. The inboard door is usually referred to as the breech or rear door, and the outboard one the muzzle door, or in British boats the bow or stern cap. From the beginning, safety interlocks were devised to prevent opening both the rear door and the bow or stern cap simultaneously and to preclude firing with the bow cap shut.

Originally, one or two torpedo tubes were mounted in the bows only. As experience was gained, additional tubes were provided in the stern and, in some classes, across the width of the boat amidships to provide firing on both beams. These were desirable when attacking ranges were short, submarines slow to respond and the target was liable to be fast moving. The additional tubes allowed the submarine, using a minimum of manoeuvre, to fire as the target approached, passed by and steamed away. Beam tubes disappeared after the First

HMS *Spiteful*, 1943. Embarking torpedoes from the depot ship. (RNSM)

World War but stern torpedo tubes persisted until recent times. These were made redundant when it became possible to set an independent course on the torpedo. Spare torpedoes are carried inside the submarine in the compartments adjacent to the rear doors. Torpedo-handling arrangements such as hoists, overhead rails and travelling chain-purchases were installed for loading the tubes.

The French and Russian navies tried carrying torpedoes in external stowage cradles fitted on the sides of the casing or ballast-tank tops. These had hinged collars that dropped to release the torpedo instead of ejecting them from torpedo tubes. The Russians also experimented with a similar mechanism that mechanically ejected the torpedo sideways so they could be launched on the surface. These novel devices were unreliable, prone to damage and proved unsatisfactory in service. They were discontinued after the First World War.

To provide additional firepower, external torpedo tubes were fitted in many submarines, particularly in wartime. There were many variations to the arrangement of these tubes. Some German minelayers had no internal torpedo tubes but were fitted with two external tubes. On some boats these were arranged with one pointing forward, the other aft. Reloads for these were carried in cradles immediately behind the rear-end of the tube and weather permitting, these could be loaded quickly while on the surface.

The British *T* class boats of the Second World War boasted eleven 21-inch torpedo tubes altogether, six internal in the bows with one reload per tube, and five fixed externals. In the final configuration, the externals were arranged with two facing forward in the bows and three facing aft, one each side amidships and one in the stern. Some French submarines at that time carried external mountings that could be trained to point on the bearing of the target, much like the rotating torpedo tubes used on destroyers. These were provided in two sizes, 21-inch (533.4 mm) and 15-inch (381.0 mm), sometimes both in the same mounting. In the Atlantic, these mountings had a tendency to freeze up when on the surface in cold weather and the 15-inch torpedoes were an operational failure. There was usually no provision for loading external tubes at sea.

Some of the long-range submarines from both world wars carried spare torpedoes in watertight cylinders in the external superstructure. Given the right circumstances, these could be hauled out of their stowages and struck below. The advent of extensive air cover and radar, which made it dangerous to remain stopped in one place for any length of time, brought an end to this practice. Most postwar designs provided for an increased supply of reloads inside the boat.

Until the advent of the nuclear-powered submarine, most torpedoes were ejected from the torpedo tube using compressed air. To launch, or fire the torpedo, a measured amount of HP air was released into the tube behind it. As it expanded, the air pushed the weapon out of the tube and this movement tripped a mechanism to start the torpedo engine. Some smaller torpedoes are capable of propelling themselves out of a full-sized tube, but this is not possible with the full-diameter heavyweight weapons.

Up to the end of the Second World War, most attacks were carried out at periscope depth against targets on the surface. During the war, a number of underwater submarine-versus-submarine encounters demonstrated the desirability of being able to fire when deep. However, neither the target-location technology, weapon-ejection systems nor the torpedoes were up to the task. After the war, the development of the sonar-directed attack against submerged targets and the provision of electrically powered, acoustic homing, deep running torpedoes were given a high priority. These developments made it both desirable and possible to fire torpedoes from below periscope depth. The air-impulse system was further refined to achieve deep firing and the resulting Dual Pressure Firing Gear (British) could fire torpedoes down to about 600 feet (180 m).

However, the demands of modern anti-submarine warfare necessitated the creation of a more efficient, quieter method of discharge. Two means are currently in use, both using a form of positive discharge, which means pushing the torpedo out using water. These are the water ram discharge (WRD) and the air-turbine pump (ATP). The WRD is a powerful air-driven piston that pressurizes sea water in the water transfer-tank that surrounds the rear ends of the torpedo tubes. A valve in the appropriate tube, or tubes, is opened to allow sufficient pressurized water from the transfer tank to pass through the tube at the force necessary to expel the torpedo. Although efficient and effective, the ram is built into the ship's structure and has proven difficult to maintain in service.

Developed by the USN as a less bulky, more accessible option to the ram, the ATP is a high-speed, high-volume, air-turbine driven water pump. In operation, air is admitted to the turbine which drives the pump impeller. The impeller spins, drawing in sea water from the outside and discharging it under considerable pressure into the water-transfer tank. As in the WRD system, a slide valve on the torpedo tube is opened to admit the pressurized water and eject the torpedo. The big advantage of the ATP is that it can be removed for maintenance with relative ease. A British-developed and -manufactured version of this equipment is installed in the *Victoria* class submarines purchased by the Canadian government in 1998.

By the eve of the First World War, the most common torpedo used aboard Allied submarines was based on an 18-inch (457.2 mm) diameter weapon developed by the Whitehead Torpedo Factory in Fiume, Austria. These were manufactured under licence in both Britain and the United States. A typical Whitehead torpedo of the 1914-1918 period, was around 16 feet (4.88 m) in length, weighed in the neighbourhood of 1,500-pounds (680 kg) and had to be ejected from the torpedo tube with a blast of compressed air.

By the outbreak of war these torpedoes were propelled by a hot gas engine. In this system, compressed air was fed to a combustion chamber where atomized shale oil was added and ignited. The resultant pressurized hot gas was fed into the cylinders of a four-cylinder radial engine. The engine drove two contra-rotating propellers through a gearbox and inner and outer propeller shafts. The hollow inner shaft also acted as the exhaust pipe. Typically, these torpedoes ran at a speed of 30 to 40 kts for a distance of approximately 3,000 yards (approximately 2743 m).

Warheads contained between 200 and 320 pounds (90.2 to 145 kg) of explosives. The torpedo was kept on a straight course by a gyroscope driven by compressed air. Depth was maintained by a hydrostatically controlled, mechanical, depth-keeping mechanism. Many torpedoes had two speed settings, the slower speed being used to gain range. Running depth and speed settings were manually set before loading the weapon into the tube.

In Germany, the Schwartzkopf torpedo factory produced its own line of steam turbine powered torpedoes. Typical of these was the CO6D, a 45-cm (17.7-inch) torpedo 5.65 m (18 ft 6 in) long, capable of travelling 5900 m (6,450 yards) at 27 kts. This torpedo carried a 122 kg (269 lb.) warhead.

The torpedo, which actually began development as a mobile mine, had the distinct advantage of hitting the target below the waterline. In the case of large warships, this meant below the protection of the armoured belt. The effect of the explosion of a torpedo warhead on an unprotected hull was devastating. During the First World War, warships of cruiser size—3,000 to 10,000 tons—and older battleships were often sunk after only one hit from an 18-inch weapon. Few merchant ships including large passenger liners, could survive a torpedo hit. However, modern warships, with good subdivision and damage control facilities, proved on a number of occasions that they could survive hits from the 18-inch weapons. This gave rise to the development of the 21-inch weapon carrying a much heavier warhead.

During the First World War, torpedoes were fired singly. The number fired depended on the size of the target. For the average target, one torpedo would suffice, and for larger ones, two. The ideal firing range was about 500 yards (450 m) or less from the target. Many commanding officers (COs) fired at much less than this in order to guarantee a hit. Even at 500 yards, the submarine was very vulnerable to counterattack. In the event either the submarine or the torpedo were sighted, there was ample distance for a nimble destroyer to avoid the torpedo and make an attack by ramming or dropping depth charges. At that close a range, the chances of the submarine making a second attack were almost non-existent.

By 1939 considerable development had taken place. Accuracy had improved to the point where the attacking range had tripled while speed and range had both increased. Tactics had also been developed to include the firing of salvoes of two or more torpedoes in order to increase the likelihood of a hit first time, if not several hits almost simultaneously.

During both wars nearly all attacks were carried out by aiming through the periscope while dived. During the early stages of the Second World War, German U-boats often attacked convoys at night, at close range, on the surface using a portable, bridge-mounted, optical sight. This tactic required a high standard of seamanship and a very steady nerve. Wartime attrition of experienced U-boat COs, and the use of RDF and radar by the

Allies, eventually forced the U-boat captains to adopt more traditional but less productive tactics.

For the submerged submarine, invisible until the moment of firing, the big splash of the torpedo discharge air exiting the tube and the telltale trail of exhaust bubbles left behind by the torpedo engine exhaust, were deadly give-aways. Attacks in calm seas were made with considerable risk to the attacker. However, just a little chop was usually enough to hide the signs and many ships thought they had hit a mine when they had actually been torpedoed, while others, having been missed, steamed away oblivious of either their good fortune or their deadly danger.

Another hazard was the possibility of the submarine broaching as the firing of the negatively buoyant torpedo suddenly made one end of the boat light. To counter this tendency, a measured quantity of sea water was flooded into an internal tank, or tanks, to compensate for the loss of weight at the time of firing. In British boats, this was accomplished by leaving the torpedo tube vent open for a measured length of time immediately after firing. Special compensating tanks were included in submarine designs for this purpose from Holland *No.1* onwards.

By the Second World War the torpedo used by submarines was a 21-inch (533.4 mm) weapon weighing over 1.25 tons, running at 45 kts with a maximum range of 15,000 yards (13,716 m) and carrying an 800-pound (362.8-kg) warhead. It was still straight running, but depth and course keeping were more accurate. Propulsion systems varied: the USN favoured a hot-gas-driven turbine engine, while the Japanese had developed a wakeless torpedo-propulsion system using pure oxygen. The British remained faithful to the hot-gas radial engine, which had been improved considerably in the intervening years. The very reliable and efficient Brotherhood-cycle torpedo engine delivered the highest horsepower-to-weight ratio of all hot gas engines, piston or turbine.

In some navies, but not the RN, an electrically driven mechanical spindle that dropped through a watertight gland in the top of the torpedo tube was provided so that the gyro could be offset at will during an attack. This allowed several torpedoes to be fired in an accurately spread fan-like salvo without having to swing the submarine. Another spindle was provided so that the running depth of the torpedo could be adjusted manually up to the time of firing.

Between the wars, most navies devised a means to prevent the discharge air from making a big splash on the surface. The RN developed the Automatic Inboard Vent (AIV) system which was first installed in a submarine in 1928. In this system, after the torpedo was expelled a power-operated valve automatically opened to vent the impulse air back into the boat through a large-bore pipe before it could escape out the torpedo tube muzzle. The valve remained open long enough to admit a measured quantity of water through the same pipe to an internal tank to compensate for the loss of the weight of the torpedo. This automatic compensation was essential when firing a salvo as the loss of weight in the bows was considerable. A salvo of six 21-inch torpedoes typically required just over a ton of compensating water.

Asdic, called *sonar* post-war, was able to detect the noise of the torpedo engine, and sonar-equipped ships could sometimes avoid being hit, especially if the weapon was fired at long-range. In order to eliminate the noise and the exhaust trail, straight-running electrically powered torpedoes were produced. The first of these was developed by the Germans in Sweden between 1923 and 1927 and entered service with the German navy in 1938. The Americans and British were slow off the mark and developed their own versions from captured German torpedoes. One example was actually removed from the side of a ship in which it had imbedded itself but failed to explode. These were somewhat slower than their hot-gas brethren, but were very effective, especially in calm seas.

Once a quiet-running torpedo had been perfected it was only a short step to the acoustically controlled torpedo that homed in on target noises. These were being used with considerable success by the Germans in the last two years of the Second World War.

The British, German and American navies suffered a relatively high number of torpedo failures early in the war. For different reasons, they all suffered from poorly designed exploder mechanisms. How these problems were discovered, analysed and corrected would fill a small book and the Germans never did completely overcome their deficiencies.

After the war torpedo development was continued, particularly by the American, British and Soviet navies. Using all of the knowledge gathered during the war, a succession of faster, quieter, deeper running, more accurate and more destructive torpedoes was soon being produced. This activity was accelerated to new heights when it became necessary to counter the challenges posed by nuclear propelled submarines having deep diving and high speed capabilities far in excess of those posed by conventional diesel boats.

Today's torpedoes feature solid-state electronics, on-board computers and space-age-fuelled high-performance pump-jet propulsion engines that produce speeds in excess of 50 kts and ranges beyond twenty nautical miles. Prior to launch these torpedoes receive target information through a watertight umbilical connection. This information is updated during the run to the target by transmitting fire-control data along fine wires laid in the wake of the weapon from an onboard wire dispenser. Weapon-performance information is relayed back to the firing vessel so that the firing submarine knows where the torpedo is and what it is doing in relation to itself and the target. Using this exchange of data, the torpedo is set to keep a running depth that takes advantage of thermal and density layers to mask engine noise. Deep-running torpedoes are quieter and leave no discernible wake. As torpedoes can vary their depth almost at will, they can be run out to the target area at depth, only coming shallow to attack a surface ship or going deeper to strike another submarine.

Torpedoes are able to utilize either active or passive acoustic homing modes, or even both depending on the circumstances. In the active mode the electronic homing system transmits an acoustic signal ahead of the weapon and listens for a return echo from the target. This information is analysed by on-board logic circuits, and the course and depth are adjusted to achieve a hit on the target. In the passive mode, the homing system listens for noises radiated from the target. Propeller and machinery noises usually provide a good point of reference. These sounds are analysed and the torpedo steers itself into the target. As the acoustic signal emitted by the torpedo in the active mode can be detected, the weapon is often steered towards the target using a combination of information from the firing vessel's fire-control system and the weapon's own passive acoustic homing system. Should one of these torpedoes miss, they are capable of reattacking until a hit is achieved or fuel is exhausted. The possible permutations of weapon control, attack and re-attack modes are numerous.

## GUNS AND MINES

To augment the relatively expensive, and at first not very accurate, torpedo armament, most submarines carried guns. These ranged in size from a .303-calibre light machine gun, to 150 mm (5.9-inch) guns carried by World War One German U-cruisers, to the 12-inch (304.8 mm) monsters mounted in three experimental British boats at the end of that war. British boats became particularly adept at using the gun during both world wars.

With the perfection of the snorkel towards the end of the Second World War, which allowed submarines to remain submerged for extended periods, the gun became redundant. The deck gun was rapidly disappearing by the end of the war but persisted in a limited way until the early 1980s. The last use of the deck gun by British submarines was on anti-piracy patrols conducted from Singapore during the late 1960s. During both world wars, all submarines carried a variety of medium-calibre automatic anti-aircraft weapons and a selection of small arms with which to arm boarding and landing parties.

Submarines are ideally suited for laying mines. Dedicated minelaying submarines were developed first by the Germans and later by the British navies in the First World War. These boats carried the same type of moored spherical mine as was being laid by surface ships.

The long-range 1,512-ton German UE-II type of the First World War was an interesting example of the long-range omnibus submarine that emerged during the war. These U-boats had four internal 457.2 mm (18-inch) bow torpedo tubes and eight reloads, a 150 mm (5.9-inch) deck gun as well as two special mine ejection tubes, or chutes, in the stern. Up to seventy 100-cm (40-inch) spherical mines were carried. Forty of these were stowed internally for launching through the stern chutes, and the balance in containers built into the casing for laying from the surface using external launching rails.

Between the wars, mines were developed for ejection from normal torpedo tubes, giving all submarines a minelaying capability. Both types of submarine minelaying were available during the Second World War. One type of British submarine minelayer carried fifty spherical moored mines externally in addition to the usual torpedo and gun armament.

A wide variety of mines is available to the modern submarine. One interesting hybrid is a mine that is propelled to its position by a redundant electric torpedo. With the advent of electronics, the fuses used in mines have become very sophisticated. Theoretically, a mine can be programmed to detonate under one particular ship. As a consequence, both minelaying and minesweeping have become highly specialized fields.

## MISSILES

The modern submarine weapon is the surface-to-surface, air-flight, anti-ship missile. A typical example is the McDonnell Douglas UGM-84A Harpoon SSM. In use aboard surface ships since 1973, the submarine-launched version was first deployed in 1981. Since its introduction, the weapon has gone through a wide range of improvements and today is carried aboard approximately seventy-five US and fifty Allied submarines, including all British nuclear-powered attack submarines (SSNs) and Australian conventional hunter-killer submarines (SSKs). The submarine-launched weapon is carried inside an unpowered, buoyant capsule that fits in a standard 21-inch torpedo tube. Prior to ejection, the weapon is connected to the submarine fire control by an umbilical cable so that the weapon can be programmed prior to launch. The encapsulated assembly is ejected from the torpedo tube like a torpedo, after which the buoyant capsule assumes an inclined launch position, ascends to the surface and acts as a launching tube. The missile is launched by a rocket booster and propelled in flight by a turbojet engine. Harpoon travels at a speed of Mach 0.85 (around 1044 km/h) has a range of 240 km and delivers a 221.6 kg warhead to which can be added the explosive effects of residual fuel. The weapon is programmed with a variety of search-and-attack patterns, and accuracy is described as pinpoint. The ship-launched version of this SSM is currently in Canadian service as the main armament of the Canadian Patrol Frigates.

## FIRE CONTROL

Primitive, hand-held mechanical computers first appeared in submarines when a mechanical computational device known as the IS-WAS was introduced in British submarines during the First World War. This was used for calculating the firing angle solution needed for aiming and firing torpedoes at a moving target from a moving platform. Because of the computational difficulties encountered in firing straight-running torpedoes at longer and longer ranges, these mechanical slide-rule-type instruments were improved between the wars. Nevertheless, the successful outcome of the attack still relied on the commanding officer's abilities with the periscope, his mathematical aptitude and good judgement.

By the end of the Second World War, most submarines were using electro-mechanical geared calculators for solving the firing equation. Many of these were capable of accepting and utilizing bearings and ranges input electronically from the periscopes and radar. Today these hybrid calculators have been replaced by sophisticated electronic computers of relatively small physical size but possessing immense computational capabilities.

Modern submarines are highly computerized. This is particularly so in the area of weapons control. Sensors of all kinds feed their signals into a data base which supplies one central analytical computer. This data is analyzed, filtered and output to provide target identification and tracking as well as integrated weapons setting, firing and running data. Computers can track numerous targets at a time and can handle several attacking situations simultaneously. Almost all aspects of weapon launching are now handled by the computer from the control room.

During the First World War the all-important periscope evolved from being a simple, monocular, single magnification viewing device to one having high and low magnifications, a split-image range-finder and the ability to look upwards as well as outwards.

Even in this day and age of highly sophisticated sensors, the periscope has been retained. This is because the combination of the human eye and brain is incredibly efficient, and the periscope does not need to emit any kind of signal in order to gather critical data.

Most submarines are provided with two periscopes. A search periscope that provides a wide field of view, a wide range of accessories and the greatest magnification, and an attack periscope that features a very small upper tube and lens and somewhat fewer accessories. The exposed portions of all modern periscopes are provided with radar-suppression coatings. Because of their size and weight these periscopes are power hoisted and power driven to prevent physical stress on the operator.

Periscopes are as high-tech as everything else in the modern submarine. In addition to their advanced optical capabilities, today's periscopes incorporate such features as thermal imaging, infrared detection and ranging, a low-light television camera that displays its image in the eyepiece or on a remote monitor and range and bearing displays. Search periscopes also include a sextant and most periscopes will accept a camera for taking still pictures. Typically, magnification varies between 1.6-power to 12-power and the viewing angle is variable between −10 degrees and as high as +75 degrees with a viewing field that varies in width between 8 degrees and 32 degrees.

# SURVIVAL AND ESCAPE

Like any other warships, submarines can be destroyed through the actions of an adversary. In these cases, there is little likelihood that any of the crew will survive. Distasteful though this may be, it is an inescapable fact of submarine life. However, to a much greater degree than surface vessels submarines are vulnerable to material failure, malfunctions of their own internal systems or to human error. Submarines are too small to carry much in the way of life-saving equipment and as they usually travel alone, abandoning ship is, more often than not, a futile option. In every case, the surest means of survival is the submarine itself, and submarines are built to survive.

In order to ensure the integrity of the submarine, every crew member must be trained and thoroughly drilled in all aspects of equipment operation and damage control. Most submariners conduct the bulk of their duties in one or two main compartments and so come to know these best through on-the-job familiarity. However, there is no guarantee that when an emergency arises everybody will be in their usual place of duty. Consequently, all hands are made intimately familiar with their own equipment and possess a working knowledge of all the equipment and systems throughout the boat. This is not just a theoretical familiarity, but the hands-on, make-it-go kind of familiarity. The golden rule of submarine survival is "Know your boat."

As survival at sea depends primarily on the preservation of the submarine, the submarine itself has been made as robust as possible. Provided the boat can be kept within its designed depth limits, it can absorb, and recover from an incredible range of abuse.

All systems are provided with control redundancy, and for critical systems this includes alternative control modes as well as semi-automated, local, and manual operation. In the layout of the systems and auxiliary machinery, all critical services are duplicated, usually forward and aft of the control room, and these can be operated independently or cross connected so that either section can service both. Where there are two or more machines to a system, one will be sufficient to maintain the service in an emergency. Where the machines are electrically driven, they can be supplied with power from more than one source and all DC machinery can fall back on the battery if necessary. In some critical systems, one electric drive motor will be AC, the other DC. Wherever there are similar systems in the same compartment, such as the trim line and the main line, they can be cross-connected and the services of one used to provide for both or to provide an alternate route around a damaged area. All remotely operated valves critical to the survival of the boat can be operated by power locally and, if necessary, by hand.

Redundancy of basic controls such as depth-keeping, steering and propulsion is multilevel. When centralized, automated computer control fails, a manual computer mode can be initiated. Should this fail, semi-automated control can be assumed at the local control consoles such as the one-man steering and hydroplane control console and the main motor switchboard. When power operation fails, manual local control can be effected.

Breakdown drills are a way of life in operational submarines. Equipment and system failures are practised on a regular basis. Submariners under training, and even experienced hands, frequently indulge in quizzing one another on how to achieve the ordinary by the most extraordinary means. It is through this intimate hands-on knowledge of their boat and its systems that submariners reinforce the combat abilities of their ship and, in so doing, maximize their own chances of survival.

## ESCAPE

All submarines are fitted for escape and are provided with the necessary equipment, while all crew members receive escape training. Where escape from a sunken submarine is possible, success will depend largely on where the incident takes place. Provided the boat is lying within the limits of its own diving depth, the chances of survival are good. To mark the position of the submarine indicator buoys are provided, usually one forward and one aft. These can be released from any compartment inside the submarine. Typically, the buoys are painted a fluorescent orange and are fitted with a flashing beacon, and often a means to communicate with the submarine. Modern marker buoys contain a Global Positioning System distress-locating device similar to those fitted in aircraft. The buoys are tethered to the boat with a stainless-steel wire rope.

Submerged signal and decoy ejectors are usually fitted forward and aft. These are provided with special pyrotechnic stores for indicating the position of a submarine in distress and for sending messages to rescuers. Communications between the sunken submarine and the surface can be as sophisticated as underwater telephony or as crude as banging on the hull with a solid object.

There are three methods by which survivors can escape. Ideally, they will be retrieved by a deep submergence rescue vehicle (DSRV). These small, deep-diving, totally independent mini-submarines are on call twenty-four hours a day and can be used in any weather. They are road, air and ship transportable and can even be piggybacked on another submarine using a special docking cradle. Typically, DSRVs are manned by a crew of two to four operators and can carry between fifteen and twenty survivors. Propulsion control is provided by a computerized positioning system and they can hover with pinpoint accuracy. Using a special skirt, the DSRV secures itself to an escape hatch coaming. This can be accomplished even when the sunken submarine is lying at angles of up to forty-five degrees. Once the skirt is secure and pumped out, the submarine escape hatch and DSRV entry hatches are opened and the survivors can transfer to the DSRV and be carried to safety.

As a feasibility demonstration, HMCS *Ojibwa* conducted the first Canadian submarine trials with a DSRV in the Gareloch in 1975. All three Canadian O-boats have completed numerous DSRV exercises, both to give the crew experience and to verify the procedures and equipment. More recently, *Ojibwa* conducted a mating exercise with a USN DSRV off San Diego while returning home from her problem-plagued 1997 west coast deployment. With the submarine on the bottom at 273 feet (83.2 m) the DSRV made a successful mating on an escape hatch and personnel were transferred to the rescue submersible without difficulty.

One escape alternative is the individual free ascent method. This is accomplished using the hood-inflation-system personal escape and survival equipment and by exiting the wreck one man at a time through small escape chambers situated fore and aft. Individual practice escapes have been made by experienced instructors using standard equipment from as deep as 600 feet (182.8 m) and by crewmen with basic training from 300 feet (91.4 m).

A variation on this method is the compartment, or mass, escape. In this procedure, the crew don their escape and survival equipment and the entire escape compartment is flooded and equalized with the surrounding sea. The survivors then exit through a specially fitted escape hatch one after the other in rapid succession. A pressure compensated, built-in breathing system (BIBS) is provided in the escape compartments so that escapees can continue to breathe air at the correct pressure even as the compartment fills with water. Although this escape procedure is effective it is considered the method of last resort. As the escape compartment must be completely filled with water, personnel can be exposed to pressure for a prolonged period. The longer the exposure to pressure, the greater the likelihood of escapees contracting the bends or suffering other deleterious effects. All submariners receive training in this method and in the one-man escape procedure.

Canada does not possess any special submarine rescue equipment beyond a portable decompression chamber that would be used to treat survivors for the bends. There is also an emergency organization that can be brought into immediate operation to provide assistance in the event of an accident involving a Canadian submarine. However, as a member of NATO, and an ally of both Britain and the United States, Canada has agreements in place whereby the navy can call on these two countries for assistance. Immediately a SUBSMASH message, indicating that a submarine is in trouble; or a SUBMISS message, indicating that a submarine is overdue, is broadcast, all available rescue facilities in that geographical area are placed on standby and the nearest DSRV is dispatched to the vicinity. Once the submarine in distress is located, a SUBSUNK message is initiated and the rescue equipment is concentrated at the scene.

Speed is of the essence. A submarine in distress has only a restricted amount of electrical power, a severely limited capacity for maintaining air quality and may be fighting a losing battle against flooding. However, too hasty an evacuation using free ascent can also be hazardous. If there are no rescue vessels on the scene the survivors, provided they avoid getting the bends in their ascent, are likely to succumb to exposure whether or not they are wearing survival suits. To this end Canada is currently developing a modular, ship-transportable means for supplying air and other survival essentials to a submarine in distress. The objective being to sustain the survivors inside the submarine until they can be removed from the wreck in the best way possible, preferably using a DSRV.

## THE LIFE

Life aboard a modern conventional submarine such as the *Oberon* class boats with a crew of around 72 or the *Victoria* class with 48 crew, could never be described as "comfortable," regardless of one's rank or standing. The lack of space alone militates against this. Nevertheless, comfort is a relative thing and a submariner who sailed in wartime boats or the submarines of the 1950s and 1960s would probably describe conditions aboard the new *Victoria*s as absolutely cushy.

Conventional submarines, where space is always at a premium, are incredibly cramped. The interior is packed with miles of piping and wiring, hundreds of valves, equipment cabinets, engines, motors, torpedoes, a myriad of control consoles and all kinds of machinery. Every square centimetre of the boat is devoted to some purpose or other and getting around must be made with due regard. Equipment is sited with respect to the requirements of the machinery. The human occupants, being much softer than the machinery, must learn to cope with this.

Nothing else smells like a submarine. It's a smell compounded of diesel fumes, engine exhaust gases, the contents of inaccessible bilges, paint and other chemical fumes and human-related odours. Its intensity and quality varies depending on activities, but it is always present and quite unlike any other. It's also a good way to sort submariners out from a crowd.

Prior to the early 1980s it was the strident "Aroogah! Aroogah!" of the klaxon alarm that sent the entire crew scurrying to their diving stations to take the boat down as quickly and as safely as possible. This is a scene beloved of moviemakers, who insist on having the captain and other officers running about shouting all manner of strange commands, whereas in reality the klaxon alarm is all it takes. The rest of the action follows as a matter of well-practised drill, and such orders and replies as may be necessary are given in a normal speaking tone.

Klaxon alarms appear to have been introduced in the RN when transverse bulkheads were first put into submarines. In these submarines, even with the bulkhead doors open, there was a need to pass orders to all compartments simultaneously. Accordingly, commercial electric alarm horns made by a company that used the trade name Klaxon were adopted. A klaxon was installed in each major compartment and a code of alarms was established to tell the entire crew what to do. The first used, and longest lasting alarm, was two blasts for diving stations. Klaxons were certainly commonplace by 1915.

Pushbutton switches to operate the klaxons were installed in the tower near the upper lid and in the control room and were used only for the prescribed signals. As the pushbuttons were deliberately sited in exposed positions, it was agreed at an early stage that no action would be taken until the second blast. It was all too easy for someone in the tower to accidentally bump the alarm button, but they were unlikely to do it more than once in succession. Any klaxon alarm of two or more blasts sent the crew to their diving stations.

At the same time, all orders were being passed by word of mouth. Personnel were stationed in the passageways just to pass orders and replies between the central command and the compartments. The grouping of controls in the central command position or control room minimised the need to relay orders. Where the controlling station was remote from command, such as when the main motor switchboards were moved

HMS *B4* in a moderate sea. Note the substantial breakwater on the fore casing. Nevertheless, the bridge is very wet and there will be water pouring down the tower. (RNSM)

aft in the British *E* class boats, voicepipes were installed for relaying orders in addition to mechanical telegraph instruments and electric indicator lights.

Between the wars, extensive use was made of electric indicator lights. Complex switching and display arrangements were provided so that orders could be given and replies received quickly and quietly. A limited range of gongs and bells was also employed until superseded by electronic indicators and modern communications devices. Telephones were extensively used in submarines from a very early date for routine communications and for confirming complex orders.

As vacuum-tube technology developed during the 1930s, public address, or "main broadcast," systems were introduced. These were the forerunner of the more sophisticated and much more reliable electronic intercom systems in use today. The main broadcast provided an easy-to-use method of passing verbal orders and receiving replies throughout the entire boat or just between individual compartments and gradually did away with the shouting of orders up and down the passageways. Another feature of these systems was a distinctive alarm buzzer, which was used to give alarms for emergencies such as fire, flooding and the possibility of collision.

In post-war RN submarines, only two klaxon signals were used. These were two blasts for diving and three blasts to go to diving stations as the boat was going deep in an emergency. In the modernized *A* class and the *P* and *O* class boats introduced during the late 1950s, going deep was a normal occurrence requiring only the shutting-off of shallow depth gauges and some other minor services, and the three-blast signal became redundant. Instead, the raucous triple blast was replaced by a quiet voice announcing, "All compartments, shut-off for going deep" over the intercom.

Today's submarines are fitted with electronic alarms familiar to anyone who has watched modern American war movies.

The sound is very different, but very effective, and doesn't jar the senses the way that the old klaxon used to do.

The motion of a submarine on the surface in even a moderate sea is something best avoided. If that's impossible, then it must be endured in the knowledge that one will get used to it or that the boat will dive sooner or later. In the fore-ends the rise and fall of the bow is decidedly elevator-like and there is no pause top and bottom. When it's rough, the impact of the seas can be painfully jarring and moving around without hanging on to something solid is quite impossible. It is not unknown for submariners to arrive home after a rough surface passage only to discover that their hips and shoulders are black and blue from bashing from side to side in the passageways. Amidships, the effects are smoother, but still very rapid. Back aft the stern is actually whipped about as if it were elastic. Throw in the roll, which can be very sharp and steep, and all the ingredients are present to upset any stomach that's even the least bit queasy. Most experienced submariners gain their sea-legs very quickly but trainees and the unfortunate few who will never get used to it, usually succumb ignominiously after a while and end up with their heads in a bucket.

When near the surface the motion of the vessel is usually characterized by a lazy roll. In heavy weather, the seas surging over the hull adds an alternating up-and-down movement to the roll making depth keeping at periscope depth something of a struggle. The small submarines of the past used to experience a condition known as "pumping." This resulted when the action of the sea overcame the effects of the screws and hydroplanes, causing the boat to rise and fall in unison with the swell. The only way to escape it was to use speed. Severe weather can cause this to happen in a modern boat, but with the power available it is much easier to break away. When snorting in bad weather the occasional shutting of the snort head valve[12] by passing waves causes a temporary vacuum in the boat that can be hard on the ears. When shallow in severe weather, the suction created by the passing of waves over the upper deck has been known to suck fibreglass hatch covers right out of their frames leaving bits of hatch cover and the steel securing bolts

still in place. When deep, the boat is very stable and only the angles and dangles caused by sharp turns or sudden depth changes can upset one's equilibrium.

Continuous background noise is commonplace in both ships and submarines. In a submarine on the surface, it is usually provided by the ship's ventilation system, the battery ventilation system and the sea. Other machinery, such as the engines, can add to the noise, but, like the smell, some noise is nearly always present.

When under way on the surface the waves add a constant sound all their own. These can be soft and soothing or downright frightening depending on the weather. When dived everything is much quieter. Main battery ventilation is stopped, the ship's ventilation is slowed down, the wave noises are nearly inaudible and the loose fittings and things in drawers and cupboards stop banging and rattling.

Submarines can be uncannily quiet. There is a condition known as the ultra quiet state which is assumed when trying to avoid detection or when searching for an equally quiet or very distant adversary. When assuming this condition, a near perfect trim is achieved, propulsion is reduced to one screw (or the screw) running very slowly and all other machinery is stopped. Even fluorescent lighting is switched off because of the hum created by the starters. All hands not needed on watch either turn in or find something to do that does not make a noise. (The sailors like that part.) All automatic machinery controls are set to manual; even the refrigeration machinery is shut down. It is so quiet that people have been known to wake up in a sweat wondering where they are. From the sonar operator's perspective, the ultra quiet state is ideal because it eliminates all background noises and the sensitive equipment has a chance to work at its best. For everyone else, it is positively eerie. This sense of eeriness is enhanced by the natural sounds of the sea and sea life which can be heard very clearly on the underwater telephone speaker and through the hull itself.

Working inside a submarine is, without doubt, a real challenge. According to the naval architects and builders, all equipment is designed and installed with "...an adequate mainte-

---

12    The valve in the top of the air intake pipe that shuts the pipe off when the top becomes submerged.

nance envelope," which is to say it is designed to be easily accessible. However, as anyone whose job it is to maintain this electro-mechanical jungle will attest, it just isn't true. In a perfect world, submariners would all be small, skinny and double-jointed. In the real world, maintainers become contortionists and go to great lengths to devise special tools for otherwise impossible jobs. The compact arrangement of systems and their components means that the maintainer must have a complete understanding of the other systems in the vicinity of the equipment being attended to. Thoughtlessly operating the wrong switch, shutting or opening a valve or leaning against a not-so-stationary object, could have disastrous results.

Domestic arrangements are necessarily basic. Passageways are narrow; living areas cramped and privacy is at a premium. The cafeteria facilities, messes or bunk spaces, heads and washplaces are divided up to cater to the needs of the three primary groups, officers, senior rates and junior rates. The officers' mess is better known as the wardroom. In *Okanagan,* the most up-to-date of the O-boats, the main cafeteria was used as the principal gathering place. Aboard the other two O-boats, *Ojibwa* and *Onondaga*, there was no cafeteria and the crew slept, ate and socialized in the individual messes. In the new *Victoria*s, the domestic spaces are grouped in two adjacent areas on 2 Deck either side of bulkhead 35. The wardroom, senior rates' and junior rates' cafeterias are all located adjacent to the galley while the main storeroom is directly below the galley on 3 Deck. Heads and washplaces and the ratings' sleeping quarters are all forward on 2 Deck. Except for the cold room, heads and washplaces and a large equipment room, the bunk spaces are completely separate from most other activities.

Sanitary facilities in the O-boats consisted of four stainless-steel appliances (toilets or heads) arranged in a row of stalls along the after port side of the control room in the busiest passageway in the ship. It is rumoured that the same type of equipment has been installed in the *Victoria*s. Each head is provided with a foot-operated flap-valve that releases the contents of the bowl into the gravity-fed sewage-collection system. A hand-operated sea-water hose is used to wash out the bowl and send the contents down the pipe and into the sewage tank. Because of their tiny size and batwing doors, the stalls in the O-boats were popularly known as *traps*. When perched on the throne, the average-sized occupant's knees touched the doors. Because

the heads were ranged along the ship's side, the curvature of the hull prevented a normal posture whichever way the user was facing. When it was rough and nature called and the sitting position had to be assumed, one could wedge oneself into position fairly securely. One head was assigned to the chiefs and POs, two to the junior rates while the officers' head co-existed along with their only washbasin in a slightly larger enclosure. Important valves were situated in the deckhead inside these stalls and during certain drills the occupant could be rudely interrupted by the second panel watchkeeper who would burst open the doors to attend to the valves.

Aboard the O-boats, washplaces were located in the same general area as the heads. Washbasins were provided at a ratio of about one for every ten men. Shower facilities consisted of dedicated hot-and cold-water taps and a mixer valve that supplied a flexible hose with a hand-held spray nozzle on the end. There was no separate shower stall for the hands or officers. The bathroom fittings were stainless steel, the bulkheads had waterproof panelling while the decks were tiled and provided with drainage so that the entire bathroom became the shower stall. A plastic curtain could be pulled across the entrance to avoid splashing passers-by, but there was no door. Aboard *Ojibwa*, the senior rates' washplace, which was integral with the mess, featured an actual shower stall, but it was far too small for the purpose and usually served as a beer store. The valves and flexible hose were left accessible just in case someone actually wanted a shower.

The heads discharged into a large sewage tank, which was emptied daily after sunset during a procedure known as "domestic routines." This was accomplished by first flushing the collection pipe to clear it, then isolating the inlets and pressurizing the tank with air to blow the contents overboard through a hull valve. In order to restore the tank to use, the air used to blow the tank was vented off and the only way to do that was to release it back into the boat. The activated charcoal filter on the vent pipe outlet might just as well have been left inboard for all the good it did. With any luck the engines were running flat out and most of the stench was sucked into the engines. If not, it was a case of taking shallow breaths for a while.

Sinks and washbasins discharged into smaller slop drain tanks and these too were blown overboard and vented inboard. The boat became somewhat hummy for a while every evening.

At the same time, the bilges were pumped, and the day's accumulated garbage, or gash, as it's known in the navy, was disposed of. Gash collection and disposal is something of an art at sea. Dry waste, such as cardboard and packaging, is torn into small pieces, sorted, flattened and stored in tightly compacted bundles for later disposal. A hydraulic can crusher is fitted in the galley for flattening tins and, during the course of the day, these are flattened, collected and temporarily stored. All wet gash such as food slops, wet rags, paper towels and the like is collected in special fabric bags placed in shaped stainless steel containers. When the bags are full they are tied-off and replaced, the full ones being stored near the gash ejector.

The gash ejector is a large-bore tube that points outwards or downwards, depending on the boat. It is provided with a muzzle door, breech door and a connection to the main line. Gash can be ditched at any depth. It is important that the gash bags sink to the bottom and are not left bobbing in the wake of the otherwise covert submarine. When it is time to ditch gash, the bags of garbage are collected and sorted by weight. Those that are too light have crushed tins or other weighty trash added to them to give the necessary minimum mass. Several bags are loaded into the gash ejector at a time with the heaviest on top. The breech door is shut and the tube filled with water from the sea to equalize the pressure. The muzzle door is opened, the main line connection opened and the ballast pump is ordered to flush forward. The pressurized stream of water entering the top of the tube forces the contents down and out and the bags sink to the bottom.

Using the Chatham gash ejector fitted in the O-boats, the whole operation was controlled from a single operating position. The muzzle door and valves were operated by an ingenious, fully interlocked, lever-operated mechanism. Some submariners take a certain delight in acting the part of underwater garbage men. Like all other drills, ditching gash has to be accomplished speedily and safely.

Many boats carried a small domestic washing machine but doing laundry at sea was not practical. There was seldom enough water to permit running the machine and when there was, the only place clothing could be strung-up to dry was in the engine room. It was one thing to allow the drying of foul-weather gear and clothing soaked in bad weather, but the Chief ERA was usu-

ally averse to having his engine room turned into a sailors' drying room. In any case, clothing dried in the engine room acquired a distinct diesel-engine aroma. Submariners soon learn to spread their available wardrobe over the number of days and weeks at sea.

At sea, food is generally plain but hot, plentiful and properly prepared. The submarine service learned long ago that a well-fed submariner is a happier submariner, and that good food is a relatively inexpensive inducement to good crew morale, not to mention the benefits of its nutritional value. Modern submarines are provided with freezers, refrigerated spaces called cold rooms and dry storerooms adequate to the needs of the average trip to sea. When storing for a maximum-length patrol, the entire submarine becomes a deep-diving warehouse.

With the exception of a daily beer allowance, spirits are forbidden at sea. When alongside away from home port, all three messes have access to full bar facilities during leisure hours.

The only real personal space crew members have to themselves is their bunk. The submariner's bunk is known as his *pit* and that is where he *crashes*. Bunks are generally stacked three high with the top one very close to the deckhead and the bottom one practically on the deck. The space between bunks is just sufficient for a slim person's shoulders to scrape by under the bunk above when rolling over. Besides a mattress, sleeping bag and pillow, each bunk is provided with a curtain to keep out the light, a punkha louvre (ventilation outlet), a reading light and a steaming bag that clips on the bunk frame in which to stow the odds and ends of one's personal gear. Bedding and any loose clothing is stowed inside a waterproof mattress cover that is always zipped-up when the bunk is unoccupied. This keeps the bunk dry and helps control the proliferation of junk in the bunk space. Sailors have a tendency to store things—magazines, pictures, DND manuals, important files, an assortment of favourite tools, scarce spare parts and the like—under their mattresses.

Today's submariners crash in sleeping bags, usually with most of their clothes on. Any emergency in a submarine is an all-hands affair, and things happen too quickly for there to be any time in which to dress. Sheets, pillowcases and pyjamas are unheard of. Sleeping bags are dry cleaned between trips to sea.

Every crew member has a locker in which to stow kit. Typically this has the capacity of one medium-size bureau drawer. Some hanging space is available for shore-going attire and the like, and the experienced keep such items in waterproof bags. The more junior the crew members, the less personal space they will have available to them and the more adept they become at hiding things in the frames, and behind the piping and wiring runs.

The supply of fresh water is no longer the problem it was in the wartime submarines when it often had to be strictly rationed. It was because of this that World War One submariners were allowed to take bottled beer to sea. Ostensibly the beer was carried to augment the meagre water supply. Enough fresh water is now carried in the tanks to meet normal domestic demands including a minimal level of personal hygiene. If necessary, rationing can be imposed simply by shutting off the supply to high-volume outlets such as showers and washbasins. Fresh water making machinery, like the distillers in the O-boats or the reverse-osmosis desalinators in the *Victoria*s, can produce high-quality fresh water quickly and in quantity. However, these machines are electrically driven and they create noise. When the need for stealth or electrical power is uppermost, water conservation becomes a way of life.

The presence of water anywhere it shouldn't be is a matter of urgent concern and is always investigated with keen interest, as is the presence of fuel oil, or the sound of air escaping. Smoke of any kind is always treated as a very urgent matter. Submariners quickly become very conscious of these things. Even when asleep, experienced submariners have an uncanny awareness of what is happening around them. Sounds, smells, the tone in which orders and reports are being given over the intercom and the angle of the boat all serve to keep the crew informed, whatever their conscious state.

Conversation among submariners is often about the boat and its systems and the way things are done in one boat compared to another. Submariners take a keen interest in the these things; their very lives depend on their knowledge. They also talk about one another and about the usual topics young men discuss—sex, money, cars, time off, and how much of each they have, want, and hope to get. Inter-departmental matters generally receive a good airing, usually in a pub in a foreign port.

Terminology has changed considerably in the surface fleet since the introduction of the O-boats nearly forty years ago. Remarkably, the submariners have retained many of the older terms, especially those still in common use in the RN. In the Canadian Armed Forces (CAF) generally, personnel below officer rank are now collectively referred to as non-commissioned members (NCMs), or just members. These are divided into senior NCMs for the chiefs and POs, and junior NCMs for the master seaman and below ranks. After unification, the old term "rating," which encompassed all non-commissioned ranks, somehow acquired an offensive connotation. During the 1980s the term NCM was officially substituted. In submarines, however, rating is still widely used to describe the non-commissioned ranks and these are divided into senior rates and junior rates, or simply the hands, for junior members.

Smoking is now actively discouraged throughout the CAF. In submarines, smoking is restricted and likely someday will be eliminated altogether. When on the surface, smoking is allowed on the bridge at any time but is restricted to certain areas inside the boat both by order and by circumstances. For safety's sake, it has always been standard procedure to forbid smoking when the battery reaches the gassing point during a charge. The battery gives off hydrogen, which, under the right circumstances, is explosive. When dived, smoking is generally forbidden, but periodically permission is given for smokers to light up. This is announced over the intercom by the pipe[13] "One all 'round," which means that smokers may smoke one cigarette apiece in an approved smoking area. This is a throwback to the pre-1950s when the maintenance of air quality in submarines was a real problem, the deleterious effects of tobacco smoke less well understood and cigarettes cost fifteen cents a pack.

---

13  A pipe in this sense, is an announcement made over the ship's intercom. Traditionally, some orders are given by the blowing of a distinctive series of notes on a whistle known as a bosun's call, or pipe, hence the term. Aboard ships the bosun's call is still used to give orders and to precede announcements but is not used below decks in submarines.

At sea, all hands are in two watches and spend six hours on watch at a stretch. The watches are changed at 0100, 0700, 1300 and 1900 hours. As much as possible during the watch, personnel are rotated among the available duties depending on their trade and experience. Only the cooks and the steward and one or two day workers are exempt from standing watches.

In home port, only the minimum number of hands are required to remain aboard overnight. These men take turns making the rounds of the boat, or boats, tending to the safety of the ships and their machinery. In home port the batteries are normally charged from ashore, but, if necessary, the generators can be run. The requirement for there to be sufficient crew on board to sail the boat was discontinued in the early 1970s.

Submarines spend a great deal of time at sea, often more than the average surface ship. One submarine in a training area can provide services to a succession of ships and aircraft and it is seldom operationally convenient to put into harbour between exercises, except when everyone else does. When bad weather delays a training schedule, the submarine will usual-ly wait it out on station until its playmates are able to return, or the operation is cancelled altogether. Frequently, by the time an exercise is called off, it's too late to put into port and the submarine patiently carries on to the next exercise area and waits. When on the surface, submarines are slower than ships. Consequently they arrive later and must depart earlier to be in position at start time.

Only the necessary, minimum amount of work and maintenance is carried out at sea. Cleanliness and tidiness are safety matters. Loose gear tends to end up in the very worst places when there is an emergency. A rag or piece of clothing wrapped around a bilge strainer can spell disaster.

The real reward comes when one day the realization dawns on the submariner that he is a valued and important member of a close-knit, highly professional, team that actually makes its black upholstered sewer pipe run smoothly, efficiently and effectively. Now that's something in which to take a bit of pride.

To paraphrase a once popular recruiting jingle, there really is "No life like it."

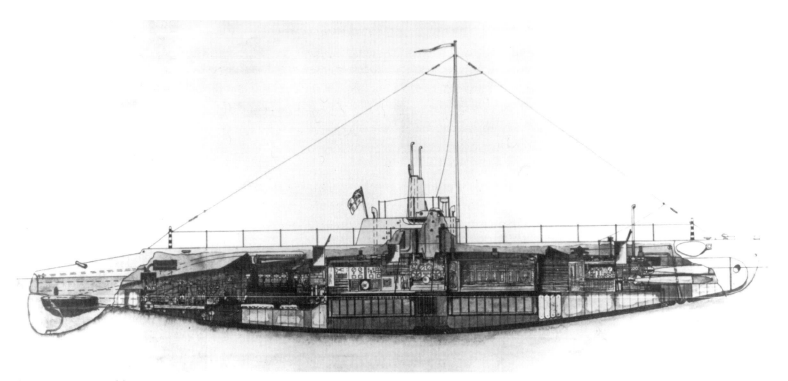

A cutaway diagram of *CC1*, used for training. (Maritime Museum)

THE STRATEGIC use of submarines and the tactics they employ were developed during the First World War, exploited in the Second World War and redefined during the Cold War. Submarine capabilities and tactics are constantly being perfected and updated.

As the world enters the second millennium, the nuclear-powered submarines of the first-class navies of the world—those of the United States, Great Britain, France and Russia—are without question the most powerful and potentially the most destructive mobile weapons systems known to mankind. At a secondary level of seapower, the conventional submarine still plays a critical role in the defence strategies of a host of maritime nations. All non-nuclear navies of any consequence possess modern conventional submarines and their capabilities and numbers are increasing steadily. Today, NATO countries alone maintain over ninety conventional attack submarines in the western hemisphere while non-NATO countries can field approximately seventy-five more. In the Asia-Pacific region, there are over two hundred conventional submarines in operation. The vast majority of these submarines, both western and eastern, were built during the past twenty years. Today, the conventional submarine is a fully accredited asset to most of the navies of the world.

On the eve of the First World War, the submarine was a novel and untried weapon. With the possible exception of Britain's First Sea Lord, Admiral "Jacky" Fisher, very few senior officers in any navy understood quite how it could be used, other than for harbour and coastal defence. In August 1914, there were only a handful of submarines in existence, many of them experimental and as much a threat to their crews as to their foes. It was Germany, a comparative latecomer to the "sub-marine club," who would utilize the new weapon to project seapower in the most effective and ruthless way possible, and set the world stage for the future use of the new weapon.

## THE KAISER'S U-BOATS

In 1914, the U-boat arm of the Kreigsmarine had been in existence for a little over six years. There were only twenty-four operational seagoing U-boats available, and in accordance with the mobilization plan, these were to be kept close to base. During the first few weeks of the war, the U-boats were stationed, twelve at a time, in a line across the Heligoland Bight where they waited for the British Grand Fleet to attack the High Seas Fleet in its anchorage in the Jade. When this attack failed to materialize, a select few were sent on attack sweeps into areas frequented by British shipping.

The young COs were eager to test their machines and prove their abilities. One U-boat returned to harbour after an unprecedented fifteen days on patrol and her proud captain reported that she was fully operational and could have remained at sea much longer. Another boat, too damaged by bad weather to attempt the heavily patrolled Dover Strait, circumnavigated the British Isles to arrive home after eighteen days at sea. These and similar incidents served to prove the long-range capabilities of the U-boats, and confidence in the new arm developed quickly.

The U-boats dispatched on hunting missions headed for heavily trafficked areas along the British coast and were quick to demonstrate their effectiveness against warships and merchant vessels alike. The first ship ever sunk by a submarine-launched torpedo was the light cruiser HMS *Pathfinder*. She was torpedoed on 5

## OPERATIONS

U-boats of No.2 Half-Flotilla at Kiel. 1914. (Author's collection)

September 1914 while patrolling in the approaches to the Firth of Forth by *U21* under the command of Kptlt Otto Hersing. The torpedo caused a magazine explosion and the ship sank quickly, taking most of her crew.

The vulnerability of British ships to attack by submarines was tragically demonstrated when *U9,* commanded by Kptlt Otto Weddigen, torpedoed three, 12,000-ton, British armoured cruisers in a single action. During the forenoon of 22 September, while *U9* was patrolling off the Hook of Holland, Weddigen's lookouts spotted mastheads and smoke in the distance. The submarine dived and headed for the area. It soon became obvious that there were three armoured cruisers steaming on a straight course in-line ahead. It was the opportunity of a lifetime.

Taking up a good attacking position without being spotted, Weddigen selected the middle ship, HMS *Aboukir,* as his first target. She was hit by a single torpedo, which set off a magazine explosion. The ship sank quickly. The second, HMS *Hogue,* apparently assuming her consort had hit a mine and acting on orders of the senior ship, came to the aid of *Aboukir. Hogue* too was struck by a single torpedo. She settled slowly by the bows and after about twenty minutes rolled onto her side and went under.

With his two bow tubes empty *U9* went deep to reload. When ready to resume his attack, Weddigen returned to periscope depth to survey the scene. To his astonishment, the remaining cruiser, HMS *Cressy,* was stopped amidst the wreckage of her consorts apparently rescuing survivors. When she caught sight of the U-boat's periscope *Cressy* got under way, steered a zigzag course and opened fire with her light armament. Stubbornly remaining near the two sunken ships, she continued firing wildly all the while transmitting a distress call on her wireless. Taking no chances, *U9* fired two torpedoes, both of which hit the frantic cruiser. Like her late squadron mates, she too sank quickly, capsizing in the process.

The success of this attack was due in no small part to the ineptitude of the British commanders who presented sitting-duck targets to the U-boat in the first place and then stopped to rescue survivors after the first ship was hit. Quite clearly, they didn't know any better. This incident also served as an unfortunate demonstration of the poor quality and inadequate supply of life-saving equipment then current in the RN. The only life jackets were those personally owned by individual officers, which left most of the crew literally swimming for their lives. Because of the speed with which the ships sank it was impossible to get any boats away except for those at the davit heads or already lowered to recover survivors from the first ship hit. There were no liferafts of any kind. In addition, the order to abandon ship was not given until it was far to late for survivors to get clear and many men were sucked into the powerful vortex created by the ships as they sank. Between them, the three ships took the lives of more than fourteen hundred officers and men.

*U9* sank a fourth cruiser, HMS *Hawke,* off Peterhead three weeks later.

The first merchant vessel ever sunk by a U-boat was the 866-ton SS *Glitra.* Outward-bound from Grangemouth for Stavanger with a load of coal, oil and iron plate, she was intercepted by *U17* off the Norwegian coast near Skudesnes on 20 October 1914. In accordance with the provisions of Article 112 of the German Naval Prize Regulations, the steamer was boarded, her papers seized, the crew sent off in their lifeboats with adequate provisions, and the ship scuttled by opening the seacocks.

On 23 November, in a superb demonstration of seamanship, *U18* under the command of Kptlt Hans von Hennig, actually penetrated the Grand Fleet anchorage at Scapa Flow. Having braved the currents of the Pentland Firth, Hennig entered Hoxa Sound, one of the entrances to Scapa, by following in the wake of a steamer. In a real twist of irony, the Grand Fleet was away making a sweep of the North Sea and the anchorage was virtually empty. While making her way seawards, the U-boat's periscope was spotted by a patrol vessel. In the pursuit that followed, the U-boat was rammed twice and damaged. Out of control in the treacherous currents of Pentland Firth, *U18* had the misfortune to run aground on the Skerries where Hennig and his crew scuttled the boat. Nevertheless, by her very daring *U18* had won an enormous psychological victory. Because it was nearly five hundred miles to the German base at Wilhelmshaven, Scapa had to that time been considered to be beyond the range of the U-boats.

To complete the opening phase of the U-boat war, *U24* torpedoed the pre-Dreadnought battleship HMS *Formidable* when she was making a Channel patrol on New Year's Day, 1915. The old battleship went down off Portland Bill, once again with a heavy loss of life.

As the British themselves wryly observed, their ships seemed to be giving the Germans every opportunity to sink them. In the first four months of warfare, a mere handful of U-boats had caused as much damage as a major sea battle. They had destroyed an obsolete battleship, three obsolescent armoured cruisers, two smaller cruisers as well as a submarine, a number of minor warships and several merchant vessels. On two occasions, submarine false alarms had caused the Grand Fleet to evacuate its supposedly safe anchorage at Scapa Flow and seek temporary shelter well out of range of the worrisome U-boats. All of this took place in a period when there were, on average, only four U-boats at sea per day. On the other side of the balance sheet, German losses had been unexpectedly high. Five boats were lost, two having been rammed and three from causes that could never be satisfactorily explained.[14]

By the end of 1914, the Admiralstab had come to the realization that the submarine was the most effective warship in their arsenal. From then onwards, the success or failure of the German war at sea would depend on the U-boats.

As early as August 1908, a German admiral had published an article that examined the idea of attacking Britain's merchant marine using seagoing U-boats. In his article, the admiral concluded that this would be far more valuable to the German war effort than would winning a major sea battle. Little heed was paid to his ideas at the time, but as the war gained momentum his strategic concept was revived. In October 1914, a prominent officer in the submarine organization suggested that the efforts of the U-boats should be directed against the weakest link in the British line of defence, the British merchant marine. At first, the Admiralstab expressed reluctance. Such a move, they maintained, would antagonize the European neutrals upon which Germany was depending for supplies from abroad.

On 2 November 1914, Britain declared the entire North Sea a war zone. According to international law, this was illegal, but Britain took the unprecedented move in order to prevent seaborne supplies, particularly those being carried in neutral bottoms and destined for neutral ports for transshipment overland, from reaching Germany.

Faced with the spectre of starvation through total blockade, the response came on 5 February 1915 when Germany declared a state of unrestricted warfare for all marine areas around the British Isles. This meant that the U-boats could torpedo Allied merchant ships at will and without warning. Flying the flag of a neutral country was no guarantee of safety. Only if the submarine CO was absolutely convinced the ship was a neutral and involved in neutral activities would it be spared. In effect, Germany had declared unrestricted U-boat warfare. Germany was conducting the same blockade of the British Isles using U-boats as the British were conducting around Germany using the ships and submarines of the Royal Navy.

When U-boat attacks on ships carrying American citizens angered the American government and aroused a strong anti-German sentiment among the American populace, Germany withdrew the U-boats from British waters. That was in April 1916. However, as their numbers increased and quality improved, the U-boats began roving further afield, attacking Allied merchant ships as far away as the American Eastern Seaboard and throughout the Mediterranean where they joined forces with U-boats of the Austro-Hungarian navy[15] and exacted a staggering toll.

In October 1916, the U-boats returned to British waters where, for a time, they abided by the rules of prize law. Early in 1917, Germany reinstated unrestricted U-boat warfare, balancing the risk of bringing America into the war against the possibility of actually winning. In this, they very nearly succeeded. At the height of the carnage, shipping losses far exceeded the ability of the shipyards to build replacement tonnage. On a global scale, the British Empire was losing four ships for every one added to the mercantile fleet. At that loss rate, defeat was predicted by November 1917.

Britain tried everything in its power to contain and destroy the U-boats but nothing seemed to have any really significant impact, certainly not in the short term. A three-pronged anti-submarine offensive was instituted consisting of building additional escort vessels, laying more minefields and trying experimental convoys in the North Atlantic.

---

14  Some historians blame these losses on mines, but as the British had yet to lay any in those areas, this is hardly likely.

15  The captain of one of those Austro-Hungarian U-boats was Georg Ritter von Trapp, patriarch of the Trapp Family Singers made famous by the Hollywood musical *The Sound of Music*. The mother of von Trapp's children was a granddaughter of Robert Whitehead, the inventor of the modern torpedo. Some time after her death, von Trapp married the rebellious novitiate Maria.

Escort vessels were turned out at a record rate; many equipped with hydrophones, an early form of asdic. The minefields in the Dover Strait were strengthened and patrolled day and night. Minefields were laid and re-laid in the Bight and around the ports used by the U-boats while British submarines lurked in the known traffic lanes. The biggest minefield of them all, the Northern Barrage, was laid between the Orkneys and the Norwegian coast. Although it accounted for a number of U-boats, this barrage was routinely penetrated. Not until 1918 did the U-boat loss rate rise significantly, but at no time were losses alone enough to demoralize or stop the U-boats. Throughout the war, production of U-boats exceeded losses in every year except 1918. On the other hand, the Royal Navy anti-submarine offensive was almost a complete failure.

Only the reluctant institution of convoy, beginning on the North Atlantic shipping routes in April 1917, saved the day for British commerce. By the end of 1917, ninety percent of British shipping sailed in convoy, and thereafter losses dropped dramatically. The U-boat had been confounded, if not actually beaten.

Germany lost the First World War on the battlefields of Europe and through social upheaval brought about by the reactions of a starving and disillusioned population. Germany had been forced into surrender, but her U-boat arm had not been defeated on the high seas, nor did it succumb to the mutinies that crippled the once proud High Seas Fleet.

A total of 178 U-boats were lost in action during the First World War.

Under the terms of the November 1918 naval armistice, the German navy immediately surrendered 114 seaworthy U-boats to the Allies. This left the Kreigsmarine with 62 seagoing boats in various states of repair and a further 149 under construction. However, as a condition of the Treaty of Versailles imposed by the Allies in June 1919, the German navy was stripped of all submarines and forbidden to possess any. To all intents and purposes, the German U-boat arm had been eradicated.

In German eyes, the U-boat offensive had been outstandingly successful, and, predictably, undersea warfare was given a significant priority in the reconstituted Kreigsmarine. As early as 1922 a U-boat technical department was secretly established in a German-run shipyard in Holland. To test their new designs, several prototype submarines were built for other European navies, while torpedo development was carried out in the factories of sympathetic nations. With the ascendancy of the National Socialist Party[16] to power in 1933, construction of sixteen submarines was surreptitiously commenced in German shipyards. Hitler repudiated the Treaty of Versailles in March 1935 and three months later entered into a Naval Agreement with Great Britain that allowed Germany once again to possess submarines. Eleven days after the agreement was signed, Germany launched her first submarine since 1918. In September 1939, after a twenty-one-year hiatus, the U-boat war was resumed, this time under a very different political regime.

## U-BOATS IN THE SECOND WORLD WAR

In the second round, known to history as the Battle of the Atlantic, the underseas assault on Britain's transoceanic lifeline was renewed with a terrible vigour. Again, as in the previous war, there was an initial shortage of submarines. As before, the Admiralstab had opted for a powerful surface fleet and, as before, would eventually be forced into relying on U-boats. Germany opened hostilities with fifty-seven U-boats of which only thirty-nine were suitable for action. Unrestricted submarine warfare was instituted from the beginning and eighteen U-boats were already at sea and on station when war was declared.

Surprised and alarmed by the intensity of the renewed U-boat campaign, the British responded by instituting redundant 1918 anti-submarine containment methods. The Dover Strait was quickly sealed with minefields and submarine nets while thousands of mines were laid in dozens of fields in a largely futile attempt to contain the U-boats. Germany occupied Denmark at an early date, sealed the Baltic and mined the Skagerrak and Kattegat. Once Norway and France had been invaded and occupied, the Germans set up submarine bases in both countries, circumventing the British minefields altogether.

---

16  The so-called Nazi Party.

Submarines of No.1 U-Boat Flotilla "Weddingen" at Wilhelmshaven, 1936. (Author's collection)

These bases provided them with relatively easy access to the North Atlantic.

Britain assumed the defensive at sea and instituted convoy from the beginning. The first outward-bound convoy left England only four days after the British declaration of war. However, the outmoded anti-submarine warfare tactics and weapons proved inadequate and mercantile losses climbed steadily. The RN had to completely rebuild its expertise in anti-submarine warfare before the U-boats could be brought to bay.

Only through the ability of Britain and the Allies to make good the losses in ships was the vital transatlantic supply route sustained during the first three years of the war. Even so, losses exceeded production most of the time. The shipping losses for 1942, the heaviest of the war, provide a chilling example of the devastation that took place at sea. In that blackest year of the Battle of the Atlantic, 1,155 merchant ships totalling 6,149,473 tons were sunk by U-boats in the North Atlantic alone. But the tide was turning.

Eventually a combination of long-range air support, the provision of small aircraft carriers to accompany the convoys, enlightened developments in anti-submarine warfare tactics, improved ships and weaponry, the breaking of the German naval codes and the inability of Germany to modernize its U-boat forces proved decisive. In the spring of 1943, after a desperate three-and-a-half-year struggle, the Allied navies inflicted such severe losses that the U-boats were temporarily withdrawn from the North Atlantic. Forty-three U-boats were lost

HM Submarine *H4* in the Mediterranean, 1917. (Author's collection)

during the month of May alone, a devastating blow to the Reichsmarine. Despite this setback, the U-boats returned to the fray and continued to harass Allied shipping until the ultimate capitulation in May 1945. However, never again would they enjoy the successes of the first phase of the Second World War, a period known to German submariners as the "Happy Time." Even the production of super U-boats near the end of the war came too late to have any significant effect on the outcome.

## The Cost

The casualties and shipping losses directly incurred by the U-boat campaigns in both World Wars are staggering, and should never be forgotten. During the course of both wars, Germany employed 1,150 U-boats on 6,274 operations. A total of 999 U-boats were destroyed (866 in action).[17]

The U-boats destroyed a total of 8,209 Allied ships totalling 27,200,678 tons, taking thousands of Allied seamen to their deaths.

17  V.E. Tarrant, *The U-Boat Offensive*, 1914-1945. Annapolis, Maryland: Naval Institute Press, 1989.

# BRITISH SUBMARINES IN THE FIRST WORLD WAR

Long before war was declared, the British submarine captains knew that their primary targets would be German warships. Despite the fact that Germany entered the war with the second largest merchant fleet in the world, mercantile targets would be rare. German merchant ships were quickly swept from the high seas, being interned, sunk, driven into port or confined to the Baltic. Much of Germany's seaborne commerce had to be carried in neutral bottoms. Throughout the First World War, British commanders were confined to the strict observance of the prize law.

At the outbreak of war, British submarine resources were divided into two broad groups: the overseas flotilla of eight *D* and nine *E* class boats based at Harwich, and a further 47 smaller *B* and *C* class boats divided among five coastal flotillas stationed at ports along the east coast, half a dozen more in the Mediterranean at Malta and Gibraltar and three were stationed in China.

Within hours of the expiration of the British ultimatum, British submarines were steaming for the Heligoland Bight (always "the Bight" to the British) to observe and report on the movements of the High Seas Fleet. The British submarines excelled in intelligence gathering, and Whitehall perfected an incredibly effective intelligence analysis operation as the war progressed.

Even this early reconnaissance provided the Admiralty with the data needed to plan and execute an attack that would be known in British annals as the Battle of Heligoland Bight. In this, the first naval engagement of the war, the British sent submarines supported at a distance by destroyers and a squadron of cruisers into the Bight to lure German forces into attacking them. The plan worked admirably and the battle unexpectedly escalated from destroyers chasing submarines into a full blown battlecruiser engagement. Germany lost two cruisers and a destroyer in this encounter. Losses would have been worse had not a heavy mist protected several badly damaged ships from the attentions of a pair of British submarines lurking along the route to their refuge in the Jade.

At the Battle of Heligoland, and on one other occasion early in the war, the British tried mixing surface ships and submarines in action but very quickly discovered that this was both dangerous and ineffective. The dived submarines were too slow to keep up with the high-speed manoeuvres of the surface ships, and there was no way to distinguish between a friendly submarine and an enemy one. The submarines also had difficulty distinguishing between friend and foe and almost attacked their own cruisers. Although the practice ceased, the concept was not forgotten and was resurrected towards the end of the war with the construction of the steam-driven 26-kt *K* class fleet submarines.

HMS *E9*, commanded by Lt Cdr Max Horton, scored the first sinking for the British submarine service on 13 September while patrolling in the Bight. As the story goes, *E9* had lain on the bottom most of the day about six miles south of the fortified island of Heligoland waiting for German ships to close her position. Unfortunately, the first lieutenant fell ill and experienced a severe bout of diarrhoea. After he made a few trips to the only head, the atmosphere became unbearable, and the CO decided to surface to air out the boat. When his periscope broke surface, Horton found himself staring at a German warship. His target was the *Hela*, an old cruiser used as the commander-in-chief's yacht. He fired two torpedoes, one of which found its target.

Throughout the war, Britain used her home-based submarines for reconnaissance and blockade in European waters and for local defence. British submarines soon settled down to waiting, watching, reporting and attacking at every opportunity. Theirs was to be a war of patient endurance interspersed with sudden and sometimes furious action, mostly against German warships.

## THE BALTIC FLOTILLA

There were some interesting side-shows for the keen British submarine captains. Seeking ways of taking the war to the enemy, the British offered to support the Russian Baltic fleet with submarines. The Russians, who were no match for the Kriegsmarine, agreed. During October, three *E* class submarines set out for the Baltic. Two, *E1* and *E9*, slipped into the Baltic via the Belts, the narrow passage of water between the

Danish islands lying between Denmark and Sweden. The third boat, which tried a different route, was detected and had to abandon the attempt.

Operating at first from Lapvik in the Gulf of Finland, *E1* and *E9* took the war to the Germans in their own waters. Despite having to follow the international rules of prize law when attacking merchant vessels, they nevertheless managed to temporarily dislocate the iron ore trade with Sweden and frequently disrupted German warship movements.

During the summer of 1915, four more *E* class and four *C* class boats were dispatched as reinforcements. The *E* class made the journey under their own power and slipped into the Baltic through the Sound, the narrow channel between the Danish island of Zealand and the Swedish mainland. This route was treacherous and the fourth E-boat ran aground in Swedish territorial waters. In contravention of international rules, she was shelled by a German destroyer before the Swedes could intervene. The boat was destroyed, half her complement killed and the survivors interned.

The small C-boats were towed to Murmansk and then transported overland on barges via the inland waterways to the Baltic. There they were reactivated in the Russian dockyard at Petrograd.

Despite enormous difficulties and the loss of two of their boats, the British submarine flotilla harried German shipping until the Bolshevik Revolution of November 1917 forced them to cease operations for want of support. When the Bolsheviks seized power, one of the first things they did was to negotiate an armistice with Germany. A condition of the treaty of Brest Litovsk that followed was the surrender of the British flotilla to the Germans. When they heard of this the British made preparations to leave Russia and scuttled their submarines. The crews then made their own way overland by rail to Murmansk where they boarded a British AMC sent to bring them home.

### THE DARDENELLES

The other show took place in the Aegean Sea during the Gallipoli Campaign of 1915. The objective there was to force the narrow, heavily defended Dardenelles Strait, enter the Sea of Marmara and attack Turkish shipping to prevent supplies from reaching the forces on the Gallipoli peninsula. After one partially successful attempt and several failures, an Australian submarine, HMAS *AE2* commanded by Lt Percy Stoker, RN, succeeded in penetrating the Strait to reach the Sea of Marmara. Unfortunately, *AE2* was sunk by a Turkish patrol vessel only three days later.[18] Nevertheless, she was followed by a regular succession of British submarines. These wrought havoc with shipping, virtually halting the flow of seaborne supplies to the Turkish forces. One of these submarines even gained fame by engaging cavalry and another by destroying trains with gunfire.

The Baltic and Dardenelles adventures were comparatively minor operations, but they proved highly effective in disrupting the enemy in their own waters, attracting disproportionate enemy resources from more important operations and in boosting Allied morale. Above all, they proved that the men and ships of the submarine service were capable of carrying out distant operations with only a minimum of support.

Fifty-three British submarines were lost at sea during the First World War, thirty-three from direct enemy action.

## BRITISH SUBMARINES IN THE SECOND WORLD WAR

Britain entered the Second World War with fifty-nine submarines. Many of these were obsolete and unsuited to the demands of modern warfare but new construction would provide a series of very rugged submarines, well suited to Mediterranean and North Atlantic conditions.

Home-based boats set up patrol lines and began laying minefields in the Bight even as war was declared. Attempts were also made to penetrate the Kattegat, with little success and several losses. Early in the war the RN suffered heavy casualties in the Bight, and had to pull back into the North Sea. At the same time, as many boats as could be spared from operations were assigned to training the anti-submarine ships that soon came streaming out of the shipyards.

As Europe fell under the Nazi heel so the British submarine flotillas were augmented by Polish, Dutch, Norwegian, Greek and Free French submarines. Before the fall of France, RN and

---

18   The wreck of *AE2* was discovered in 1998 and a joint Australian-Turkish operation is being launched to salvage her.

French submarines were used as convoy escorts between Britain and Halifax. Patrol activities were expanded to cover Norway and the coast of France, particularly the Bay of Biscay which was the route into and out of the newly established French bases. A year later when there was an acute shortage of escorts, RN boats were again assigned to the Halifax–UK and Gibraltar–UK convoys as escorts. With the Soviet Union's entry into the war, British submarines were called upon to act as surface escorts on the notorious Murmansk convoys. British home waters submarine reconnaissance and containment operations continued unabated throughout the war.

Meanwhile, three British flotillas assembled in the Mediterranean, one at Gibraltar, one at Malta and the third at Alexandria in Egypt. A handful of Allied submarines was attached to these flotillas, mostly to the one at Malta. In what is considered by many to be the most intense submarine offensive of the war, these submarines effectively crippled the German-led offensive in North Africa for want of fuel, reinforcements and supplies of all kinds.

In the Indian Ocean, British boats operating from the port of Trincomalee in Ceylon established patrols along the Malay Peninsula, laid minefields in strategic waterways and harassed Japanese shipping at every opportunity. A handful of valiant Dutch submarines, originally based in the Dutch East Indies, pursued a hit-and-run offensive in Indonesian waters even as their bases were being overrun. These, and British submarines from the Indian Ocean flotillas, eventually concentrated at Fremantle, Australia, and formed a valued adjunct to the large-scale American effort that developed in the Southwest Pacific from late 1943 onwards.

Seventy-four British submarines were lost in action during the Second World War.

## THE USN

American submarines played only a small part in operations at sea during the First World War and no USN submarines were lost in action. Only one American submariner was actually killed in action. He perished while undergoing operational familiarization training aboard a British submarine when it was sunk in error at night in the Irish Sea by a British steamer.

In the Second World War however, things were very different. After the Japanese attack on Pearl Harbor on 7 December, 1941, brought America into the war, USN submarines took the offensive in the Pacific with all the forces available. After losing their forward base of operations in the Philippines in early 1942, the USN submarines established a temporary forward base near Fremantle on the west coast of Australia and continued the war from there.

Despite some initial organizational and materiel setbacks, the Americans took a leaf from the German book and exploited it brilliantly in the Pacific, where they conducted the most successful submarine offensive in history. By war's end, the Japanese merchant marine had virtually ceased to exist, largely through the efforts of the fleets of modern, purpose-built American submarines and the use of innovative and aggressive tactics. American submarines also took a heavy toll of Japanese warships.

American operational submarines were almost totally absent from the Atlantic.

The USN lost 60 submarines during the Second World War, 42 to direct enemy action.

## OTHER NAVIES

The French and Italian navies entered the Second World War with large submarine fleets but both failed to exploit their potential. The Italian submarines were not particularly successful in either the Atlantic under German command or in their native Mediterranean, and suffered heavy casualties.

After the fall of France in June 1940, the majority of the surviving French submarines remained with the Vichy regime and were based in North Africa. Some of these showed their mettle when the British raided Dakar in 1940 and again in 1943 when the Allies, spearheaded by a strong American force, landed at several points along the coast of North Africa.

Several Free French submarines served under British command with considerable distinction. After the Italian surrender in the autumn of 1943, a number of Italian submarines were assigned to anti-submarine training duties on behalf of the Allies, particularly at Bermuda.

The USSR entered the war with a strong submarine force, but the political purges carried out by Stalin just prior to the war had stripped the navy of most of the best officers. Considering its size and the potential inherent in the Soviet submarine arm, its accomplishments were comparatively modest.

In December 1941, the Imperial Japanese Navy possessed a large, modern submarine fleet. The Japanese designed and built their submarines for a variety of purposes, including a class of large aircraft-carrying submarines and others purpose-built for the transport of supplies. They also built midget submarines at a very early date as well as the traditional attack types. A number of these were used in the attack on Pearl Harbor but without success. However, the Japanese high command was slow in defining the role of their submarines at the beginning of the war and much effort was wasted in ineffective attempts to use submarines in conjunction with the surface forces.

Japanese submarine forces were most effective in the Indian Ocean where they were able to operate independently. IJN submarines probably achieved their highest success rates during the battle of Guadalcanal at the end of 1942. In this protracted action, they were used aggressively for the single purpose of sinking enemy shipping. As the surface fleets were decimated by superior American air, surface and submarine forces, much of the IJN submarine effort was diverted to supporting their beleaguered and widespread network of island fortresses and as a consequence, the submarine offensive rapidly deteriorated. At the same time, USN anti-submarine capabilities improved enormously. As well, throughout the war the Americans led the Japanese in the development of electronic devices such as radio-direction-finding (RDF) and radar. As a result, Japanese submarine losses were horrendous, particularly when the losses are compared to their relative lack of success.

## THE COLD WAR

Throughout the three-decades-long Cold War, both NATO and the USSR maintained large submarine forces and developed strong anti-submarine warfare resources as well. NATO and Soviet submarines alike followed established convention by conducting long-range reconnaissance missions and through being deployed as underseas fleets in being ready to take the offensive against the opposing fleets and mercantile marine should the war turn hot.

It was in the middle of the Cold War that submarines took on a new and more sinister role in becoming strategic, mobile, long-range nuclear-missile-launching platforms. During the 1960s, atomic missiles first appeared at sea carried in external launching pods aboard diesel-electric submarines. The submarines had to surface to launch and guide them, and the missiles only had a range of a few hundred miles, but they were a precursor of the immense destructive power that is still being deployed at sea today.

It was during this period that the nuclear-powered submarine revolution took place, particularly in the USA and the USSR but also in Britain and France. These were the first true submarines, able to remain submerged indefinitely and totally independent of the surface.

Almost from the beginning nuclear-powered submarines were built in two basic configurations: hunter-killer attack submarines (SSNs), and intercontinental ballistic-missile-launching submarines (SSBNs), the so-called "Boomers." By the late 1980's, both the USSR and the United States were deploying nuclear-powered SSBNs carrying nests of vertical launched intercontinental ballistic missiles (ICBMs).

### NUCLEAR PERIL

With the advent of marine nuclear power plants and the deployment of nuclear warheads, came the problems associated with submarine accidents at sea and the subsequent release of radioactive materials into the world's oceans. Misadventure has already claimed a number of nuclear-powered submarines belonging to both the USA and the USSR. The potential for pollution of an insidious and dangerous kind from the wrecks of these submarines is a serious problem that is very much with us today and will be for the foreseeable future. So too are the difficulties associated with the disposal of worn-out reactors and redundant nuclear warheads now that the Cold War is over. This problem is particularly acute in the old USSR where the rusting hulks of discarded nuclear submarines line the jetties of the bases in Litsa Fjord and at Gremikha and where there is no money for modern nuclear waste disposal facilities.

WHEN the Canadian navy was established in 1910, it would have been impractical for the fledgling force to even consider operating submarines. Theoretically, possession of submarines would have had a deterrent effect on the aspirations of a prospective enemy, but the likelihood of Canada ever having to face such an enemy was negligible. During the First World War, the relative isolation of Canada's coasts served to provide a real measure of protection. In 1914, when a German cruiser squadron was loose in the Pacific, it never ventured within a thousand miles of Canadian waters, despite the fact that Canada was the only enemy territory along the entire Pacific Seaboard. On the east coast, a few German U-boats did operate off the Halifax approaches, but only for a brief period towards the end of the war. The east coast ports, like those on the west coast, were never directly threatened by German surface forces against which submarines could have been deployed effectively.

Considering the state of the country's finances between the wars, Canada had much more to gain in operating destroyers than submarines. However, there was a strong case to be made for having submarines for anti-submarine training, although this was not appreciated until the war was well under way.

The strategic situation in 1939 was considerably different than in 1914. Although neither coast was ever directly threatened by enemy surface forces, there was an effective threat from submarines. This was particularly so on the east coast where U-boats landed agents in the Bay of Fundy region and penetrated the Gulf of St. Lawrence and the St. Lawrence River itself, with seeming impunity. It became necessary to close the Gulf of St. Lawrence to shipping for a period during 1942 to the detriment of the movement of goods. The only enemy action on the west coast was the shelling of Point Estavan lighthouse on 20 June 1942 by the Japanese submarine *I-126*.

In the period between the wars, it was accepted that the U-boat arm of the German navy had been vanquished, and that U-boats would never again become a significant force in a future German war. Only when German rearmament began in earnest was this fallacy exposed. Because of this state of public denial, and the slow pace of naval weapons development between the wars, the RN was ill prepared for the U-boat onslaught that took place during the first three years of the Second World War.

To help redress the balance, Canada undertook to build, and ultimately to man, a fleet of anti-submarine escorts, the famous (or infamous, depending on your experiences) corvettes. When these ships began entering service, it was quickly realized that there was a real need for submarines with which to train them. The RCN had none, but training submarines were eventually provided by Britain through various means. At the same time Canadian officers were afforded an opportunity to serve in British submarines on an equal footing with their RN and other Commonwealth counterparts, as they had been throughout the First World War.

With the advent of NATO in the late 1940s and the intensification of the Cold War during the 1950s, the Canadian navy took on an increasing responsibility for anti-submarine warfare (ASW), reprising its Second World War role. However, during the war, ASW had been a specialty of the naval reserves and these had long been demobilized. The navy found itself having to scramble for expertise and manpower as well as for suitable ships.

With the regular incursion of Soviet submarines and intelligence-gathering vessels into Canadian waters, a new need for submarines became apparent. The RCN would have liked to

Port side of the "operating compartment" of a CC-boat. (Author's collection)

have been able to station operational submarines along Canada's maritime frontiers for surveillance and possible defensive operations, but this was never possible. Ultimately a joint Canada-USA underwater monitoring and airborne surveillance system was established, elements of which continue in operation to this day.

Along with the acceleration of ASW training that began in the early 1950s came a renewed requirement for seagoing training submarines. These were needed to provide ASW training services for RCN ships, carrier-borne anti-submarine aircraft and the long-range patrol aircraft of the RCAF.

It was the story of the war all over again: the RCN had no submarines. However, this time, surplus submarines and submarine building capacity were available, but the RCN was in the midst of rebuilding and the Canadian government steadfastly refused to consider the acquisition of submarines. Fortunately, Britain and the United States were able to provide training submarine services to the RCN on a part-time loan or rental basis for the next twenty years. Not until the mid 1960s did Canada acquire submarines of its own.

## POST-COLD WAR

It has long been recognized in diplomatic and military circles that Canada can ill afford to ignore the underwater dimension. Canada has the longest coastline of any nation, including a vast underwater Exclusive Economic Zone (EEZ) that extends for 320 km offshore. Beyond the east coast EEZ is the continuation of the continental shelf over which Canada also exercises stewardship under international agreements. Canada's economic welfare is very closely linked to its coastal waters and offshore resources. These waters support national inshore and offshore fisheries and an important international deep-sea fishery as well. The seabed holds an enormous, almost untapped wealth of oil, natural gas and minerals that is rapidly growing in importance as technology finds environmentally acceptable ways to extract them. Through these same waters sail the ships carrying the 350 million tons of cargo that are processed through Canadian ports every year. All of this ocean-dependent trade represents about forty percent of the Canadian gross domestic product.

Canada's maritime forces are responsible for the guardianship of this vast territory in all three maritime elements—on the surface, in the air and below the surface. These forces are dedicated to representing Canada's interests at sea in the maintenance of national sovereignty, the enforcement of international law and in the fulfilment of international security agreements. To meet these obligations, Canada's maritime forces must be capable of responding effectively in all three elements. As has been demonstrated in recent years, this is best accomplished through the deployment of a balanced maritime force, including ships, aircraft and submarines.

Canadian governments of the past have never been comfortable with the concept of the Canadian navy owning and operating submarines. To some extent, this is tied to an abhorrence for submarines that was created in the public consciousness by the experiences of the two world wars. Canadian politicians have used this public aversion to advantage on several occasions. Citing among other things a lack of public support for the concept, Conservative and Liberal governments alike have resisted repeated efforts over the years to equip the Canadian navy with submarines. Eventually, the military necessity of having submarines and the financial and diplomatic realities of renting submarine services from other governments made an impression in a way Canadian governments have always understood—in dollars and cents. Not until then were the naval authorities able to convince the government of the cost effectiveness of Canada owning its own submarines. However, even when submarines were eventually acquired, both quality and numbers were sacrificed on the altar of politics and short-sighted fiscal restraints.

One would like to think that the Canadian navy today possesses submarines because of a genuine conviction on the part of government that they are a necessary component of a modern, balanced Canadian navy. However, an examination of the performance of Canadian governments, past and present, reveals a less than reassuring story. From a layman's perspective, it appears that the navy has submarines at all only because of internal pressure from certain elements within the bureaucracy, and that it was expedient for the government to be seen to be co-operating with its allies. This was as true in 1964 when the O-boats were purchased as it was in 1998 when their replacements were acquired. Consequently, Canada's submarine service is destined by longstanding political tradition to occupy a somewhat tenuous existence in the eyes and minds of its political masters.

## THE WEST COAST

DURING the last week of July 1914, the possibility of global war came as a shock to the communities scattered along Canada's Pacific coast. A powerful German naval force, the German Pacific Squadron, was loose in the Pacific, and British Columbia had little in the way of seaward defences. When they pulled out in 1910 the British had left behind a small battery of obsolete coast defence guns at Esquimalt, a pair of antiquated gunboats, and a shed full of mines that no one knew how to prepare or lay. The four-year-old Royal Canadian Navy was represented by a solitary warship, HMCS *Rainbow*, a small, obsolete, protected cruiser originally bought for training purposes. Except for the equally obsolescent heavy cruiser, HMCS *Niobe* on the east coast, Canada possessed no other warships. From the public perspective, neither the British nor the Canadian governments appeared to be very concerned for the security of Canada's west coast.

In order to provide against a possible attack by Japan, then a rapidly growing Pacific naval power, a survey of the defence needs of the area had been carried out by the Colonial Defence Committee. Their findings were submitted in a report to the Colonial Office in 1905. The report recommended the construction of a naval base at Vancouver and the acquisition of a combined force of cruisers, destroyers, submarines and coastal artillery for the protection of Vancouver and Prince Rupert. The survey concluded that Esquimalt was too exposed to be used as a primary base, but that the defences there should be strengthened.

The British withdrew their forces a few years later, and the Canadian government had neither the will nor the resources to implement the findings of the committee. The only recommendation acted on was the acquisition of a pair of modern 9.2-inch guns for Esquimalt. By 1914, a protected emplacement had been built on Signal Hill, but the guns had not been mounted nor had proper range-finding equipment been provided.

In accordance with the terms of the Naval Service Act of Canada, which was enacted on 4 May 1910, the British Admiralty became responsible for the defence of all Canadian maritime interests once war was declared. However, in August 1914, the nearest British warships were on the other side of the Pacific. Meanwhile the German cruiser squadron had virtually disappeared from sight. The popular press ensured that the good citizens of British Columbia were made well aware that, to the Germans, their province and its fifteen hundred miles of coastline was the only enemy territory on the entire Pacific Western Seaboard. The United States and all of Central and South America were neutral, while both Chile and Argentina were openly pro-German. There was even a strong pro-German bias in certain parts of the United States. Given the circumstances, British Columbia had every right to be concerned about its security.

In fairness to the Admiralty, Naval Intelligence had predicted, correctly as it turned out, that the German Pacific Squadron would make for the South Atlantic and the River Plate area. There, they could join forces with cruisers already positioned in the West Indies and attack British shipping off Buenos Aires and along the west coast of Africa. As soon as war became imminent, a British squadron was assembled and dispatched to the South Atlantic to intercept the German cruisers should they follow their predicted course.

# PART 2
# THE CANADIAN SUBMARINE SERVICE

## THE FIRST WORLD WAR

*CC1* on her cradle at Yarrow's, Esquimalt in July 1916. (DND)

The Chilean submarines
*Iquique* and *Antofagasta*
at Seattle Washington,
August 1914.
(MARCOM Museum)

On their way south, two of these ships, the armoured cruisers HMS *Good Hope* and HMS *Monmouth,* called at Halifax to take on coal and fresh provisions. It was during that stop that the flagship embarked four Canadian midshipmen, recent graduates of the first class to complete their training at the Royal Naval College of Canada in Halifax.

## THE CC BOATS

The Premier of British Columbia, Richard McBride, was under intense public pressure to provide some form of defence for the Victoria–Esquimalt area and the Strait of Georgia, the inland waterway between Vancouver Island and the mainland. He wanted destroyers, as recommended in the Colonial Defence Committee survey, but none were to be had. When a Seattle shipbuilder, James Venn Paterson, offered to sell him a pair of brand-new submarines, the premier immediately began negotiations with Ottawa and the builder. Ottawa consulted with the Admiralty, which recommended their acquisition, provided Canada could man them.

Ordered by the government of Chile at a cost of $412,000 each, the two boats were built at Seattle, Washington, in the Moran Bros. Shipyard by Paterson's Seattle Construction and Drydock Company. They were constructed using machinery and drawings provided by the Electric Boat Company of New Jersey. In the shipyard they were known as *Chile 1* and *Chile 2*, or simply *C1* and *C2*. They were nearly identical and had a dived displacement of 420 tons. Both were armed with 18-inch-diameter torpedo tubes, four forward in *C1*, two forward in *C2* and one aft in both. When launched, they were given the names of Chilean cities; *C1* became *Iquique,* and *C2, Antofagasta.*

After attending their trials, the Chilean naval officials declared that the boats had failed to meet contract specifications. The purchase was put on hold, and the Chilean government stopped making payments to the builder. Negotiations were arranged to resolve the impasse, but by the end of July, no progress had been made. It was then that Paterson seized the opportunity and made his pitch to the authorities in Victoria.

While the diplomatic situation in Europe deteriorated, Naval Service Headquarters (NSHQ) went looking for officers with submarine experience. Remarkably, two retired RN submarine captains had already reported themselves for duty: Lieutenant Adrian St. Vincent Keyes, RN, in Toronto, and Lieutenant Bertram E. Jones, RN, in Victoria. Both had left the navy prematurely during the personnel reductions that took place in the RN early in the twentieth century. Both were on the British Admiralty's Emergency List. Accordingly, they were under an obligation to report for service should a war threaten. This they had done several days before the call went out for submarine officers, and both agreed to accept temporary commissions in the RCN. Somewhat reluctantly, NSHQ gave the BC Premier the go-ahead to negotiate for the purchase of the two submarines on behalf of the Naval Service.

After a series of clandestine negotiations with the builder, that involved neither the American nor the Chilean governments, the deal was completed on the day war was declared. The price by this time had risen to $575,000 per submarine, including a hefty brokerage fee for Paterson. During the day, a contractor's steaming crew unobtrusively slipped aboard the boats, topped-up the fuel tanks and made ready for sea. On the evening of 4 August, under cover of darkness and a light fog, Paterson spirited the submarines out of the shipyard on their silent electric motors. This was only hours before war was declared and the USA confirmed its neutrality. It was even before approval for the actual purchase was received from Ottawa.

Early the following morning Lieutenant Jones and an inspection party embarked in the tug *Salvor* and met the two boats in the Strait of Juan de Fuca in neutral waters. After a very thorough inspection of both submarines, he handed Paterson a British Columbia provincial government cheque for $1,150,000. The two submarines arrived at Esquimalt during the forenoon of the first day of the war. Their appearance off Esquimalt put the wind up the locals, and they narrowly escaped being shelled by the militia guarding the harbour approaches. The two boats arrived only hours ahead of an American cruiser that had been dispatched to stop the transfer. Some hours after their arrival, Premier McBride received a telegram from Ottawa authorizing him to proceed with the purchase.

When it came to naming the two boats the naval authorities at Esquimalt suggested calling them after the two principals in the deal, McBride and Paterson, but NSHQ had its own ideas about names. A few days later, on 7 August, they were commis-

HMCS *Shearwater*, 1915, with CC1 and CC2 alongside. (Maritime Museum of BC)

sioned into the Royal Canadian Navy as HMC Submarines *C1* and *C2*[19] (later changed by the addition of the word Canadian to *CC1* and *CC2*).

Two crews were assembled from a mixture of regular and reserve volunteers drawn from *Rainbow* and the base at Esquimalt. Only the two captains, one of the coxswains and a stoker petty officer had any previous experience in submarines.

However, what the remainder lacked in knowledge they made up for in eagerness and hard work. One of their first jobs was the changing of hundreds of Spanish tally plates for English ones. Within a few weeks the decommissioned RN sloop, HMS *Shearwater*, was converted into a depot ship for the two submarines and recommissioned in the Canadian navy. The little flotilla was now complete.

19  It is sometimes claimed that this was because of their resemblance to the British *C* class but there was no such similarity. As both COs had commanded *C* class boats and knew better, this explanation must be discounted altogether.

One eye witness to all of this was Barney Johnson, a Master Mariner and marine pilot. Born into a seafaring family at Birkenhead, England, on 22 February 1878, Bernard Leitch Johnson had been raised to the ways of the sea. Soon after turning twelve he was apprenticed to a Liverpool firm of ship owners and, on his fifteenth birthday, signed aboard the sailing ship *Benmore* as an apprentice seaman to begin the long haul from the fo'c'sle to a command of his own. It was aboard the square rigger *Borrowdale* in July of 1894 that he first sighted, and fell in love with, the lush, wild beauty of the British Columbia coast.

When the ship sailed from Vancouver harbour, young Johnson stayed behind to make his own way in his newly adopted homeland. By 1899 he had won a mate's position aboard the tiny steamer *City of Columbia*. In 1902 he was granted his coastwise master's certificate and the command of the steamship *Capilano*. Five years later he received his master's certificate, foreign-going, for both steam and sail and, by 1910, was captain of the *Prince Rupert*, a brand new Grand Trunk Pacific fast passenger steamer. In 1913, by then ten years married, Johnson took a position as a marine pilot at Vancouver so as to be able to spend more time with his wife and young son. They were just getting settled when Johnson became aware that war with Germany was imminent.

The day before that fateful 4 August 1914, Johnson had volunteered his services as a pilot for the cruiser HMCS *Rainbow*, but only for a month. He never sailed in *Rainbow*. Instead, he offered to help out with the newly arrived submarines. He was about to embark on a four-year career as a submarine officer of some distinction.

As he remembered in his memoirs:

Selecting the submarine crews was an interesting procedure. About fifty loosely screened recruits were mustered and were told by Keyes that we were selecting crews for the submarines which was a voluntary service and there would be no loss of respect if any man did not wish to volunteer. They all stood fast. Keyes then said a few words about the responsibilities of submarine personnel, pointing out that the failure of any one to do his job correctly and quickly could jeopardize the safety of the ship and of all hands. Orders were then given "Seamen, one step forward, Stokers one step back, march. Electricians fall-out on the right, steamfitters on the left." Those who did not fall into those categories were told that their volunteering was appreciated and were dismissed. Then came the careful screening of the selected volunteers and fortunately several Royal Navy deserters were located, who, with a King's Pardon, and together with some personnel from HMS *Shearwater*, gave us one strand of disciplined men but not a thread of submarine experience. The Base Engineering Officer found our Engine Room Artificers and a retired Lieutenant, RN, a Midshipman and a Cadet, both RCN, showed up to complete the officer personnel.[20]

The two captains and officers for the CC-boats and *Shearwater* came from a variety of sources including the RN, the RCN and the RNCVR. The junior submarine CO and both first lieutenants were usually RNCVR officers. Each boat also carried a junior officer under training. During the first two years these were RCN midshipmen preparing to serve aboard RN submarines overseas, and later, junior RNCVR officers.

The senior CO, Adrian St. Vincent Keyes, was a gifted and charismatic leader who immediately set to work making his submarines operational. An American submarine captain was hired to help with learning how to handle the new boats. All leave was stopped. Training classes were started and on-job-training organized. Eight 18-inch torpedoes were shipped to Esquimalt by rail from *Niobe*. These were modified to fit the American torpedo tubes, embarked and test fired using cork-filled practice heads. Escape training, such as it was, was conducted in the public swimming pool in Victoria. Practice dives and torpedo firings were made in full view of the Victoria waterfront, much to the delight of the locals who gathered on the Dallas Road to watch. In only a few hectic weeks Keyes and Jones had the crews trained and the submarines armed and running effectively.

20  B. L. Johnson, *Naval Events 1914-1918*, Vancouver City Archives, Add. MS 581.

Where it all began. Central command in one of the CC boats looking forward. It was not really a control room, there was no after bulkhead. The hand pump on the left supplies fresh water to the galley sink.
(Maritime Museum of BC)

The forward torpedo compartment of *CC2*, with the radio operator's stool in front of the radio cabinet, left.
(MARCOM Museum)

For as long as the German squadron remained at large in the Pacific the submarines conducted patrols in the Strait of Juan de Fuca. They also made visits to the small communities along the coast to show the flag and provide a measure of reassurance. Within the month HMS *Newcastle,* a modern British cruiser, and the Imperial Japanese cruiser *Idzumo* arrived to bolster local defences. The presence of these warships was particularly appreciated when reports began arriving describing the trail of destruction left by the German cruiser *Emden* in the Indian Ocean. During a 70-day rampage, she single-handedly sank 68,000 tons of shipping. Far away perhaps, but a dramatic demonstration of what could happen, especially as one of *Emden's* sisters had detached from the squadron and had made an appearance as close to British Columbia as Honolulu.

Tensions rose to near panic when, on 1 November, *Good Hope* and *Monmouth* intercepted the German squadron and were both sunk in a short, one-sided battle off the coast of Chile near a place called Coronel. The two cruisers went down in rough seas after dark and there were no survivors in either crew.

The Royal Navy had suffered a decisive defeat at sea—its first in almost a century— and the RCN its first battle casualties.[21] Retribution was swift and decisive. Within days of the news, a powerful battlecruiser squadron was dispatched from England. In a running battle off the Falkland Islands on 8 December 1914, four of the remaining five German warships were destroyed. With the destruction of the last German ship in March 1915, the crisis evaporated entirely.

Once the threat to the west coast had been eliminated the submarines were laid-up for the winter while NSHQ and the government decided their fate. After the exciting days of the first five months of the war, this was to prove a depressing time for all concerned. Early in 1915, Adrian Keyes resigned his Canadian commission and returned to England to become a decorated destroyer and Q-ship captain. In the spring, the government made the decision to keep the little submarines and their depot ship in operation as a contribution to the overall imperial maritime defence effort. Command of the flotilla then fell to Bertram Jones.

Shortly after their purchase, the acquisition of the CC-boats became a politically contentious issue. On 11 February 1915, the Honourable William Pugsley, Member for Saint John, rose in the House to present a scathing report implicating McBride and Paterson in a web of intrigue and financial wrongdoing. His presentation was based on a combination of fact, supposition and guesswork, but it drew enough attention to instigate an official investigation.

Some of the facts seemed particularly damning. The first was that the Chilean naval authorities had rejected the boats because of their poor performance. This made it seem as if the submarines were inferior, whereas in fact it was really a matter of failing to meet the contractual definition. The second problem occurred when McBride reported the purchase of the boats to the prime minister by telegraph. The message stated he had paid a price of "one million and fifty thousand dollars." Apparently a clerical error, this was quickly amended to $1,150,000, but the damage had been done and the opposition took full advantage. When it was discovered that Paterson had padded the price to include a generous commission for himself, the proverbial fat was in the fire. As well, the repair costs and maintenance expenses for the boats seemed to be very high. Subsequent investigation revealed that the boats had been built using inferior materials and that some of the workmanship was sloppy. When a report mentioning that the boats were difficult to handle when dived was revealed, the matter of their safety also became an issue. Most of these technical problems had been cleared up in the first dockings, but the political stage was set and the play must out.

The submarines were included in an auditor general's investigation into purchases made under the War Appropriations Act. Although damning allegations were made, nothing was proven. Eventually a Royal Commission (the Davidson Commission) was established to investigate wartime appropriations, again including the submarines. The outcome of this investigation, in which plenty of detailed expert evidence was given, cleared McBride of any actual wrongdoing but characterized Paterson as a rank opportunist.

21  Midshipmen Cann, Hatheway, Palmer and Silver.

In 1917, the Admiralty asked that *CC1* and *CC2* be sent to the Mediterranean. Accompanied by *Shearwater*, the two boats undertook the seven-thousand-mile journey to Halifax. During the voyage, they became the first ships flying the White Ensign to pass through the recently opened Panama Canal.

The trip was fraught with hardships. Heavy seas, constant mechanical and electrical breakdown and blistering heat all contributed to the misery. That the boats made it as far as Halifax is a tribute to the sheer doggedness of the crews and the ingenuity of the engineers. However, by then it was obvious that the primitive diesel engines were too badly worn to make the rest of the long journey. The boats were refitted and retained at Halifax for local defence while *Shearwater* was re-armed for use as a patrol vessel.

## THE CANADIAN-BUILT BRITISH H-BOATS

As early as the end of August 1914, Canadian Vickers placed a proposal[22] before the Deputy Minister for the Naval Service to build two or three Electric Boat Company submarines for the RCN at Montreal. At 400 tons dived displacement and mounting four 18-inch torpedo tubes in the bow, they were similar to *CC1* but with improved engines. Vickers was offering to have the first two boats completed by the 1915 opening of navigation on the St. Lawrence River for a price of $572,000 each. This was $2,800 less than the amount paid for the CC-boats, plus a considerable return to the Canadian economy through wages paid to Canadian workers and materials purchased in Canada. A further $50,000, it was claimed, would have been recoverable from customs duties. The third vessel, it was predicted, could be ready for trials a month after the first pair.

As they had done in the case of the CC-boats, the Canadian government sought the advice of the Admiralty. This time Whitehall advised they reject the offer on the grounds that the design was unsound, and that the boats could not possibly be built that quickly. The Canadian government acquiesced and turned down the offer. This whole affair provided a precedent that would typify the performance of successive Canadian governments with respect to the acquisition of submarines, even to the present day.

On 3 November 1914, Charles M. Schwabb, President and Chairman of the Board of the Bethlehem Steel Corporation of Pittsburgh, Pennsylvania, struck an extraordinary deal with Admiral "Jackie" Fisher, First Sea Lord, to supply twenty submarines "of the latest design" to the Royal Navy. Bethlehem Steel subcontracted the building of the submarines to the Electric Boat Company. Electric Boat in turn proposed their latest medium-sized submarine. Three of a similar type had already been built for the USN, which called them the *H* class. At 440 tons dived displacement they were not the biggest available by any means, but because of the USN contract the parts could be produced quickly and in quantity. They were almost identical to the boats turned down by the Canadian government but two months before. The design was good enough for Jackie Fisher and his boss, Winston Churchill, First Lord of the Admiralty. Churchill, like Fisher, fully appreciated that secretly adding twenty submarines to the Royal Navy's strength inside six months would be quite a coup.

Originally, the submarines were to be shipped to Britain in kit form for completion in British shipyards at a cost of $500,000 apiece. Electric Boat had perfected this system during the Sino-Japanese war of 1905 when they supplied both Russia and Japan with prefabricated submarines. Construction was begun almost immediately, some at the Fore River shipyard in Quincy, Massachusetts, and the rest at the Union Iron Works shipyard in San Francisco. When the American government threatened to take Electric Boat to court for possible violation of American neutrality laws, a new deal—and a new price—was negotiated with the Admiralty. The first ten boats would be built under Contract 602E at the Canadian Vickers shipyard near Montreal. As Electric Boat was fifty percent owned by Vickers, their Canadian operation was the obvious choice. The first pair was to be built, tested and ready to sail in four and a half months, with the remainder following at a rate of two per month. The price was $600,000 per boat, or about double the price of a standard British *E* class boat that was taking more

---

22  PAC RG 24 Vol. 4018, 1062-4-2. Canadian Vickers tender to build Design 20E Holland boats for the Naval Service of Canada.

The bell from *H6*, now in the MARCOM museum. The inscription reads "H.M. Submarine H6, launched by Mrs. Campbell-McGregor May 12 1915." Campbell-McGregor is believed to have been the Admiralty Naval Overseer. (MARCOM Museum)

Royal Navy *H* Class submarines *H1*, *H2* and *H3* at St. John's Newfoundland June 1915, en route to Gibraltar. (Author's collection)

than twice as long to build. The second batch of ten was to be built at the Fore River shipyard and handed over when the diplomatic situation permitted.

On New Years Day 1915, the British Admiralty arbitrarily took over the Canadian Vickers Shipyard and stopped all other work, including an important icebreaker contract. An Admiralty Overseer's Party and an Electric Boat Company management team arrived and, under their direction, the Vickers workforce began an around-the-clock submarine-building program.

Raw materials from Bethlehem Steel, and castings and machinery from Electric Boat were shipped in from the United States. Contracts were let locally for parts that could be produced in Canada. The project was kept secret. A high fence was erected around the shipyard property and the Canadian Militia provided guards. The entire workforce was provided with identity cards, and security at the gates was rigidly enforced. The first keel was laid in the building sheds at Canadian Vickers on 11 January 1915.

All of this activity took place without the consent, or even the official knowledge, of Ottawa. Eventually the Foreign Office informed the Canadian government via the Governor General that Canadian Vickers had been commandeered by the

Admiralty to build submarines for the RN. By that time the work was already well advanced. Relationships between Ottawa and the British Foreign Office were severely strained by this blatant act of imperial arrogance. However, Canadian Vickers was owned by the British parent company and there was nothing Ottawa could do about it without compromising the war effort. In the end, it was just one more incident that served to wean Canada away from its last ties with British colonialism.

The situation became even more strained when Ottawa's request that two of the boats be diverted to the Canadian navy for the defence of the Halifax area was refused by Churchill. The First Lord curtly insisted that Halifax was not in any danger, and that furthermore, the RN would ensure its protection.

The ten submarines were all built, put through their trials and commissioned well within the time stipulated in the contract, thus earning Electric Boat a considerable sum in early-completion bonuses. The construction of these submarines was an extraordinary industrial accomplishment for Canada and much of the credit must go to the Electric Boat Company management team and the workforce at Canadian Vickers.

The boats were commissioned in two groups. *H1* to *H4* were finished first. They completed builder's trials in the St. Lawrence with deep-diving trials being conducted at Murray Bay (La Malbaie). On 25 May 1915, the Governor General, accompanied by Her Royal Highness Princess Patricia, presided at the commissioning of HMS *H1* at Quebec City. The other three followed within days, but with less ceremony. Following a short stopover at St. John's, Newfoundland, the four boats sailed for the Mediterranean in company with the armed merchant cruiser (AMC) HMS *Calgarian* carrying a contingent of Newfoundland infantry.

The remaining six boats, *H5* to *H10,* also completed their trials in the St. Lawrence and were commissioned at Quebec City about a month later. After a two-week stay at Halifax they crossed the Atlantic in company with the cruiser HMS *Carnarvon* and two freighters carrying spare gear, emergency fuel and general cargo. The submarines arrived in England on the first anniversary of the beginning of the war. The transat-lantic crossings made by the H-boats were the first ever undertaken by submarines.

As the submarines neared completion, the two officers and fifteen men in each crew were drawn from among the flotillas in England and sent over by steamer. In order to alleviate the heavy demand on British manning resources, NSHQ offered one complete passage crew. When the Admiralty indicated that they preferred to keep the crew for the duration of the war, the offer was withdrawn on the prime minister's insistence. Three Canadian officers joined the second group of boats and one able seaman was borrowed by the RN to replace a man taken ill. During construction three diesel mechanics were recruited into the RNVR as engine room artificers at Montreal, but it is not known whether they sailed in the submarines. As far as is known no Canadian navy ratings served in RN submarines overseas. Intriguingly, Commander John G. Bower, RN,[23] himself a submarine captain, mentions that the crew in *H8* commanded by Barney Johnson, contained a high proportion of Canadians and Scots, but this has not been substantiated.

The building and manning of the H-boats is well documented, both in personal accounts and on the official level. The Admiralty, with Canadian concurrence, transferred Barney Johnson to the Royal Navy Volunteer Reserve (RNVR) and gave him command of *H8*. Following his arrival in England he was transferred to the Royal Navy Reserve (RNR)—where he rightly belonged— and he remained in submarines until the end of the war.

One of the most candid descriptions of the commissioning of these submarines comes in the form of a collection of letters written by Lieutenant Sam Brooks, RN. Brooks was First Lieutenant in *H9* under the command of Lieutenant Frederick Williams-Freeman, DSO, RN.

Sam Brooks was first lieutenant in an *A* class boat at Devonport when he was posted to Canada. Most of *H9*'s crew had sailed together before, and Williams-Freeman had just completed his qualifying period as a new CO. They boarded the Allan Line steamer RMS *Corsican* at Glasgow and set sail on 5 June for the ten-day crossing to Canada. They were looking forward to a

23 J.G. Bower, *The Story of Our Submarines.* London: William Blackwood and Sons, 1919.

Building H-boats at Canadian Vickers. (PAC)

leisurely four to six weeks at Montreal while the boats were being finished before they had to get down to some serious work.

*Corsican* only had two classes of passenger: cabin and third, which meant that the two officers were thrown in with the ERAs and everyone else except for the seamen, stokers and civilian commoners. Once the passengers had recovered from the initial bout of seasickness and made one another's acquaintance the trip became more bearable. This was especially so when the two young officers discovered some female telephone operators among the cabin-class passengers, and struck up a friendship with one of the barmaids. Meanwhile, the sailors befriended a group of female domestics amongst the third-class passengers.

The party came to an abrupt end, however, when the ship made its scheduled stopover at Quebec City on Tuesday, 14 June, and the entire submarine crew was whisked off the ship. Sam described the moment in a letter to one of his female relatives:

> As the Corsican came alongside at Quebec we perceived several seamen on the quay following a wildly gesticulating Commander, RN. In about half a jiff we were simply snatched out of the ship, bag and baggage (half packed)—rushed round the dockyard—told the boats were ready for us, and we should probably sail for England on Sunday! That was some jar, wasn't it?

The H-boats, now wearing their coded pennant numbers, are joined by *H4* and ready to depart for the Mediterranean, June 1915. From inboard: *H2, H4, H1, H3*.
( F. Gordon Bradley)

The final lot of H-boat hull kits being built at Vancouver. The Russian revolution would preclude their delivery and they ended up in the USN as *H4-H7*.
(UBC Archives)

It was then they were told which submarine they were taking over. As it turned out, they were going to join their boat the next day while she was undergoing builder's trials. The crew would have a week to ten days in which to learn their way around the boat before they commissioned her and set sail. They joined *H9* at 6:00 a.m. the following morning, never having seen a submarine of the type before. Shortly afterwards she set sail down the St. Lawrence on a four-hour full-power trial. The remarkable thing is that nobody seemed particularly perturbed by the whole proceeding. As Sam Brooks remarked at the end of his letter:

> The contractor's people, of course, ran the boat as she is not turned over to us yet, we are just passenger-pupils. Now there is something to make up for the rush & panic & no Montreal—and that is the boat. She is top hole and thank goodness I got this job. I had a good grovel around her works this afternoon and then came ashore.

Because all ten submarines completed their trials within a two-month period, there was a large civilian trials party living ashore in the hotels at Murray Bay. The officers were put up in the same hotels. Sam described the situation at Murray Bay in a letter to his sister Mary written from the Chateau Murray two days after the previous one:

> This is the strangest spot on earth. It is on the north shore of the St. Lawrence about 80 miles below Quebec and quite 'in the wilds'. There is no railway for miles and miles; all communication is by steamer and telegraph. There are lots of houses here and two large hotels (this being one) but they are all built very roughly of wood,—plank walls inside with no paper or varnish and fitted throughout with electric light, even the wee cottages have electric light and the main street, containing about four shops, has lovely lamp posts.

> I must say they feed us well at this place, salmon and trout and cream galore. Not one of the natives can speak English but they speak French with a Yankee accent [Sam spoke schoolboy French]. However, there are quite a colony of Yankees and English, with wives and families, in this hotel, bossing the submarine trials.

We did a 200-feet dive this afternoon & leaked like a sieve, so that means another day here and another test. When all is correct we commission and go back to Quebec to paint and store & square up. It is really marvellous to compare the workmen here with the English dockyardmen. They do things in about one hundredth the time here with less men & better work. The building of these boats must have been a record I should think.

Some things are much the same no matter who is involved or when, and getting a submarine ready for sea is much the same in any day and age. They formally commissioned on 27 June and Sam described what it was like for him the following day, only a few days before sailing for Halifax.

> It is very strenuous work on the boats now, the very last of the firm's workmen are leaving to-morrow and *H9* is a solid mass of wet paint & inches of rubble and dirt on the decks, and piles and piles of packing cases of stores on the quay.

> How we are ever going to square things off in 4 days goodness only knows. We are booked to push off on Saturday [3 July].

And sail they did, all six submarines, on schedule except for one boat that damaged a screw getting away from her berth. The crew changed the screw on the spot without the aid of a dock. The boats and their escort, HMCS *Canada,* enjoyed an uneventful voyage until stopped by a pea-soup fog just after clearing the Strait of Canso. They spent the night anchored in Arichat Bay. That evening *H9* held an impromptu concert party on the casing for the local fisherfolk who came out in their boats. They played the gramophone they had received from Vickers as a commissioning present. The fishermen came only as close as was necessary to hear the music and none of them ventured so much as to touch the submarines. Weighing anchor in the morning they chased the fog banks towards Halifax but managed to stay in the clear. In his final letter, Sam describes the culinary arrangements aboard *H9:*

> We have got a most excellent cook in the shape of the senior Able Seaman & Freeman & I have been living like fighting cocks. Had a fine rush 'round Saturday

morning shopping and dashed on board for the last time just before we shoved off with a leg of mutton in one hand & a silver basket in the other. He [the AB] cooked that mutton just fine and has made a jam tart & buttered egg gadgets with fried ham & toasted sardines—lovely!

## MORE H-BOATS

In an attempt to employ the submarine-building capacity that had been established at their shipyard, Canadian Vickers submitted another proposal to the Canadian government[24] at the beginning of June 1915. Vickers proposed the construction of two *H* class submarines at a cost of $600,000 apiece with a further bonus of $50,000 per boat for finishing construction before freeze-up. NSHQ fully supported the proposal and passed it on the minister who forwarded it to the prime minister. Overcome by the enormous cost, lacking the will to again consult with the Admiralty and beset by an impending investigation into the purchase of the CC-boats, the prime minister abruptly terminated any further discussion about building submarines.

In the autumn of 1915, another of James Paterson's enterprises, the British Pacific Construction & Engineering Company, was created to assemble five *H* class submarines in kit form on the Canadian west coast. They were built to fulfil an Electric Boat Company order from the Russian government. Construction took place in a temporary building yard at Barnet, on the south shore of Burrard Inlet near Vancouver. These submarines were to be shipped to Russia as prefabricated kits. The steel plate and rib sections for the hulls were cut to dimension, punched for riveting, rolled or bent to shape and then assembled using nuts and bolts instead of rivets. The parts were checked for fit, labelled, then disassembled, crated, and loaded onto railway cars for delivery to Vancouver along with the remaining machinery and other fittings sent to Canada from Electric Boat Company suppliers all across the United States. Shipped to Russia, these five submarines were completed before the end of 1916 by the Baltic Works shipyard in St. Petersburg to become *AG11* to *AG15* in the Imperial Russian Navy.

Following completion of the British order, a further six hull kits were completed by Canadian Vickers and shipped to Vancouver along with the remaining parts, also for delivery to the Imperial Russian Navy. These were completed by Baltic Works at Nikolayev becoming *AG21* to *AG26*. Some of the Russian H-boats survived both World Wars, the last one being scrapped in 1947.

Canadian Vickers then proceeded to build eight more complete H-boats for the Italian navy. This contract was actually brokered by the Admiralty, which convinced the Italian government to take advantage of the capability available at Canadian Vickers. These were commissioned in two groups. The first pair left Montreal in the autumn of 1916 ahead of the St. Lawrence River freeze-up and completed their trials at Halifax. They sailed for Italy in December. The remaining six commissioned at Montreal in the spring of 1917.

A final six kits were built for another Russian order by the British Pacific Construction & Engineering Company in a temporary yard on Canadian Pacific Railway property at Vancouver. The Russian revolution precluded delivery of these kits, which were to have been *AG17* to *AG20, AG27* and *AG28*. After languishing in storage in Vancouver for over a year, they were eventually purchased by the USN. Completed in the Puget Sound Navy Yard at Bremerton, Washington, they were commissioned in 1918 as USS *H4* to *H9*.

## H-BOATS AT WAR

The H-boats were popular among the crews. The British sailors dubbed them "Ford submersibles" because of the way they were mass-produced and for the reliability of their engines. As designed, the H-boats provided a bunk and a small locker for every man. Although they were provided with lockers, British submariners were expected to sleep on the deck or in hammocks. If there was room, bunks were provided for the captain and first lieutenant only. In British service the pipe-framed canvas bunks in the H-boat wardroom area

---

24   PAC RG24, Vol. 4020 1062-12-2. Canadian Vickers proposal and description of Contract 602E submarines.

*H* class forward battery space, the aftward continuation of the fore-ends. In the centre foreground is the HP air bottle well with the deck plates removed. Beyond that is the forward battery covered with a planked deck. The only head is in the far right corner. The wardroom will be on the right, the Chief & PO's mess on the left and a dozen men will bunk in among the torpedoes.
(PAC)

*H* class. After end of the after battery. Door to engine room in the centre, port and starboard main motor switchboards to left and right, battery charging panel in right foreground. This area also served as the cafeteria for all hands and six men bunked here.
(PAC)

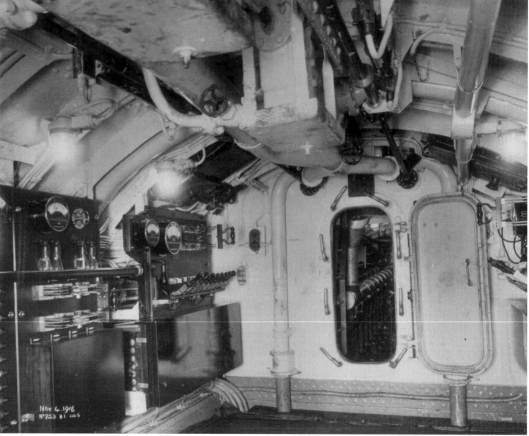

The damage to *H8* after being mined looked bad enough on the surface—it was even worse under water. (RNSM)

were soon replaced by built-in wooden bunks. Other well-liked features were the fully enclosed head located in the forward battery compartment, which even boasted its own ventilation exhaust that was trunked into the battery ventilation system. In British-built boats the head was exposed, except perhaps for a curtain. A novelty for the British was the cafeteria-style messing with full galley facilities in the after battery compartment.

Another handy feature was the ventilator pipe enclosed within the dual periscope fairing. Originally installed to provide for the redundant tactic of running on the surface in a trimmed-down condition, it proved particularly useful for steaming on the surface in rough weather. When the shut-off valve at the top of the pipe was opened, the submarine could continue running the engines with the upper lid shut to keep the seas from pouring down the conning tower. In this con-dition, the boat was conned using the conning tower periscope.

Barney Johnson of *H8* preferred that the watch be kept on the bridge and had a steel tractor seat bolted to the after side of the periscope fairing. Perched in his seat, from where he could keep a good lookout, the officer of the watch was well clear even of waves breaking over the tower and could communicate with the interior of the boat by shouting down the ventilator. The idea must have caught on because a tractor seat appears in photographs of several of the UK-based H-boats. It was also used by Johnson in a demonstration of conning the boat from this position while dived but the Admiralty observers were not impressed. They rightfully pointed out that the occupant of the seat was very vulnerable on his lonely perch and that periscopes were perhaps a better, and safer means of conning while dived.

The mine damage to Cap Johnson's *H8* was extensive. The big bowcap has been blown away and all tanks forward of the pressure hull flattened.
(RNSM)

Before joining their flotillas, all of the boats were provided with Sperry gyrocompasses, a small, enclosed, wireless office and a wireless set. A portable aerial was fitted on the back of the bridge. The British later installed improved periscopes, enclosed bridges and made other modifications as the war progressed. The four H-boats in the Mediterranean were all fitted with a 6-pounder gun on the fore casing.

There were several wartime casualties among the Canadian Vickers-built H-boats. The first one in trouble was *H6*. During the night of 18 January 1916, she strayed off course and went aground on the sands of Sheirmonikoog off the Dutch coast. Half the crew was taken off by a British ship. The rest were picked up by the Dutch and spent the remainder of the war in an internment camp. The Dutch salvaged the boat, bought it from Britain and commissioned her in their own navy as the *O8*. She survived to be taken over by the Germans when they invaded and occupied Holland early in 1940. As *UD8,* the German navy used her as a training boat. She was scuttled at Kiel towards the end of the war and ultimately scrapped.

On 22 March 1916, Barney Johnson's *H8* almost met her end on the sandy bottom off the same stretch of Dutch coast. While dived on the last day of a week-long coastal reconnaissance patrol, she snagged the mooring cable of a stray British mine and set it off. Fortunately the mine detonated outside of lethal range, but considerable damage was done to the forward part of the boat. *H8* settled nose-down onto the bottom at eighty feet with water pouring into her battered fore-ends at several points. Her cool-headed captain and determined crew managed to stem the leaks, get their boat surfaced and back to England in a hair-raising overnight passage of the North Sea. Even the Germans admitted it was a gutsy escapade.

In July 1916, *H3* hit a mine while trying to make a dived penetration of the well-protected Austrian anchorage in the Gulf of Cattaro on the Dalmatian coast. A sentry on shore spotted the disturbance caused by an exploding mine. Nothing was ever seen of the submarine. A cutter sent to investigate retrieved papers and woodwork that provided the proof.

*H10* was the next to go. Like so many of her ilk on both sides, she failed to return from a routine patrol in the North Sea. It is presumed she hit a mine around 19 January 1918.

The next to succumb was *H5,* which had the misfortune to be mistaken for a U-boat. The submarine was run down by the British freighter SS *Rutherglen* while charging her batteries on the surface in the Irish Sea on the night of 2 March 1918. Although the steamer reported that she passed through a group of survivors struggling in the icy water, no attempt was made to pick them up. Among the casualties was an American officer[25] who was aboard for familiarization. The captain of the steamer was decorated for destroying a German U-boat, and the true circumstances were not divulged until after his death.

On 16 April 1918, while proceeding on the surface in the Mediterranean, the Italian *H5* was mistaken for a U-boat and torpedoed in error by the submerged British *H1.* The Italian boat appears to have been considerably off station.

Some of the remaining *H1* class[26] with a Canadian connection were long-lived. Those in RN service were scrapped after the war when the Admiralty decided to standardize on submarines fitted with 21-inch torpedo tubes. The six American boats with hulls made in Vancouver were all broken up in 1931. However, a few of the Russian and Italian *H1* class survived the Second World War. So too did six of the ten boats originally built for Britain at the Fore River shipyard. These had been ceded to Chile in 1917 as part-exchange for Chilean warships taken over in British shipyards when the war began. Two of this group survived until the mid 1950s.

## CANADIAN SUBMARINERS OVERSEAS

In addition to manning the two CC-boats, eleven Canadian officers served overseas where they were the only other national group serving in the Royal Navy submarine branch. (See Table 1 for a complete list.) After completing their apprenticeship in the CC-boats, these officers were actively encouraged to serve in RN submarines. Towards the end of the war, Canadian volunteers were being posted directly into RN submarines.

---

25    Lieutenant (j.g.) E. W. F. Childs, USN, junior officer aboard the USN submarine L-2.
26    *H1* class because the Admiralty later produced an improved H-boat of their own known as the *H21* class.

The CANUK boat, HMS *D3*, Cap Johnson, Captain and SLt W. M. Maitland-Dougall RCN, 1st Lieutenant. Harwich, summer 1916. (RNSM)

The first RCN volunteer, Midshipman William McKinstry Maitland-Dougall, was born and raised in the town of Duncan on Vancouver Island. He was a member of the first group of cadets to take their training at the newly opened Royal Naval College of Canada in Halifax.[27] He completed his three years of training in 1914 at the head of his class. Midshipman Maitland-Dougall volunteered for submarines even as the purchase deal was being concluded between McBride and Paterson, and joined the CC-boats at Esquimalt shortly after their arrival. When the boats were laid-up during the winter of 1914–15, he was posted to headquarters in Ottawa and later to the patrol vessel HMCS *Canada* at Montreal. When the H-boats were being built at Montreal he volunteered to serve overseas and was personally recommended by the Director of the Naval Service. He made the crossing to the UK aboard *H10,* becoming the first midshipman to ever serve in a British submarine.

He was the first Canadian to undertake his Submarine Officer Training Course (S/MOTC) at HMS *Dolphin* and on completion was posted back to the H-boats. While still a sub-lieutenant, he qualified as a first lieutenant and was later appointed captain of a submarine at the age of twenty-two.[28]

The RCN officers were well received in "The Trade," as the RN submarine branch was known. They served out the war aboard operational boats in Home waters, including the Western Approaches, as well as in the Mediterranean and Aegean. In addition to Maitland-Dougall, two other RCN officers would have their own commands before the war was over.

There were two remarkable volunteer reserve officers among the Canadians. One was Barney Johnson[29] who sailed in the CC-boats and commissioned *H8*. In all, he commanded four submarines. (See Table 2.) Early in 1916, Johnson was awarded the Distinguished Service Order for bringing the badly damaged *H8*

---

27   Which included future Admirals Murray and Jones of WW2 fame and the four midshipmen who perished aboard *Good Hope*.

28   He was the first RCN officer ever to be given command of an RN warship.

29   It was always Barney at home, but in RN submarines he was known as Cap Johnson.

home and for his continued service in submarines. Johnson was the only RNVR, and the first of only six RNR officers, to command British submarines during the First World War and ended the war with the rank of Commander. He served with distinction in the Second World War, retired as a Captain and was made an Officer of the British Empire.

The other VR submariner was Lieutenant William Lowell "Tarrybreeks" Thompson, RNVR, from Ucluelet, BC. He Joined the RNVR in Vancouver and was the first Volunteer Reserve officer to serve in RN submarines. He joined *H5* in Montreal and remained with the H-boats at Harwich and Yarmouth throughout the war, serving mostly as a spare submarine officer. Thompson qualified as a first lieutenant and is known to have made war patrols in several boats including *H5* and *H8*.

Thompson returned to the west coast after the war and tried to make a living as a fisherman. In the 1920s, when the Americans imposed prohibition, he became a rumrunner. He enjoyed a measure of success but came to an unfortunate end in 1931 when his ship, the *Chasina*, vanished at sea with all hands while on a smuggling run to the Orient. The mystery of their disappearance was never solved.

Near the end of the war, two other Canadian RNVR officers, Lieutenants George le Cas Bott of Edmonton, and Albert Brooks Watson from Montreal, completed their training at HMS *Dolphin*. However, neither officer remained in submarines long enough to serve in an operational boat.

## FIRST RCN CASUALTY

In September 1917, Lieutenant William McKinstry Maitland-Dougall was appointed to the command of HMS/M *D1*. This submarine was attached to the depot ship HMS *Platypus* which was based at Lough Swilly on the north coast of Ireland. At the age of twenty-two the young Canadian became the first RCN officer to ever command a British submarine. *D1* made one patrol in the Western Approaches before being assigned to HMS *Thames,* the newly established submarine commanding officers' training school at Portsmouth. After three months of running for HMS *Thames, D1* was paid off. Maitland-Dougall was then given command of *D3* in which he had previously served as first lieutenant under Barney Johnson.

Captain Johnson and ship's company, HMS *D3*, 1917. (RNSM)

Lt. William McKinstry-Maitland Dougall, RCN, when CO of HMS *D3*, from Duncan, Vancouver Island. (Author's Collection)

At the beginning of December, *D3* was ordered to join the Sixth Flotilla at Fort Blockhouse for Channel patrols. Though not as strenuous as working in the North Atlantic, the confined waters of the English Channel provided a unique range of problems. Allied shipping traffic was heavy, well armed and usually escorted. Out of necessity, unidentified submarines were never given the benefit of a doubt, and the British boats had learned to stay out of sight of their own forces or to exchange identities in plenty of time. Merchant vessel and patrol craft alike were noto-

riously triggerhappy. During January, *D3* was fired on twice in the same day by RN patrol boats. In February Maitland-Dougall had sighted two destroyers escorting a freighter five miles off and he dived deep to avoid detection, but one of the escorts, HMS *Achates*, had spotted his periscope and dropped six depth charges close to *D3*'s position. On returning to *Dolphin*, Maitland-Dougall was reprimanded by the Flotilla Commander for not surfacing to identify himself. As a final indignity for that month, *D3* was run over by a surfaced submarine while dived on an exercise in the Solent, a busy, narrow stretch of water between the Isle of Wight and the mainland. Luckily, she only suffered a badly bent periscope and some shattered nerves among the crew.

On the afternoon of 7 March 1918, *D3* put to sea for a seven-day patrol in the eastern part of the south Channel patrol area. Maitland-Dougall had been fully briefed regarding the movements of Allied ships and air patrols in his area, and *D3* had been supplied with all the appropriate signalling equipment necessary for exchanging identities. To provide easy recognition from the air a black-and-white bull's eye had been painted on the forehatch cover. By sunrise of 8 March, Maitland-Dougall was on station and dived. On 11 March, a British airship exchanged identities with an Allied submarine in *D3*'s billet without difficulty. Friday, 12 March, dawned clear and calm but under the heat of the spring sunshine a layer of low-lying mist developed making it impossible to keep an effective periscope watch. *D3* surfaced. Trimmed down, ready to dive and keeping a good lookout she could be under again in less than a minute if trouble threatened.

At approximately 2:30 p.m., the French airship *ATO* from LeHavre air station sighted a surfaced submarine about thirty miles north west of Fécamp. Selecting a course with the sun and breeze astern, the airship approached the westbound boat cautiously, seeking to identify it. When about a mile from their quarry, the Frenchmen were startled to observe what they took to be rockets ascending from the back of the submarine's bridge. Assuming themselves to be under attack, the airship crew opened fire with their machine gun and descended for a bombing run.

Their target was *D3*, which had waited for the airship to close in order to exchange identities and then fired the recognition signal for the day, red smoke grenades. Unknown to

Maitland-Dougall, and to the authorities back at Blockhouse, the Frenchmen were completely unaware of this method of exchanging identities and consequently thought the grenades were rockets. As their dirigible was filled with thousands of cubic metres of highly flammable hydrogen, the Frenchmen had reason to be concerned.

If *D3* had any chance of survival at all it lay beneath the surface. Remaining on the surface would have presented the dirigible with a sitting-duck target. The submarine was almost under when the first pair of 52-kilo bombs exploded astern. Passing over its target, *ATO* came around for a second run. Sighting the wake of the submerged boat, the dirigible commander aimed ahead and made a setpiece attack, bracketing the target with his last two pairs of bombs.

Having suddenly lost over 300 kilos in weight the airship soared skyward, almost out of control. At 1,200 metres the French aircrew watched and waited. After about four minutes, a mass of air bubbles erupted on the surface, to be followed by the submarine's conning tower. By the time the airship managed to descend the boat had gone leaving four widely separated men swimming in the frigid waters. Shutting off his motors the French commander tried shouting to the survivors and was astonished when one of them responded in English. Unable to get his unwieldy craft close enough to the surface to pick the men up he instructed his crew to toss their lifebelts to the floundering submariners. During the attack, he had tried to contact his base by wireless, but the airship's transmitter had insufficient power. The commander decided to get help and headed for shore to find a ship to send to the scene.

Some time later *ATO* returned with the destroyer *Typhon* and both started searching for the survivors. By 6:10 p.m., the airship was forced back to base by incoming fog. The destroyer remained until well after dark but found nothing. *D3* and her gallant crew were gone.

The airship commander submitted his report of the action to the airstation commander that evening. In it, he indicated that the submarine might not have been German. The next day word of the attack reached *Dolphin* and it was soon confirmed that the victim was *D3*. On Monday, 15 March 1918, she was officially posted as missing, presumed sunk in the English Channel. The young Canadian captain had been killed two days before his twenty-third birthday.

For the Maitland-Dougalls in faraway Duncan, BC, this was the second devastating personal tragedy of that cruel war. Eleven months before, they had lost their only other child, nineteen-year-old Hamish, a corporal in the Third Battalion, CEF, during the attack on Vimy Ridge. The loss of the boat and her twenty-nine men was mourned in homes across the United Kingdom as well as in Duncan, BC. No one would ever be told officially of the circumstances surrounding her sinking although the Maitland-Dougalls were apprised of the details privately by Commander Alexander Quicke.

In the conclusion to his report on the sinking of *D3* to the Commander in Chief, Portsmouth, Alexander Quicke remarked, "Lieutenant Maitland-Dougall… was in my opinion in the very front rank of the younger submarine captains, a most thorough, conscientious and resourceful officer." The RCN had suffered its first submariner casualty and lost its first submarine captain, an officer of great future promise and a pioneer in his profession.

## THE CH-BOATS

After the Armistice, the Admiralty ceded two Fore River-built *H1* class boats laid-up at Bermuda to Canada as replacements for the worn-out CC-boats. The two boats, *H14* and *H15,* had been commissioned during the summer of 1918 at New London under the overall command of none other than Lieutenant Commander Barney Johnson, DSO, RNR, who was CO of *H15.* They reached Bermuda the day after the Armistice was signed and berthed alongside HMCS *Shearwater.* The one-time submarine depot ship was still commanded by Johnson's shipmate from 1914, Commander Bertram Jones, RCN. As there was little point in continuing the voyage, the boats were decommissioned and placed under a care-and-maintenance party while the crews took passage to England in a homeward-bound cruiser.

In late 1919, the two boats were sailed to Halifax. Fully refitted, they were commissioned in the RCN in April 1921 as HMC ships *CH14* and *CH15.* The two captains and first lieutenants were drawn from amongst the Canadians still serving in British submarines. The crews consisted of a few exRN-trained submariners recruited into the RCN to man the boats, while the

*CH15* passing the sheerlegs at the Naval Dockyard, Bermuda, winter 1921-1922.
(Author's collection)

*CH14* and *CH15* dressed overall, 1920-1922.
(PAC)

bulk of the men were green RCN ratings, most of whom had never been to sea before.

The two submarines spent the winter of 1921–22 based at Malabar in Bermuda exercising with Canadian and British ships. Upon their return to Halifax, they, along with most of the rest of the navy, fell victim to the severe defence budget cuts of May 1922. The same cutbacks resulted in all Canadians being withdrawn from RN submarines. The two submarines lay alongside the paid off cruiser *Aurora* at moorings in the Northwest Arm for many years, an eyesore for the residents of prestigious Armdale. In 1927, all three vessels were towed away after being sold to a Montreal shipbuilder for scrap.

## THE SITUATION AT A GLANCE

CANADA'S armed forces all but disappeared in the retrenchment that followed the First World War. On two occasions the navy came very close to being abolished altogether, once in 1920 and again in 1933. For most of the period, the impoverished permanent naval establishment consisted of the dockyards and barracks at Esquimalt and Halifax and a tiny regular force manning and supporting two destroyers, one on each coast. Naval Service Headquarters (NSHQ) was housed in a few offices in downtown Ottawa. Not even the naval college, which had been moved to Esquimalt after the 1917 Halifax explosion, survived the budget slashing. Canadian officers were being trained in Britain and aboard British ships.

Following the First World War the RNCVR was disbanded and eventually abolished. In 1923, the Royal Canadian Naval Reserve (RCNR) and Royal Canadian Naval Volunteer Reserve (RCNVR) were brought into existence as purely Canadian organizations. The RCNR was originally established in nine Divisions, later reduced to five. Experienced Canadian merchant marine and fishing fleet personnel already in the RNR, and those who would have qualified to join the RNR in the past, were now obliged to join, or were transferred to, the RCNR. This ensured that these seamen and their skills would be available in Canada instead of being arbitrarily absorbed by the RN as had happened in the First World War.

In order to provide a large reserve to fill out the naval ranks in an emergency, the volunteer citizen force was revived but, as with the merchant marine, strictly for Canadian use. In 1923, twelve RCNVR companies were established in major centres across the country. A full company consisted of one hundred men. If there was insufficient local interest fifty-man half-companies were set up. Seven more RCNVR units were raised before the outbreak of the Second World War. Both reserve forces were given summer training aboard the two destroyers and in smaller vessels on local bodies of water. There were no womens' organizations until after the outbreak of war.

With the rise to power of Hitler and the National Socialists in Germany during the early 1930s, an ambitious program of naval expansion was put in hand. Four destroyers were ordered from Britain and the naval budget was increased significantly. On the eve of war, the RCN comprised six destroyers, four minesweepers, a trawler and two small training vessels. In all, there were 1,819 regular force personnel and around 2,220 reservists. In accordance with the terms of the Naval Service Act, the destroyer force was placed at the disposal of the Admiralty as reinforcement for the RN. The Admiralty still held responsibility for the security of Canadian waters in wartime.

Prior to the actual outbreak of war, it had been the avowed intention of the Canadian government that no Canadian lives would ever again be sacrificed in a European war. The Canadian Parliament debated the matter for over a week before declaring war on Germany.

The Admiralty, and by inference NSHQ as well, was convinced that Germany would not resort to the large-scale use of submarines as they had done in the First World War. The Admiralty gave every assurance that the U-boat menace could be contained using the asdic submarine detection gear and powerful depth charges. Consequently, little heed had been paid to the demands of modern anti-submarine warfare (ASW). Only one of the RCN destroyers was equipped with asdic and only one officer in the RCN had received any specialized training in ASW.

## THE SECOND WORLD WAR

**Detail of HMS *Spiteful*'s control room. (RNSM)**

Britain however had learned a bitter lesson in the First World War and convoy was introduced in the North Atlantic from the very beginning. Germany had a powerful and modern surface fleet, which was something the British could respect. As well, German merchant raiders were at work in the North and South Atlantic sealanes from the outset. The first eastbound convoy, HX 1, left Halifax on 16 September, six days after Canada's declaration of war. Canada's direct participation in the Battle of the Atlantic had begun.

On the ASW front, early encounters with the enemy quickly demonstrated the limitations of the much-vaunted asdic while intelligence sources warned that large numbers of U-boats were under construction. At the Admiralty, the now famous whale-catcher-cum-corvette was quickly settled on as a suitable stop-gap anti-submarine (A/S) escort vessel. Cheap, quick and easy to build, it utilized commercially available engines and boilers, carried simple weapons and could be manned by reservists. In 1940 alone, orders were placed in fifteen Canadian shipyards for sixty-four corvettes and eighteen minesweepers, while an additional destroyer was immediately transferred from the RN.

From the beginning, the Canadian government insisted that Canada would run its own military show. History has shown that, although the government arguably adopted the right policy, Canada lacked the resources for anything like complete military independence. This decision and the lack of flexibility then existing at NDHQ effectively cut the RCN off from British facilities as far as training and equipment development were concerned. The United States had adopted a neutral stance and so could offer little in the way of assistance on this side of the Atlantic. In all fairness, no one in Canada could have visualized that the war was going to create the 400 percent expansion of the naval forces that it did.

Along with the large fleet of A/S escorts that soon streamed out of Canadian shipyards came an urgent demand for training. In addition, as the war developed, coastal patrol aircraft of three air forces were soon operating from bases in the Maritimes[30] and Newfoundland and all needed the services of submarines for ASW training.

The RCN had no submarines. NSHQ did not consider there was a need for any, nor could the peacetime navy have afforded them. Britain had none to spare either. During the first two years of the war, even obsolete 1920s-vintage *H21* and *L* class submarines were being used on operations in emergencies. The RN was suffering unexpectedly high losses and submarines for any purpose were in short supply. It was far too late to build any and the RCN was forced to make do with whatever the RN could spare. The Admiralty was aware of, and in sympathy with, the Canadian ASW training situation, but was hard put to find the resources. Relief was on the way, but in the meantime, some interesting operational developments took place on Canada's east coast.

## ANGLO-FRENCH ESCORT SUBMARINES

It was almost a year before U-boats became a serious menace in the North Atlantic. In the early stages of the Battle of the Atlantic, heavily armed surface raiders posed the main threat to the convoys. During that first year most Halifax–UK convoys were escorted by a battleship, a heavy cruiser or an AMC and, for some convoys, between December 1939 and July 1941, a submarine.(For a complete listing of the submarines involved, see Table 8.)

The French had long advocated the use of submarines as convoy escorts. On paper at least, their heavy armament, endurance and good sea-keeping ability seemed to qualify them for the task. During talks held with French naval authorities in October 1939, the Admiralty reluctantly agreed to allocate a small number of suitable British submarines to escort duties in support of a French squadron assigned to the job.

On 12 November, the French *deuxième Division de sous-marin*, consisting of four 1500-tonne first class submarines and a small depot ship, the AMC *Quercy,* sailed from Brest, arriving at Halifax thirteen days later. The French crews and shore support staff were temporarily quartered aboard the CNR passenger liner *Prince David* that was lying alongside at Halifax awaiting conversion. These submarines provided a return trip escort service for convoys where the only other escort was an AMC. In all,

---

30   RCAF from Pennfield Ridge in New Brunswick and the air station at Eastern Passage, Nova Scotia, the USAF from Argentia, Newfoundland; and the RAF from Greenwood, Nova Scotia.

The 2nd Flotilla, Halifax, April 1941. Alongside the depot ship HMS *Forth* are, from inboard: HMS *Porpoise*, HMS *Talisman*, and the Dutch O-15. Three short foc'sle corvettes are secured alongside the CNR jetty on the Dartmouth side. (Author's collection)

eight French submarines arrived at Halifax to pick up a convoy and return to their base in France.

The *Quercy* was not equipped for Canadian winter conditions and within days of her arrival headed south for the West Indies. Designed primarily for use in the Mediterranean, the French submarines were no better off. During the winter, the crews experienced considerable hardship. A large part of the armament of these submarines consisted of external, trainable torpedo tubes, which had a tendency to freeze up. The French boats were withdrawn in June 1940 when the fall of France became imminent.

The British contribution consisted of three *Porpoise* class minelaying submarines, *Seal, Cachalot* and *Narwhal,* which arrived at Halifax in late November. When employed in these duties the minelayers did not carry their allotment of fifty or so mines. Each returned to England with a convoy but did not repeat the exercise.

The British, who were not happy with the arrangement, were quick to withdraw their boats. One of the reasons given was that they were unhappy with the stationing of the escort submarines in rear of the convoy on the flank from which an attack seemed most likely. It was concluded they would be of little use in countering a serious surface attack, especially from that quarter. Another was the weather, which was so consistently bad that attacks seemed most unlikely. On at least one occasion, the escorting submarine failed to make contact with its convoy at all because of the non-stop gales. It was also felt they could be more usefully employed on reconnaissance patrols and minelaying operations. Contributing factors to the decision to withdraw were the lack of diesel-engine maintenance and repair facilities and the shortage of suitable accommodations for shore support staff and submarine crews at Halifax.

## THE SECOND FLOTILLA

As late as November 1940 surface raiders continued to pose a serious threat. Suitable escorts were still in short supply and the Admiralty, despite the misgivings of Flag Officer Submarines, decided once again to reinforce the Halifax-based escort forces with submarines.[31] At the end of November the minelayer HMS *Porpoise* was withdrawn from Biscay patrols and sent to Halifax. She made three trips to the mid-ocean meeting point with convoys and conducted several independent anti-U-boat patrols before returning to the UK in April 1941. In March, *Porpoise* was joined for a few weeks by the fleet submarine *Severn* from Freetown, South Africa.

In late February 1941, the Second Flotilla, consisting of the brand-new depot ship HMS *Forth* and her attached submarines, was sent to Halifax to reinforce *Porpoise* and to provide a support base. The ships were sailed independently. *Forth* herself arrived on 3 March 1941 carrying £1.75 million in gold bullion destined for the safety of the Bank of Canada vaults in Ottawa.

The large depot ship was particularly welcome in Halifax because of her battery of high-angle 4.5-inch (114.3 mm) guns which provided a much sought-after defence against the perceived possibility of German air raids.[32] *Forth* was soon joined by three *T* class boats, *Thunderbolt, Tribune* and *Talisman,* and the large French cruiser submarine *Surcouf*. During their passage to Canada *Talisman* and *Thunderbolt* were diverted, along with *Severn,* which was returning to Freetown, to join in a fruitless search for the powerful German surface raiders *Scharnhorst* and *Gneisenau*.

When *Talisman* arrived in the Halifax approaches on 26 March, the lookouts sighted debris and survivors in the water. Four men were rescued alive. Their ship, the armed yacht HMCS *Otter,* had suffered an accidental explosion and fire. Events happened so quickly there was no way to get off a distress message, nor was it possible to get the boats away. She burned out and eventually sank. Two officers and seventeen men were lost as a result.

*Taku,* a fourth Second Flotilla T-boat, had to be towed back to England when she encountered bad weather and developed serious defects. *Cachalot* had also been assigned to accompany *Forth* but was diverted to minelaying operations in the Bay of Biscay and never did return to Halifax. Second Flotilla submarines carried out convoy escort and patrol duties until withdrawn in July. (For details see Table 8.)

After the experiences of the previous winter, new tactics had been devised. This time the submarine took position ahead of the columns of ships on the side from which an attack seemed most likely. Should a surface raider appear, the submarine would dive before it was spotted. The convoy, meanwhile, was to turn in a direction that would draw a pursuing attacker into range of the submerged submarine.

The submariners had strong reservations about the plan, as it was all too easy for the raider never to come within range of the slow moving dived defender. Perhaps fortunately, these tactics were never tested in action. Even so, when one convoy was attacked by U-boats at night and carried out evasive manoeuvres, the escorting submarine found itself having to steer between the columns of blacked-out merchant ships and in grave danger of being attacked or run down.

At that point in the war, British submarines could only accompany the convoys about halfway across the North Atlantic. This was known as the mid-ocean meeting point, or MOMP, which was where the UK-based anti-submarine forces took over from the Canadian–Newfoundland-based escorts to shepherd the convoys through the Western Approaches. It was too risky for the submarines to continue beyond the MOMP with the ships because of the presence of U-boat packs. It would have been all too easy for the British boats to be mistaken for the enemy. Before beginning the return voyage to Halifax, the submarines made an anti-submarine sweep astern of the convoy just in case there were shadowing U-boats. On a number of occasions, the submarine was the only escort and on others, a submarine and an AMC provided the total escort force.

In June, *Thunderbolt*[33] was dispatched to a position southeast of the Grand Banks to intercept a supply U-boat. On the 15th she sighted and attacked *U557*. The U-boat spotted the torpedo tracks, dived to safety and later reported *Thunderbolt* as a *Thames* class submarine. In the official report it was noted that high seas foiled an eight-torpedo spread.

The steady advance of the U-boats into the North Atlantic from their new bases on the French Biscay coast made it too

---

31   As well as those based at Gibraltar for UK-Gibraltar convoys.
32   Remarkable as this may seem today, the Halifax Civil Defence authorities took the possibility of an air raid seriously at that stage in the war. All available mobile AA guns had already been sent to Britain.
33   The salvaged HMS *Thetis* which sank with heavy loss of life while on trials just prior to the outbreak of war.

HMS *Thunderbolt* docked down alongside the depot ship HMS *Forth*, showing her bow torpedo tubes. (Author's collection)

HMS *Cachalot*, Halifax, December 1939. The big minelayer appears to be slipping for sea from alongside a destroyer. Note that she is flying two ensigns—no sense taking chances.
(MARCOM Museum)

HMS *Thunderbolt*, 2nd Flotilla, off Halifax in spring 1941. She had started life as HMS *Thetis* which accidentally sank in Liverpool Bay on builders' trials. There were only four survivors. Being necessary for the war, she was rebuilt and manned by a volunteer crew.
(Author's collection)

dangerous to continue using submarines as escorts. In July, it was decided to disband the Second Flotilla. After a brief docking at Saint John, New Brunswick, *Forth* was sent to St. John's, Newfoundland, where she provided a support base for anti-submarine escorts for three months. The submarines were dispersed to other commands in the UK and Mediterranean.

## THE INVASION OF ST. PIERRE AND MIQUELON

Towards the end of June 1941, *Surcouf* arrived at Portsmouth, New Hampshire, for a refit which was completed by the end of October. After a series of post-refit trials, she reached Bermuda in mid-November. By mid-December, she had returned to Halifax to join up with three Free French corvettes, *Mimosa, Alysse* and *Aconit,* all under the command of Admiral Muselier.

In the last week in December, the four ships sailed from Halifax under Free French control bound for the west coast of Newfoundland. After a rough passage, the flotilla appeared off the Vichy French islands of St. Pierre and Miquelon. Here, Admiral Muselier led an uncontested take-over under the protection of his little fleet, which included *Surcouf*'s pair of 203 mm (8-inch) guns. By the middle of January 1942, *Surcouf*

had returned to Halifax to attend to a never-ending list of defects. Near the end of the month, she sailed for Bermuda on the first leg of her final, fatal, voyage.

## RCNVR SUBMARINERS

Twenty-three RCNVR officer volunteers were accepted for service in RN submarines during the course of the Second World War and there was one known non-volunteer. (See Table 3 for a complete list.) Two of the volunteers returned to General Service on completion of their training, two others were invalided out and another opted out after only a short period of service. The remainder served in submarines for the duration of the war. The non-volunteer was posted to the training boats operating under RCN control where he remained for the rest of the war. He never learned if there was any particular reason why he was posted into submarines, but apparently accepted that it was as good as anywhere else to serve. During the war approximately 20 percent of all personnel in RN submarines were drafted, or posted in, and did not offer their services as volunteers.

All of these officers were originally posted to the UK to serve on loan with the RN. Upon arrival, they were sent to HMS *King Alfred* at Hove, near Brighton on the south coast.

The Free French cruiser submarine *Surcouf* at Halifax, December 1941. (Maritime Museum of the Atlantic)

There they were formed into class-size groups mostly made up of junior officers belonging to the RNVR and RNR to which were added a handful of Commonwealth personnel. All were given an indoctrination course to familiarize them with the RN. Following that phase, they were given an opportunity to take basic specialist training in subjects such as navigation and signalling. On completion, they were offered a variety of postings, including motor torpedo boats, coastal patrol boats, defensively equipped merchant ships and submarines.

At *King Alfred*, and elsewhere in the RN, there was a tendency to classify all non-British personnel as colonials. The Canadians, and no doubt other commonwealth personnel, found this stereotyping somewhat irritating and for the most part stood their ground against it. By the time they reached the flotillas most had become inured to this kind of annoyance. Pay, however, was always a potential sore point; Canadians were considerably better off than their RN counterparts. By all accounts, it seldom became an issue.

Once they were accepted for submarines, the volunteers were placed on waiting lists for their S/M OTC. Sometimes there were long delays, and, in the interim they were sent to sea in surface ships. Until the summer of 1942, S/M OTCs were conducted at HMS *Dolphin,* the spiritual home of the RN Submarine Branch. *Dolphin* occupied the grounds of Fort Blockhouse, one of the old fortresses guarding the entrance to Portsmouth harbour. The base is located on a spit of land on the seaward side of Haslar Creek in Gosport, on the "other" side of Portsmouth harbour. Because of disruptions caused by the heavy air raids on the south coast and in the London area during the Blitz, basic training was moved to HMS *Elfin* at Blyth on the north-east coast, home of the Sixth Flotilla. The training operation was set up in what was normally a boy's training school.

The RCNVR officers served in all theatres where RN submarines operated including Home waters, the Canadian east coast, the Mediterranean, the Indian Ocean and the south-west Pacific. As the focus of the war shifted from Europe to the Pacific and Japan, there was a tendency to concentrate them on the boats running from Digby, Nova Scotia, preparatory to the Canadians taking over some of the training submarines. At the end of the war, the CO of one of the Digby boats was a Canadian, as were two of his officers, while one of the coxswains was a Newfoundlander. In a similar vein, by the time HMS *Truculent* reached the end of her 1944 refit in Philadelphia, all of the officers except the CO were Canadians. Whether it was by sheer coincidence or by design is not known. *Truculent* was destined for service in a Home waters flotilla.

Three other RCNVR officers served in the Special Services. Two were the original volunteers chosen for the Chariots (so-called human torpedoes) and a third served in the X-craft mini-subs. Although they endured many hardships and spent long hours perfecting their dangerous craft, only one of these officers was ever actually engaged in actions against an enemy target.

Officially, no RCN ratings served aboard RN or Allied submarines during the Second World War. However, there are three known exceptions. The first was Leading Signalman Arthur Hardy, who served aboard the Dutch submarine *O15* during the two years she was based at Halifax. Later, Petty Officer Electrical Artificer Ken Walters of Victoria, BC, served in HMS *Truculent*, which he joined without the benefit of any submarine training during her 1944 refit at Philadelphia. He was later drafted to HMS *Unruffled* at Bermuda where he remained until she stopped at Digby on her way home at the end of the war. As well, a petty officer asdic rating served aboard HMS *Unseen* at Digby. He originally went aboard as a temporary replacement for an injured crew member but remained until the boats left Canada.

Ten Newfoundland ratings, all of whom enlisted in the RN, served in submarines during the war. Two of these men lost their lives, both in Canadian waters. (See Table 5 for details.)

## MEMORIES OF THE MED

From late 1940 until September 1943, the submarines of three British flotillas waged a continuous and aggressive submarine campaign against Axis shipping supplying the Italian and German armies in North Africa. The Eighth Flotilla, based on Gibraltar, operated in the western part of the Mediterranean between Gibraltar and the islands of Corsica and Sardinia. The First Flotilla, which had moved from China to Malta early in the war and then set up base at Alexandria, operated mostly in the eastern end of the Mediterranean and supported the Tenth Flotilla. The brunt of this work fell to the British, two Polish, and three Dutch submarines of the Tenth Flotilla based on the belea-

Commander Ben Bryant's HMS *Safari*. Fred Sherwood of Ottawa was the First Lieutenant. (RNSM)

guered island of Malta. From their base on Manoel Island in Lazaretto harbour, these submarines maintained a full schedule of offensive operations despite the constant siege of their home base by Axis sea and air forces.

Their area of operation extended throughout the central Mediterranean basin from Corsica to Crete. When the British surface forces were withdrawn from Malta, the Tenth Flotilla hung on, even after losing four submarines in the harbour to bombing. Eventually, they too were forced out. Nevertheless, they continued to operate from Alexandria and Beirut until they were able to return to Malta. The combined efforts of the three Mediterranean flotillas exerted a constant pressure on the Axis supply lines to the point that shortages of all kinds significantly hastened the defeat of the German forces in North Africa.

Four Canadian officers were in the Mediterranean flotillas during the height of the campaign. The very first was Lieutenant J. D. Woods from Toronto. He lost the toss of a coin with his classmate Freddy Sherwood of Ottawa. Leaving England in November 1940, Woods took the long route to Alexandria, going by sea via the Cape and the Suez Canal. He made one particularly unpleasant patrol and decided submarines were not for him.

Freddy Sherwood, after a series of patrols in Home waters, arrived in the Mediterranean in May 1942. By then, he was First Lieutenant in Commander Ben Bryant's *Safari*. At first she was assigned to the Eighth Flotilla at Gibraltar and later the Tenth at Malta. Freddy was aboard for six patrols, three from each base. When he left *Safari* in November, it was to return to England for his Commanding Officer Qualifying Course (COQC).

At the end of September 1942, Lieutenant Hugh D. S. Russel joined HMS *Traveller;* a First Flotilla boat then based at Beirut, Lebanon. Along with most of the boats from the First, *Traveller* was loaned to the Tenth to cover Operation Torch, the American landings near Oran in North Africa. On completion of the landings, she remained attached to the Tenth.

Operation Principal was originally planned as a concentrated Chariot attack against Italian battleships in Taranto harbour. Three *T* class submarines carrying Chariots in watertight containers on their upper deck were to surface in the harbour approaches after dark, launch their Chariots and clear out. The Chariots were to make their way into the harbour, lay charges under the ships or attach magnetic charges to their hulls, and either escape to seaward or take refuge with the underground ashore. Surviving Chariot crews were to be picked up by the handier *U* class boats. Because of shipping movements, the plan had to be changed several times. In the end, it was decided that one T-boat would attack two large cruisers in Maddelena har-

A close-up of *P34*s hull, showing the ruptures caused by her encounter with a mine off the toe of Italy on 12 April 1942. The photo was taken at Port Said, May 1942. (Author's collection)

bour in northern Sardinia while the other two struck at a heavy concentration of shipping in Palermo. Other submarines would be ready on patrol to take advantage of any naval activity arising as a result of the attacks.

In preparation for Operation Principal, *Traveller*, commanded by Lieutenant Commander D. St. Clair-Ford, left Malta on 8 November to carry out a reconnaissance of the Gulf of Taranto. The submarine was never heard from again. Post-war investigations have concluded she hit a mine in the approaches to the Gulf. Lieutenant Russel was the only Canadian submariner killed in action in the Second World War.

At the same time, HMS *P311* (an unnamed T-boat, she was unofficially christened *Tutenkahmen* by her CO) set out to attack the cruisers in Maddelena harbour. She was commanded by Commander R. D. Cayley, RN, a three-time DSO winner. One of the ten Charioteers aboard *P311* was Lieutenant C. E. "Chuck" Bonnell, DSC, RCNVR. He was one of the two original Chariot pioneers. The submarine was last heard from on 31 December when she reported she had cleared the dangerous Sicilian Channel. The assumption is that she hit a mine in the Strait of Bonifacio during her approach to the target area.

Considering the cost, the raid on Palermo harbour was at best a qualified success. Of the five Chariots launched, two made successful attacks, resulting in the loss of a brand-new Italian cruiser and a large merchant ship.

In June 1941, after a short period in an H-boat, Sub-Lieutenant Keith Forbes of Wolfville, Nova Scotia, joined the *U* class boat *P34*,[34] when she was under construction at Barrow. *P34* was commanded by Lieutenant P. R. H. "Soft Joe" Harrison, RN. After trials and work-ups at Dunoon, they sailed directly for the Mediterranean to join the Tenth Flotilla. They reached Malta near the end of August. For most of this time, Keith was the only Canadian in the flotilla. *P34* carried out twelve war patrols in the Mediterranean theatre during which she sank two enemy submarines and several merchant ships.

In the sixteen months that *P34* was with the Tenth, a dozen boats were lost. On two occasions, *P34*'s own survival was in serious jeopardy. On the first, she detonated a deep-laid mine while dived off the toe of Italy and was literally blown to the sur-

face. All of the torpedo tubes and both periscopes had been rendered useless, and she hightailed it back to Malta. On the second occasion, she sprang a serious leak when a tail-shaft gland, damaged in the mining incident, let go while she was being depth charged off North Africa. On that occasion the boat made an excursion to 450 feet, far below her 250-foot safe diving depth.

Incidents like this were all part of the normal hazards of war in a submarine. These included depth charging and gunfire from irate merchant ships and their escorts, the attentions of a variety of aircraft all intent on the submarine's destruction; minefields that could not be avoided, minefields no one knew about until it was too late and daytime and nighttime air raids while in harbour.

In April 1942, shortly after *P34* limped back to base following her encounter with the mine, Malta was abandoned. The lack of air cover for the minesweepers trying to keep the channels clear forced the Tenth Flotilla to seek temporary refuge with the First Flotilla at Alexandria. *P34* went into dock to have the ripples taken out of her hull. A month later the submarines had to evacuate that port when the Afrika Korps came too close for comfort during its unsuccessful bid to take the Suez Canal. During the short voyage to Palestine, the First Flotilla depot ship HMS *Medway* was torpedoed by a U-boat. Although the loss of life was small, the sinking of the depot ship was a serious blow. Considered the best of the depot ships in commission, she provided the workshops and accommodations and was carrying all of the spare gear and spare torpedoes for both flotillas. Being buoyant, many of the spare torpedoes floated clear of the wreck and were recovered. However, most of the personnel in the submarines, which had been routed independently, lost all of their kit and personal possessions. After this setback, a temporary depot called *Medway II* was set-up ashore at Haifa in Palestine, where it became the new home of the First Flotilla. This base was later moved to Beirut in Lebanon.

By May 1942, Keith, who went aboard as navigator, had worked his way up to First Lieutenant (or Jimmy). *P34*'s Jimmy was not one to stand on ceremony. As a Canadian RCNVR officer he always reckoned he had a certain advantage over his

---

34   *P34* was given the name *Ultimatum* just prior to her return to the UK. She survived a second commission in the Med.

Royal Naval College trained counterparts, in that he had never been exposed to the formal rules. As a young civil engineering student and part-time hard-rock miner he had already learned the value of delegating responsibility. Providing they kept him informed, he had the good sense to leave the chiefs and POs to run their departments. He quickly appreciated that by establishing a good rapport with his senior rates he had achieved something of value.

Early in July 1942, when *P34* was lying alongside the cruiser HMS *Cleopatra* at Haifa, the Jimmy returned aboard late one night to discover the trot sentry sound asleep leaning against the deck gun mounting. Leaving the unsuspecting seaman to his slumber, Keith went below, turned out the duty PO and instructed him to bring the sailor up before him on defaulters next day. Off went the PO to do his unpleasant duty.

Next morning Keith briefed the coxswain telling him that he wanted to make an example of the seaman but did not intend punishing him according to the extent allowed for in the regulations. In the usual fashion, the wardroom table was covered in green baize, copies of *King's Regulations and Admiralty Instructions* and the *Articles of War* were laid out, as also was a .45-calibre revolver. The latter was not usual, nor was it loaded, but sleeping on watch was a serious offence, and Forbes wanted to impress the miscreant.

At the appointed time, the defaulter was mustered outside the wardroom, his cap on his head. The coxswain called the man's name and official number, the sailor took two steps into the wardroom, took one look at the table, blanched, and stood rigidly to attention.

"Off caps" barked the coxswain in the prescribed manner. The seaman whipped off his cap and the coxswain read out the charge. The whole ceremony was very impressive. Following the coxswain's litany, Forbes placed his hand lightly on the revolver lying on the table in front of him and proceeded to lecture the unfortunate seaman on the seriousness of his offence. In the process he pointed out that, according to the regulations laid out in front of him, sleeping on watch could be punishable by death.

At this point Forbes observed two things. The defaulter was almost in shock and the coxswain, knowing full well the whole thing was a sham, was about to crack up.

Forbes was having a hard time keeping a straight face himself, but he had to finish. He ended his lecture by telling the seaman that, as he was new to the service, and to *P34*, he was going to let him off with a caution. The look of relief that suddenly crossed the young man's face was something to behold.

"Caution to be recorded. On caps. About turn. Get forward and get turned to," growled the coxswain, somehow managing to keep a straight face.

Once the startled sailor was out of earshot, Forbes and the coxswain cracked up completely. From that time onwards, whenever the Jimmy needed a man to carry out some unpleasant or arduous duty, he knew he could rely on one particular young seaman to get the job done smartly, and without complaint.

Amidst the dangers and seriousness of the undersea war, there were some diversionary episodes. The *boffins*, as scientists were irreverently known in the forces, kept coming up with wonderful things, like dehydrated spinach. It was compact, easy to store, very nourishing and required minimal preparation. Just the thing for submarines. While *P34* was dived, the able seaman torpedoman who was doing the cooking, put some of the dry green stuff in a big pot, added the recommended quantity of fresh water and turned on the heat. Nothing happened. He added some more water and stirred the mess up a bit. Still nothing happened. Nothing, that is, until they surfaced after sunset and opened the conning-tower hatch.

Because of the need to vent compressed-air services inboard, and because high-pressure air system pipe joints were not always as tight as they should be, a moderate pressure invariably built up inside the boat when she was dived. And so, as soon as the hatch opened and pressure inside the boat suddenly returned to normal, the stuff literally exploded into life covering the tiny galley in a thick green mush, much to the delight of the crew. The cook, however, was very unhappy and seriously considered going back to shoving torpedoes around, preferably in a different boat.

On another occasion, the flotilla commander, Captain (S) Ten, G.W.G. "Shrimp" Simpson decided that *P34* should experiment with baking bread at sea. "It's the sort of thing Canadians do at home all the time. Isn't it, Forbes?" carped Shrimp Simpson as he broke the news to *P34*'s CO and Jimmy. As it happened, in this

HMS *P34*'s crew with their skull and crossbones at the end of her first commission, showing four merchant ships and two submarines sunk, and fourteen survivors rescued from one of the submarines. The officer at bottom right is Keith Forbes from Wolfville, NS, who was the First Lieutenant. (RNSM)

particular case, Captain (S) was right. However, Keith, who had often helped his mother bake bread at home in Wolfville, was not going to admit to it. The acting cook and his Canadian Jimmy were sent inboard for a crash course in bread baking.

Electrical power was always a precious commodity in a submarine. Consequently, cooking and baking of any kind was usually done while charging the battery on the surface at night. All preparations, however, were made during the day while dived. Accordingly, the dough was mixed, the yeast added, the mixture kneaded and the loaves-to-be were set out in pans under cloths to rise. This they refused to do. More yeast, more kneading and pounding, and still no rise. The cook

was becoming increasingly frustrated, and Forbes was stymied. Until they surfaced that evening.

When the tower hatch was opened and internal pressure returned to normal, the supercharged dough rose with a vengeance—all over the galley, just as the spinach had done. Once the cook was calmed down, the mess cleaned up, and everyone appreciated what had happened, bread making became a regular and popular night-time activity aboard *P34*. They even had reconstituted spinach now and then too.

Keith Forbes was awarded the Distinguished Service Cross in December 1942, becoming the first Canadian submariner of the Second World War to be decorated.

## THE RUSSIAN VISITORS

In early October, 1942, six Soviet submarines left their bases on the Kamchatka Peninsula at Vladivostock and Petropavlovsk-Kamchatka and set out on a seven-month, 17,500-mile odyssey to Polyarny near Murmansk on the Kola Peninsula. The flotilla of six submarines was under the overall command of Captain First Rank I. Tripolsky. Submarines *L15, L16, S51, S54, S55* and *S56* travelled by way of the Aleutian Islands, San Francisco, the Panama Canal, Cuba, Halifax, Reykjavik, and the United Kingdom to reach their new base. The last pair arrived after a thorough refit in England in May 1943. During the voyage, *L16* was sunk by the Japanese submarine *I-25* off the west coast of the United States. The Soviet Union was not at war with Japan at that time. The Russian officers claimed they were attacked on several occasions, but the veracity of this cannot be confirmed nor are any such attacks mentioned in the available references.

The Soviet squadron put in at Halifax for repairs on 14 December. Dockyard assistance was requested and given for making some of the repairs. When the Canadian Flag Officer paid the submarines a visit, the Russians were delighted. According to some of the dockyard men who worked aboard the submarines, they were clean, well maintained and the crews well disciplined. It was the opinion of the engine fitters that the diesels they worked on were certainly of German design if not German manufacture. During their stay the Russian officers were allowed some shore leave, as were the men, but in small groups and always under the watchful eye of the political officer. The Soviet squadron sailed from Halifax on 29 December bound for Reykjavik.

## TRAINING SUBMARINES

From the late 1940s onwards, the rapidly increasing involvement of the RCN in ASW operations emphasized the need for live training at sea, particularly in the prosecution of the anti-submarine attack. Events to that time had demonstrated a very low level of anti-submarine efficiency in almost all RCN ships then at sea, particularly in those operating under Canadian command. With up to 140 new anti-submarine vessels scheduled to enter service during 1941, the need to give realistic training in Canadian waters had become acute. Canada sought help from both the RN and the USN. The RN had no submarines available to station in Canada for training purposes. The United States, though not yet directly involved in the war, was in the midst of a massive rearmament program and was not prepared to supply submarines, even old ones, to anyone.

The development of a towed asdic transponder by the Canadian scientific community made up somewhat for the complete lack of anti-submarine sea-training facilities. This device was streamed on a line behind a tug or harbour craft. Depth could be varied by changing speed and hauling in or paying out the towline. When the sound wave emitted from a ship's asdic set (or sonar transmitter) struck the transponder, it emitted a return signal, much as a submarine hull would reflect the signal back to the transmitter. However, the device was only suitable for giving training in very basic active acoustic procedures.

From the beginning, sea-training facilities in the UK were heavily tasked with meeting their own training requirements. Canadian destroyers and corvettes working with the RN were given training and equipment improvements as if they were part of the RN command to which they were attached, but this was exceptional. It was a rare occasion on which other RCN vessels were accommodated. The ever-increasing number of anti-submarine escorts working out of St. John's and Halifax seldom made the complete transatlantic crossing and so were forced to make do as best they could at home. The Admiralty was fully aware of the plight of the RCN, but with every submarine pressed into operational service, the RN was in no position to help.

In August 1940, a Dutch boat, HNMS *O15,* commanded by Lieutenant Hans van Oostram Soede, had to put into Halifax with engine problems while making her way to England from her peacetime station at Curaçao. Despite the state of her engines, she was practically commandeered by the Canadian authorities to provide training services to the RCN.

In August 1941, while operating from Pictou, the crew of *O15* was invited to take tea with HRH Princess Juliana of the Netherlands. The reception took place at Pictou Lodge, a Canadian National Railways holiday resort near the town of Pictou on the Northumberland Strait, where the princess and

HMS *P512* off Pictou Nova Scotia, summer 1942. (Author's collection)

HMS *P554* acting the part of a U-boat while training RCN personnel in boarding procedures, St. Margaret's Bay, 1942. (CDR L.F.L. Hill, RNR)

her children were enjoying a summer holiday. According to the recollections of the crew members, everything except tea was served, and a very enjoyable time was had by all.

Working for the Canadians had its hazards. Stories abound, but it has been reliably reported that on one occasion *O15* was fired on by the shore batteries guarding the Halifax approaches. On another, she was slightly damaged by a practice bomb dropped from an aircraft. This also happened later to one of the British boats. She also became entangled in a sweep-wire when a minesweeper passed over her position not realizing she was there.

As a final indignity, *O15* was rammed by a destroyer while moored to a buoy in Halifax harbour. One of the lend-lease four-stacker destroyers was moored to a buoy in the same trot. She was preparing for sea and had steam up. Somehow, full power was accidentally applied to one engine. She broke her moorings and slammed into *O15*, puncturing a main ballast tank. While the crew shut down the boat, the submarine assumed an alarming list, but the damage was not serious, and she was soon repaired on the Dartmouth marine slips.

Despite persistent engine problems, *O15* operated as best she could for nearly two years before undergoing repairs at Philadelphia and finally reaching England. At the same time, British submarines on passage to the United States for refits were scheduled to provide training services for a few months en route.

With the entry of the United States into the war in December 1941, help was soon forthcoming from south of the border. In the spring of 1942, the USN offered the British the loan of two—later increased to as many as eighteen—1920s-vintage submarines. In the end, the Admiralty acquired nine of these as part of the ships-for-bases lend-lease deal. Three were 569/680-ton *R* class boats and six of the larger 854/1062-ton *S* class submarines,[35] the American navy's infamous "pig-boats." The RN determined that the *S* class boats had a limited operational potential, while the *R* class were suitable only for training. Only one of the RN-operated American *S* class boats was ever used operationally. Manned by a Polish crew and named *Jastrzab*, she came to an unfortunate end at sea in May 1942, when mistaken for a U-boat by a Norwegian escort. She was

35  Not to be confused with the much more modern British *S* class submarines.

HMS *Seawolf* diving. She is depicted here in full operational trim complete with machine gun mount behind the bridge. Note the gentle dive angle, sufficient to get the fore planes under but not enough to expose the screws. (E. A. D. Holmes)

depth-charged but managed to surface and most of the crew was rescued as their boat sank. It was concluded that *Jastrzab* had strayed outside her station boundaries because of the obsolete navigation equipment she carried.

As the American submarines were reactivated and made serviceable, the British crews were sent over by sea and joined the boats at New London, Connecticut. The one feature of this period noted by the British submariners, was that the American steamers were all dry. They found the American submarines to be very similar to their own *H* and *L* classes, which considerably simplified the familiarization process. There were a few domestic problems. One of the COs discovered that his crew was making both tea and coffee in the coffee urns, with the result that neither beverage tasted quite right. He sorted that out quickly by acquiring some kettles and teapots. RN submarines were not equipped with coffee urns, nor were the American submarines provided with teapots and kettles. American torpedoes and fire-

control equipment were also something of a mystery to the British sailors, but fortunately they never had to use them except for occasional practice firings. On at least one occasion one of the vintage weapons ran in a wide circle and hit the firing submarine. The torpedo sank, and the submarine suffered only a minor dent.

Two *R* class boats *P512* and *P514,* and two *S* class, *P553* and *P554* were allocated to the RCN. Of these, *P514* and *P553* were based at St. John's, Newfoundland, to provide anti-submarine training to the ships of Flag Officer Newfoundland Force. With the arrival of the US Army Air Force maritime patrol aircraft at Argentia, one of these boats was allocated to provide anti-submarine training in Placentia Bay for the USAAF. The second boat continued to work out of St. John's with the ships. The waters around Newfoundland were notoriously bad for anti-submarine training but, as there was no opportunity for the ships to train elsewhere, they were forced to make do.

## THE LOSS OF *P514*

Just after midnight on 21 June 1942 HMS *P514* was sunk in error by the minesweeper HMCS *Georgian*. The tragedy took place off Cape Race when the path of the eastbound submarine and her corvette escort, which were heading for St. John's from Argentia, intercepted that of CL 43, a westbound convoy being escorted by the minesweeper. Problems with one of the ships in CL 43 had delayed the start of the convoy, and it was several hours behind schedule. At the same time, an eastbound convoy, SC 88, which had been blown north of its intended track, intercepted and passed through CL 43. The situation was confusing and dangerous. Visibility was poor, and the night sky was overcast with frequent mist patches.

*Georgian* detected approaching diesel-engine noises on her hydrophones and turned onto the bearing to investigate. When the lookouts spotted the submarine, the helm was immediately put over and without hesitation she rammed *P514* amidships. At 0040 hours Atlantic Time, the submarine went down in 27 fathoms. There were no survivors. A lone body was spotted in the water at the time but sank before it could be recovered. The body of Engine Room Artificer N.C. Bennett came ashore near Ferrylands a month later. He was interred in the local graveyard with full military honours.

At the enquiry, no blame was attached to anyone concerned. It was NSHQ policy then, and throughout the war, not to inform escort forces of the movements of Allied submarines for fear they would hesitate in attacking U-boats. The only measure of safety offered to Allied submarines passing through an operational area was the establishment of temporary no-attack zones for aircraft, but the submarines were always on their own when it came to both ships and aircraft.

### PICTOU, DIGBY AND BERMUDA BOATS

That same summer, *P512* and *P554*, in company with *O15*, were running from the original RCN sea-training base at Pictou, Nova Scotia, an extension of the HMCS *Stadacona* training organization. Here, engineering, gunnery, seamanship and asdic-operator training were being given aboard corvettes and minesweepers in the Northumberland Strait areas. When Pictou harbour showed signs of freezing over training operations were shifted to the sheltered, nearly ice-free, waters of St. Margaret's Bay. During the summer of 1943, all anti-submarine warfare sea training was moved to HMCS *Cornwallis,* the newly opened training base at Deep Brook, Nova Scotia, and the Bay of Fundy areas. However, Pictou continued to be used for training and work-ups[36] on a limited scale until the end of the war, and the Digby-based submarines often provided services there.

Once the British wartime building programs began producing new submarines in quantity, some of the older RN boats were released from operations, allowing the ex-USN lend-lease boats to be replaced by more up-to-date submarines. Between January and November 1943, HMS *Seawolf, L23* and *L27* arrived. These boats were assigned to HMCS *Cornwallis* and were based at nearby Digby. *L26,* later joined by *L27,* was sent to Bermuda to work with HMS *Somers Isle*, the shared RN–RCN sea-training base near St. George's. *P512, P553* and *P554* were returned to their owners. Bermuda was important to the Canadian navy because of the excellent weather and water conditions. Most new-construction work-ups were carried out from there, particularly for the new frigates and rebuilt corvettes.

Following the wind-down in the Mediterranean in late 1943, plans were made to replace *Seawolf* and the *L* class boats with a quartet of newly refitted *U* class boats, all veterans of the Mediterranean campaign. *Unseen* arrived in Canada at the end of July 1944 and was based at Digby. *Unruffled,* which had accompanied *Unseen,* went on to Bermuda. She was joined by *United* and *Upright,* which arrived during August. The Bermuda training flotilla was later augmented by their recent enemies when four Italian submarines with their crews were pressed into service to provide anti-submarine training services to Allied warships. The *L* class boats were laid up at Halifax and Digby.

---

36  Work-ups is the process by which a newly commissioned ship's crew is exercised in ship handling, damage control and action procedures by a specialized team.

This is the only known photo of the ill-fated *P514* (ex USS *R19*), Lt W.A.
Phillimore RN, under the white ensign.

(Author's collection)

## A COXSWAIN'S TALE

*Ernie Potts, who served for most of the war in submarines, vividly recalls his experiences as coxswain of a British submarine in Canada. His account has been included here in his own words.*

Early in 1944, I was sent to Sheerness in Kent to take over as Coxswain of *Unseen*. She was being refitted in the old Naval Dockyard. In May we left the dry-dock and after swinging compass and making a trim dive, left for the Holy Loch where we joined the flotilla alongside HMS *Forth*.

We only had a short stay there and then we left for Canada. As far as I can remember we had an uneventful crossing of about eight days arriving at St. John's, Newfoundland on 9 July 1944. Soon after securing alongside we were visited by a Supply Rating to take our order for victualling stores. The Canadian system of victualling was completely new to me. There seemed to be no limit to what we could order and a variety of foods that we had not known since peacetime, even to the luxury of ice cream.

Every time he asked me if I would like something, I said, "Yes." About three hours later an enormous van arrived on the quay. Where were we to stow it all I had no idea but we managed. Normally our meat arrived already boned to save valuable space. The lamb arrived in complete carcasses. I gave the job of dismembering it to the Gun Layer who attacked it with an axe, the only instrument he could lay his hands on. My only concern was the lack of rum. I was not dangerously low but would have felt happier with a few extra gallons.

After two days, we sailed again, this time for Halifax where we arrived on 14 June. I don't know why we stayed there for a few days, but it did give me a chance to top-up with rum from the RN depot there.

The next stop was Digby where we tied-up at the public jetty normally used by fishing boats and the ferry to St. John, NB. At that time, we were the only submarine at Digby. *Seawolf* was based there but was running from St. John for a few weeks. We were accommodated at the Navy League Hostel, which was at the far end of the main street of the town.

The arrangement was that we had all meals on board. The duty watch stayed aboard overnight and the off-duty hands stayed at the hostel, returning aboard for breakfast in the morning.

It wasn't until then that we were told the true reason for our visit to Canada. As the Canadian navy had no boats of their own, we were to act as target, asdic running for them each day to train RCN and RCAF personnel in anti-submarine detection and attack.

The daily routine was soon established. When the off-duty watches returned on board for 0700 hrs the crew would eat breakfast. Hands would then turn-to and clean ship until exercises were confirmed by the base, HMCS *Cornwallis*, about 15 miles away up the Annapolis Basin. Hands would then go to Harbour Stations; we would slip and steam out through Digby Gut and rendezvous with one or more converted yachts in the Bay of Fundy. Towing a float to mark our position, we would dive until attacked and then surface. An attack was signalled by the surface ship dropping hand-grenades into the water. We could also signal our position by releasing smoke candles. This would go on throughout the day until about 1700 hrs when we would return to the pier. The off-duty watches would then go ashore, the main meal of the day having been eaten while we were dived.

There was no exercising on the weekends. The hands would be turned to during the forenoons, have their tots and dinner on board and afterward the off-duty watches were allowed ashore. Most went to the hostel for the afternoon then out and about in the evening.

Fog was very prevalent during the mornings in the Bay of Fundy and if it was foggy, we did not go out to exercise until it had cleared. If it remained foggy after midday, exercises were cancelled. All the crew would pray for fog, work like mad to make the boat spotless so that the Jimmy had no alternative but to grant a Make and Mend and give leave to the off-duty watches directly exercises were cancelled.

Civilian clothes were worn most times when ashore. We were on Canadian rates of pay, which were considerably higher than the RN. Facilities at the hostel were good and all in all we had a pretty good time.

Some days aircraft from the air base at Pennfield Ridge in New Brunswick would join the surface craft and drop small practice bombs on us. On one occasion, an aircraft scored a direct hit on our periscope shattering the top of it. This entailed a trip to Halifax to have a new periscope fitted and this was

HMS *Unseen*'s Jolly Roger, Digby Nova Scotia, 1944, showing eight ships sunk, three damaged (bars), five secret agent landings (daggers and lighthouse), gun actions (crossed guns), a record-breaking deep dive (diver's helmet), and "The Saint" symbol compliments of the mystery writer Lesley Charteris.
(R. C. Foster)

done between 6 December and 1 January, 1945. While at Halifax we were fitted with a dummy snorkel mast to make us look like a German U-boat. We discovered later that it looked nothing like the German original.

In June, we were joined by *L-23* and in May by *Seawolf*. *Seawolf* went to Philadelphia for a refit in July but *L-23* continued to run with us out of Digby. By the end of the war, there were five *U* class boats at Digby. Except for *Unseen*, they had come from Bermuda. *L-23* was paid off at the end of 1944 and *Seawolf* was scrapped in Canada after the war, but the *U* class went home afterwards.

On 21 February 1945, I stayed ashore to arrange for some supplies. When I returned to the hostel, I received the news that *Unseen* and *Seawolf* had collided while both were dived. Apparently the surface vessels should have been watching the floats the boats were towing but they had not signalled them to surface when the floats showed they were on a collision course. When I arrived at the pier, I was relieved to find that it had been a glancing blow. The only damage done was a badly bent gun platform on *Unseen* and there were no injuries. This time repairs were carried out at St. John's where we arrived on 12 March '45.

While we were at Halifax over Christmas 1944, the TGM [Torpedo Gunner's Mate] was doing routines on one of the torpedoes and sitting with the pistol[37] on his lap when the detonator exploded. His whole abdomen was peppered with tiny aluminium particles but there was no serious injury. He was only out of action for about two weeks.

During the early part of the commission an Asdic rating had to return to England and was temporarily replaced by a

---

37  Part of the warhead detonating device.

*Unseen* at Digby, 1944-45. (McBride collection)

HMS *Unseen* in Digby Gut, 1944, during gun action drill. (J.A. Cross)

Canadian PO. He was a grand lad, settled in very well and liked the life so much that he remained with us until we returned to the UK at the end of the war.

Every Saturday sailing races were organized by the RCN in the Annapolis Basin. It became a regular thing for the officers to take a few ratings and sail in the cutter class while the PO Telegraphist and myself would take a crew and sail in the whaler class. Hardly a week went by without one of us winning—the prize was a silver spoon and I think the PO Tel kept them all.

Other afternoons and evenings we spent horseback riding, ice skating tobogganing, etc. The PO Tel came off a horse, I came to grief skating, and we both finished up in hospital, but not for long—our only war injuries!

Two of the ratings, AB Weeks, the gunlayer, and an Asdic rating, both married local girls. They had to return with us at war's end but both rejoined their brides in Canada on being demobbed.

Shortly after VE Day, a Sunderland caught a U-boat, the *U889*, on the surface and she was brought into Shelburne. Off Digby we put half our crew aboard the U-boat and took her CO and several of the crew aboard *Unseen* before escorting her into Shelburne.

We left Canada for home in September 1945. We ran into bad weather the second day out and it was the worst trip I had during my whole time in the service. It took us eleven days to reach Londonderry. We were pooped twice and had to slam the upper lid shut to keep from flooding the control room. The Sperry compass toppled and the magnetic compass reflector was flooded so we had to steer from the bridge. We steamed for five days on dead reckoning, as the navigator couldn't get a sight. We got a fix on the ninth day and it put us almost bang on course.

We left *Unseen* in 'Derry. As most of the crew were HOs [Hostilities Only] they demobbed in Belfast and headed for home. The rest of us went to Blockhouse. It was all over for us.

## WAR'S END

IN THE period immediately following VE-Day, two German U-boats surrendered to Canadian forces at sea. *U889* was first, hoisting the black flag of surrender to an RCAF long-range Liberator that had spotted her on the surface off Newfoundland on 10 May. Later that day the U-boat was joined by surface escorts to be taken in to Shelburne, where they arrived on 12 May. She was moored at a buoy while a crew from the boats at Digby and a twelve-man RCN boarding party were put aboard. After most of the German crew was taken off, she was brought alongside.

On the night of 11 May, *U190* reported her position by wireless and was intercepted that night by two frigates detached from a nearby convoy. Half of her crew was taken off at sea and guards were put aboard. *U190* had been responsible for the sinking of HMCS *Esquimalt*, the RCN's last casualty of the war, only weeks before. This caused some tension between the Germans and their captors aboard the frigate HMCS *Victoriaville*. The Germans apparently received some rough handling, but there were no incidents of consequence. *U190* arrived in Bay Bulls, Newfoundland, on 14 May and was secured to a buoy. The rest of her crew was removed by launch and a scratch crew of RN submariners drawn from the boats at Digby and in refit at Philadelphia was put aboard. The submarine was in a shambles and very low in the water. With the help of the German engineer, she was made seaworthy, cleaned up and commissioned in the RCN on 19 May. HMCS *U190* was taken into St. John's on 3 June.

Both U-boats were taken over by the RCN and manned by mixed RN–RCN crews. As long as the boats were capable of diving the COs were submariners and the officers were a mix of General Service and submariners. Both boats were quickly sent on victory tours around the Maritimes and up the St. Lawrence River as far as Montreal. On returning to Halifax they carried out a series of dived and surfaced technical evaluation trials for the benefit of the scientists sent down from Ottawa.

*U889* was one of the U-boats allocated to the USN and was turned over to American authorities for disposal in January 1946. *U190* had been allocated to the RN, which allowed the RCN to retain the submarine for evaluation and trials purposes.

After VE-Day, all four of the British *U* class boats were temporarily transferred to the RCN to meet the anticipated ASW training program for the war in the Pacific. It was expected that the war with Japan would last at least two more years. *Unruffled, United* and *Upright* joined *Unseen* at Digby. Having been warned that the RN was going to be short-handed, the RCN was actively preparing to help man the four boats. The RCNVR officers still serving in RN submarines overseas were being brought home, and plans were in hand to train volunteer ratings. Three of the Canadian submariners were already in HMS *Unseen*. Lieutenant Jack Cross was the CO, Lieutenant G. L. McPhee, first lieutenant, and Lieutenant W. H. Holmes the navigating officer while Lieutenant E. K. Fowler was First Lieutenant aboard *United*. The intent was that as Canadians were brought in and trained they would gradually replace the RN submariners. To facilitate this process, a fifth *U* class boat, HMS *Una*, was sent to Canada specifically to train Canadian submariners. Her coxswain was Petty Officer Tom Dower from Grand Falls, Newfoundland. She arrived at Digby early in September.

Following the sudden ending of the fighting against Japan in mid-August and the for-

## THE COLD WAR ERA

HMS *Alderney* on arrival at Halifax, 31 July 1952. (CDR E. G. Gigg)

*Seawolf*, *L23* and *Unseen* alongside the SS *Largo* at Digby, spring 1945.
(McBride collection)

mal surrender two weeks later, rapid demobilization brought the RCN to a virtual standstill. NSHQ had no option but to relinquish the Digby-based submarines. As ASW was deemed an important aspect of the post-war navy, the RCN made representation to the Admiralty for the retention of one submarine for training and work-ups. The RN obliged and the most recent arrival, HMS *Una*, was instructed to remain. For a brief time that month, all five *U* class boats congregated at Digby. *Upright* and *United* sailed for the UK at the end of the first week in September, *Unseen* and *Unruffled* followed a month later. As the RCN was unable to resume ASW training on a scale sufficient to justify the retention of the boat, *Una* sailed for England at the beginning of November, leaving her Newfoundland coxswain behind.

This left only HMCS *U190* with a mixed RCN–RN crew, almost all of whom were reservists due for demobilization. As there was never any intention of operating the boat, she was paid off on 24 July 1947 and the crew released. Stripped of useful equipment and painted a bright yellow with red stripes, *U190* was taken to sea and sunk off Halifax on Trafalgar Day, 21 October 1947, in a position close to that of her last victim. The exercise was called Operation Scuppered. Symbolically, *U190* was to be attacked by rocket-firing aircraft, fired on by destroyers and as she sank, depth-charged by the frigates. Ironically, she succumbed to the rocket attack and went down almost immediately.

The boarding party and British submariners taking over *U 889* in the approaches to Shelburne Nova Scotia. (Frank Deadman)

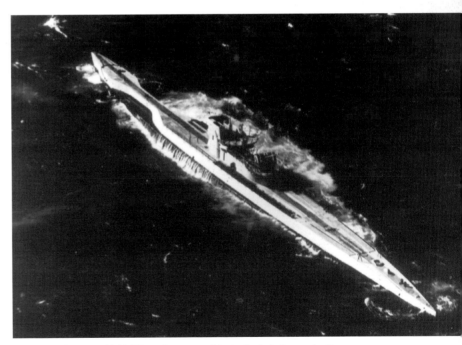

"Operation Scuppered." *U 190* as she appeared just prior to being sunk off Halifax on Trafalgar Day, 21 October 1947. (Author's collection)

A Sunderland flying boat keeping an eye on *U 889* as she heads for Shelburne Nova Scotia. The photo demonstrates how difficult it was to spot these boats in heavy seas. (E. A. D. Holmes)

HMS *Ambush, Astute* and *Alderney* alongside. A rare occurrence indeed. (CDR W. T. J. Fox RN (Ret'd))

The laid-up RN boats were all disposed of in Canada just after the end of the war. *L-26* was deliberately sunk as an anti-submarine bottom target in the approaches to Halifax about two miles southeast of Horseshoe Ledge Buoy. *Seawolf* and *L-27* were towed away and scrapped by Marine Industries of Sorel, Quebec. The same firm also bought *L-23*, but she parted her tow in a gale and sank somewhere off Nova Scotia.

## POST-WAR TRAINING BOATS

By the summer of 1946, the post-war navy had begun to stabilize, and an attempt was made to resume anti-submarine training.[38] As a temporary expedient, the RCN arranged with the Admiralty to rent HMS *Token* for a trial period of two months. On the face of it, this appeared to be an economical way of acquiring the services of a training submarine. The total running costs, which included diesel fuel, lubricants, miscella-

neous repairs, provisions and other consumables, came to less than $5,000.

When the RCN tried to renew this arrangement for the following year, they found they could have a submarine for only two months, and under much different, more expensive, terms. Not only would the RCN be expected to pay for the running costs, but also for shore accommodations, pay supplements to bring RN pay up to par with Canadian rates, as well as any docking, towage and pilotage fees. While NSHQ mulled this over, it was decided to look elsewhere—which meant to the United States, and preferably free of charge. The Americans indicated that they could provide a training boat, but in the Seattle area and only for a couple of weeks in October. This would not meet the needs of the east coast and the RCN decided to accept the Admiralty offer after all. The RN scheduled an *A* class boat for the autumn.

---

38   Remarkable as it may seem, ASW was then a specialty of the RCN(R).

The Americans, though slow to respond, did not ignore the RCN's plea for help on the east coast altogether. A much easier, less formal relationship existed with the USN than with the RN. Though somewhat restricted in what they could do for what was essentially a foreign navy, the USN actively sought opportunities to help their neighbour and wartime ally. Between June 1947 and August 1948 various American submarines provided a total of nine weeks direct training for Canadian ships in short, one-to-two-week parcels. In addition, the USN invited the RCN to participate in their own ASW training exercises held off Key West, Florida, in March 1948. This was a fortuitous opportunity as no RN submarines were available for hire in 1948. For as long as the USN retained diesel-powered submarines for training on the east coast, the RCN was given frequent training opportunities either as joint participants in USN exercises or for short periods of dedicated ASW exercise time.

It was during this time, 1946 to 1950, that the Soviet submarine threat was being fully realized. In their take-over of eastern Germany at the end of the Second World War, the Soviet Union had acquired not only examples of the most advanced German submarines, but also the technology and trained personnel to build and support them. It did not take the USSR long to begin an ambitious re-equipment program that would see the Soviet navy take a lead in submarine development and construction which it would pursue for the next three decades. Consequently, with the encouragement of Britain and the USA, the RCN began to take an interest in the importance of anti-submarine warfare.

The organizing of ASW submarine time was becoming an ongoing preoccupation for RCN training planners. No sooner had one loan been negotiated than it was time to start all over again for the next year. Beginning in 1949, a more permanent arrangement was negotiated with the RN. One submarine was to be made available for RCN and RCAF anti-submarine warfare training on the east coast for about nine months of the year. (See Table 7 for a complete listing of the submarines involved.) The west coast was left to rely on US–Canadian joint ASW exercises and occasional training-submarine services provided by the USN.

In July 1948, NSHQ had set up the RCN Submarine Committee to look into the problem of supplying training sub-

marines for the navy on a long-term basis. One of their early recommendations was to borrow an RN submarine and partially man it with Canadians, as had been intended with the Digby boats. As there was only one trained submarine officer left in the RCN, it was decided to approach the RN to see if Canadian officers could be included in the training courses given in the UK, as had been done during the war. Assuming that this was going to be a recurring situation, the RN agreed, probably in the hopes that Canada would eventually be able to acquire and man its own submarines. Little did anyone realize just how long, and tortuous, a process it was going to be!

Twenty-four candidates were initially identified. This was whittled down to six in the selection process and in the end, only three were named for the course. The first post-war Canadian submarine trainee was Sub-lieutenant G.W.S. Brookes who joined S/M OTC No. 116 in June 1950. At about the same time, a naval constructor officer was sent to the US Submarine School at New London to take the American basic submarine training course. Between then and 1983, over one hundred Canadian officers undertook their S/M OTC in the UK. Of these, twenty-eight eventually passed their COQC.

Between 1949 and 1955, RCN ASW training needs were met by rotating two British submarines per year at Halifax and taking advantage of any training opportunities offered by the USN. In an effort to provide training more efficiently, NSHQ proposed the loan of an RN boat for eighteen months at a time. Initially, the RN had reservations about this proposal. The authorities were particularly concerned with using operational submarines for ASW training for long periods. This would result in reduced operational efficiency through a lack of pro-submarine time in which the submarine could exercise its offensive skills. The RN also pointed out that using an operational boat for eighteen months would escalate the cost considerably. A deployment of that length meant that the crew would be accompanied by their families and this expense would be passed on to Canada. The three-month rotation of fresh operational submarines was more acceptable to the RN. This provided the RCN with at least a minimum of ASW training time at a modest cost of about $80,000 a year.

Nevertheless, the RCN held out for the longer-term loan. As early as 1950 the British authorities actually suggested that the RCN borrow a fully manned training submarine (as opposed to an operational boat) for eighteen months at a stretch. They indicated there would be no problem with Britain providing the boat as long as Canada fully supported and maintained it. It was even suggested that a boat could be provided for the west coast as well.

While NSHQ thought this over and did their sums, there was a change in senior personnel in Britain. This led to the imposition of new conditions and the Canadian planners revisited their proposals. In 1951, the idea of the RCN manning borrowed submarines was again explored. Temporarily at least, this proved to be impossible due to manning shortages throughout the fleet brought on by the demands of the Korean conflict. Siphoning off a hundred and fifty or so trained tradesmen and a dozen officers would cripple the surface fleet.

In the meantime, the RN was suffering another round of personnel cutbacks. The Admiralty was still prepared to provide submarines on a long-term basis but preferred that the RCN man them. As a stopgap, the RN suggested that Canada either buy or lease two *U* class boats, *Upstart* and *Untiring,* recently returned from the Greek navy. These, it was pointed out, required a crew of only thirty-one each, plus a support party and shore facilities.

The idea seemed to have some merit so the RCN examined the proposal in detail and discussions resumed early in 1953. It was revealed that the submarines required some work. They needed a refit and would have to be provided with a snort induction system and radar. As well, the work would have to be done in a private yard at greater expense than in the naval dockyards, which were booked solid. The RN indicated they were willing to provide essential personnel on loan for as long as it would take the RCN to train their own personnel. By this time, NSHQ was taking the proposal seriously. Plans were prepared for the necessary support facilities at Halifax and for the selection and training of personnel.

To senior Canadian authorities, the concept of creating a submarine service to provide only training submarines had several drawbacks, all of which had been encountered, but unresolved, during the war. The cost of buying or leasing training submarines and supporting them was prohibitive and could not be supported solely as a training expense. There was really no such thing as a training submarine. Submarines used for training were, for the most part, obsolescent operational boats such as the *U* class—inexpensive in first cost but costly to maintain. Personnel at all trade and rank levels would have to be taken from the fleet to man them, which would cause disruptions in career planning. There was also the dilemma of whether service in training submarines alone would provide sufficient incentive for men to want to serve in them. Overall, operating submarines strictly for training did not seem to be a cost-effective solution. On the other hand, the institution of an operational submarine service was adjudged politically and morally unacceptable.

Discussions continued with the British authorities in the hopes of coming to a long-term agreement whereby the RCN could acquire the services of more submarines for longer periods of time without establishing its own submarine service. As before, the RN indicated they could probably provide the boats but, faced with an ever-declining manpower ceiling, not the personnel. The whole process was gradually forcing the government up against its own wall of moral reluctance and fiscal restraints. The navy could see no solution other than to acquire the two *U* class boats and start an RCN training submarine service. The operational value of the *U* class boats was negligible in any case, even if they were armed.

## THE SIXTH SUBMARINE SQUADRON

With the advent of the *St. Laurent* class destroyer escorts in 1954 and the overall expansion of the RCN to 21,000 men, the need for long-term, realistic anti-submarine training time escalated considerably. In 1953, the maximum predicted requirement for the period 1954 to 1957 was calculated at 750 days for the east coast and 450 days for the west coast. It was estimated that it would take six submarines to meet the full demand, two at Esquimalt, four at Halifax. The assumption at the time was that one dedicated training submarine could provide 196 training days per year. In light of subsequent experience, this was to prove optimistic, to say the least.

The possession of two *U* class boats would certainly not solve the problem. Between them they could provide at the most, four hundred training days per year—but it would be a start. There was also the possibility of utilising the submarines themselves in the anti-submarine role, a consideration that had arisen as far back as 1948 but again, was something that

L-R: LtCdr T. B. Dowling (CO), Captain J. C. Littler (COS MARCOM), Cdr W. T. J. Fox (SM6), and LtCdr Bonner on the return of HMS *Astute* from exercises, 4 April 1955. (MARCOM Museum)

hinted at an operational capability. The government, however, remained stubbornly opposed to the establishment of a Canadian submarine service for any purpose.

The answer emerged unexpectedly from a meeting with the Admiralty held in May 1954. The RN proposed that a squadron of three fully operational *A* class submarines be established at Halifax on condition the RCN supplied the equivalent number of men for two crews and a support party. Canada would also be required to provide suitable shore-support facilities and to pay the bills. This kind of arrangement had been in place in Australia since December 1949, and seemed to offer an acceptable solution to the Canadian situation.

NSHQ set to work on the proposal. There were many problems to be overcome. Subsequent to the changes introduced in 1949, RCN and RN codes of discipline were now quite different

and a compromise had to be found if the two groups of personnel were to mix both at home and in the UK. Support facilities for the three boats had to be set up in the dockyard and agreements reached on which navy would pay for what. Despite setbacks and misunderstandings, the details were hammered out and the agreement written. It seemed to be the deal that Canada was looking for.

The contract with the Admiralty, known as *The Heads of Agreement for the Formation of a Royal Navy Submarine Squadron for Service in Canadian Waters*,[39] received cabinet approval in November 1954. The essential elements of the agreement were:

> The RN will form the Sixth Submarine Squadron, consisting of three *A* class Submarines, for service in Canadian waters. The first two submarines to be available in March 1955, the third submarine to be

---

39 Letter, Admiralty M.158/454 of 21 October 1954. The actual Agreement was attached to the letter as an Appendix. PAC RG24, Acc 8384/167, Vol 3924, File 8357SS, Pt. 5 and Minutes of the 424th meeting of the Naval Board, October 1954.

An ice-coated HMS *Amphion*
shortly after her arrival at Halifax,
14 January 1957.
(Author's collection)

available in June 1955. The submarines will each perform an operational tour of duty of eighteen months in Canadian waters, returning to the United Kingdom for periodic refit and to give leave to the RN members of the crews. This arrangement will ensure an average of two and one half submarines available for training in Canadian waters at any one time.

The command of the squadron and of the individual submarines will be vested in the Admiralty.

At no time will the crew of any submarine contain more than fifty percent RCN personnel.

The total manpower requirement for the squadron including spare crew and base staff will be 304. Of this, 180 will be provided by the RCN, of which not more than 152 RCN personnel will serve in Canada, the balance being employed elsewhere in the RN.

RCN personnel will be paid RCN pay and allowances at all times.

RN personnel serving in the squadron will be paid RN pay and allowances by the United Kingdom, plus an additional bonus, on a daily rate basis, to be paid by the RCN except when the submarines return to the United Kingdom for refit. The Commander of the squadron and his immediate staff consisting of two officers and three men, who will be accommodated ashore in Halifax, will be paid RN pay and allowances by the United Kingdom, plus the difference between RCN and RN pay and allowances to be paid by Canada.

The crews of the submarines will be under RN discipline and conditions of service at all times with the exception that RCN personnel serving in the squadron will be entitled to normal Canadian leave.

The RCN will pay the cost of running repairs, normal operating expenses and victualling of the crews, except when the submarines are in refit in the United Kingdom. Accommodation will be provided at RCN Barracks, Halifax, while the submarines are in harbour.

The RCN will be responsible for paying the costs of periodical refits for two out of the three sub-

marines. This is estimated at a maximum annual sum of $340,000.

In the event of total constructive loss or damage, when under the functional control of the RCN, the RCN will be financially responsible to such an extent as may be agreed to at the time between the Admiralty and the RCN.

When the submarines are operating in Bermuda waters the frigates of the British America and West Indies Squadron may join with HMC ships for joint antisubmarine training at the discretion of the Flag Officer, Atlantic Coast. If at any time the Admiralty should desire these submarines to be used for any period exclusively for training RN ships, such arrangements would be considered outside the terms of this agreement and subject to special negotiation.

The terms of this agreement are to be effective for four years, renewable for periods of two years thereafter.

The Sixth Submarine Squadron (SM6) was brought into being on 3 February 1955 when the Order in Council authorizing the expenditure of public funds on the squadron was issued. Its shore-support base, HMS *Ambrose,* opened in the basement of the old Flag Building (building D14) at Halifax on 5 March 1955. Ten days later the first SM6 submarine, HMS *Astute*, arrived. (See Table 7 for a complete listing of SM6 submarines.)

SM6 mechanical and ordnance workshops were set up in what used to be the North Machine Shop (building D2). Torpedoes were serviced and stored at the existing torpedo workshop in the Naval Armament Depot (now the Dockyard Annex) across the harbour in Dartmouth. Periscope repair facilities were also established there in conjunction with the Optical Shop. Spare torpedo warheads and gun ammunition were stored in the naval magazine at Bedford. The submarines berthed on old Jetty 5 (Jetty NK). Maintenance dockings were mostly carried out at the Dartmouth Marine Slips. Accommodations for single and unaccompanied married men were provided at HMCS *Stadacona* in C Block, one of the disused wooden barrack blocks located where the Fleet Club now stands. Officers and senior rates were accommodated in their respective messes.

"Dead-eye" Dowling, CO of HMS *Astute* poses at the attack periscope. The helmsman's position can be seen in the centre. The fire control calculator ("fruit machine") and firing levers are on the right. (MARCOM Museum)

Well in advance of the formal opening of SM6, NSHQ set the wheels in motion for the selection of personnel to be sent to the UK for training. According to armed forces press releases, at the first call over fifteen hundred men volunteered for service in submarines. The first forty-eight Canadian submarine trainees left for England at the end of November 1954. This group was quickly followed by a second of eighty ratings. Split into two parties, they flew over at the beginning of 1955. The first group left on 2 January, the second two days later. A third group of forty-two volunteers departed on 24 January. On completion of their training these men, and the smaller groups that followed in later years, were distributed throughout the RN submarine service including SM6. The term of service for RCN personnel in submarines was for an initial two and one-half years and this was renewable by mutual agreement.

The training proceeded satisfactorily, and, in April 1955, a progress report was sent to NSHQ. Although the majority of the Canadians were graded above average in ability, problems existed in compatibility between RCN and RN trade and rank structures. This was particularly so in those areas where the RCN had gone to great lengths to create its own identity after the Second World War.

One of the principal problems was that RCN junior electrician's mates did not have enough technical knowledge for submarines. Another was caused by the RN having separate Underwater Weapons (torpedo) and Underwater Control (sonar) trades, while the RCN had a joint Torpedo Anti-Submarine trade. Differences also existed in basic engine room training and the level of experience. As well, there was a need to correct some of the rank and trade imbalances caused by RCN leading seamen having petty officer equivalent trade status. This, it was suggested, could be achieved through granting local acting promotions, which were used frequently in the RN. However, the RN commented that the willingness of the RCN men to learn and adapt greatly reduced the magnitude of many of the problems. The remaining issues were quickly resolved when NSHQ agreed to allow local acting promotions and quickly upgraded the basic electrician requirement to an electrical technician. Men in the Torpedo Anti-Submarine trade were assigned to either the Underwater Weapons or the Underwater Control trade when they were taken into submarines, thereby resolving that issue. The first groups had included a number of ordinary seamen and in view of their lack of technical experience it was agreed that all personnel in future would be of able seamen rank or above. In view of the difficulties inherent in trying to integrate people of two very different navies, the initial training and absorption of the Canadians into RN submarines went remarkably well.[40]

Most Canadians, particularly the younger ones, felt very much at home in Britain. They quickly discovered that they were being quite handsomely compensated in comparison to their British messmates. A Canadian leading seaman drew wages and allowances roughly comparable to the basic pay of a junior British lieutenant! As well, Canadian personnel over nineteen years old were entitled to a duty-free ration of three 40-ounce bottles of spirits, six bottles of wine and 880 Canadian brand cigarettes per month. Those serving aboard a boat could also claim the RN cigarette ration of 440 cigarettes per month. All of this had to be paid for but the prices were very low compared to the same products at retail. Although the RN-issue "blue liner" cigarettes were not popular among the Canadians (nor among the British for that matter) they were useful for barter or to tide one over between pay-days. In addition, married personnel received a generous housing allowance. All this at a time when a pint of beer in a good pub cost one shilling, or about twenty-five cents.

Most Canadians were astute enough to manage their financial affairs so as not to alienate their less-well-off British messmates. As Canadians were paid twice monthly and the RN every two weeks, a certain amount of give-and-take took place on the messdecks, all in the interests of mutual domestic stability. In Canada, of course, the RN was brought up to Canadian rates and there was little difference in pay between equivalent ranks.

40 In the way the RCN men integrated into the various submarines and were treated by the RN, especially some of the senior officers who regarded the Canadians as "colonials," there is a whole aspect to the story of the RCN submarine experience that is not documented. In much the same way that the early days of the First Canadian Submarine Squadron were extremely difficult and fraught with personality clashes, these settling-in problems are not a matter of public record.

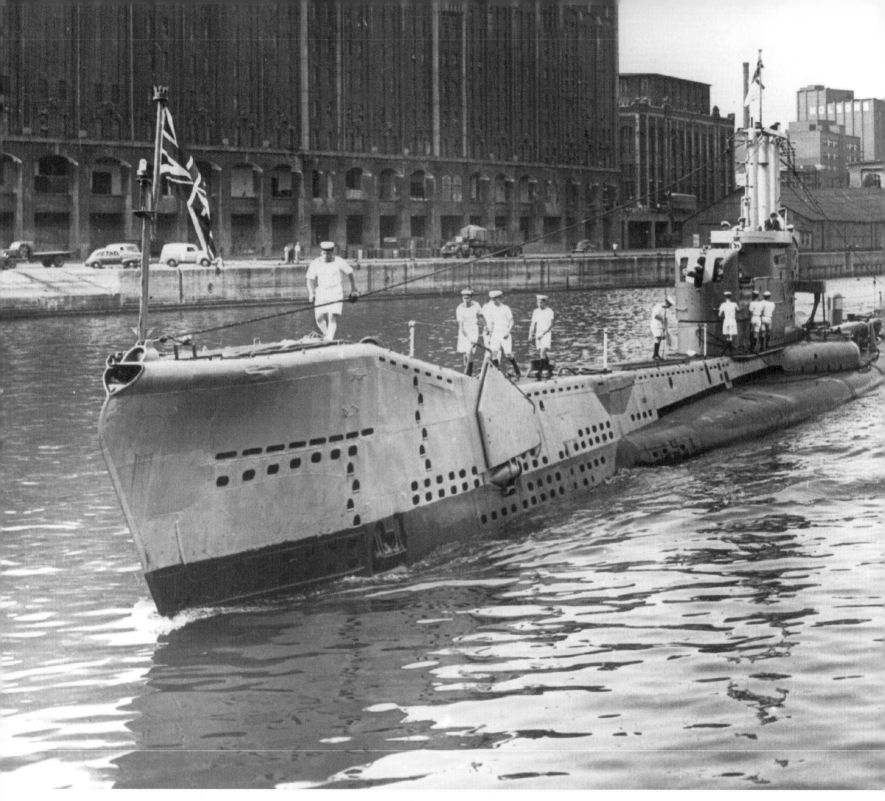

HMS *Astute* arrives at Victoria Basin, Montreal, on a recreational visit, 4 August 1955. (CF photo)

## GOING BOATS

*As one Canadian submariner recalls:*

In the winter of 1955–56, when I was an Ordinary Seaman Torpedo Detector rating aboard *Haida*, we joined in an ASW exercise off Bermuda. During the exercises we were given the opportunity to spend twenty-four hours aboard the A-boat that was working with us. I'm certain it was *Alderney*. Off we went in the whaler, and when we arrived on board I felt right at home. There was good reason for this. During my basic trades course in *Stadacona* we had been visited by a petty officer from the British submarines. He gave us a half-hour talk about submarines and the life aboard them. Most of us were impressed with his talk and many showed an interest in volunteering, myself included. It was then we discovered that we had to be rated Able Seaman before we were allowed to volunteer. As well, I had made the acquaintance of many of the crew in the old wet canteen in the basement of A block. They were a happy and roisterous bunch, and we got along well together.

Once we got below I was impressed by the boat itself. Aboard a *Tribal* life consisted mostly of polishing and scrubbing and standing lookout, lifebuoy sentry and wheelhouse watches, but we never had much to do with the ship itself or even the weapons equipment. In the submarine, you were right in with the machinery, and everyone had a real job to do—or so it seemed to me. I was also surprised at how much everyone seemed to know about the boat, and I was already familiar with that peculiar brand of comradeship found in submarines. Anyhow, two of us slapped in[41] as soon as we were back aboard *Haida*. Neither of us had our ABs, but they were just around the corner. When we saw the "old man," he granted our requests effective the date of our promotions. Within a month, we had both been rated up.

On returning to Slackers, I was sent to *Stadacona* to be tested for suitability for submarines. This entailed enduring all kinds of questions by the "shrinks," and a trip to HMCS *Granby*, then located ashore at the French Cable Wharf, for a run in the decompression chamber. Around Christmas time, *Haida* went into the floating drydock in Halifax shipyard and I went home to Cobourg on leave. When I returned, I was drafted to *Stadacona* to await a billet in submarines. Meantime I was employed at the old cellblock as a daytime cell sentry. It was there I learned that Regulating POs were almost human and that sailors did some very stupid things from time to time. Early in April I was out of there and bound for the UK by way of fourteen days leave.

I reported to HMCS *Donacona* in Montreal when I came off leave and flew out of Lachine in an RCAF North Star transport plane the next day. It was a four-engine, propeller-driven, cargo plane. Noisy as hell. There were some very uncomfortable canvas bucket seats (jump seats they called them) along the sides of the main compartment and a pile of big crates and machinery lashed down in the centre. The seven sailors, a few Wrens and five or six officers that made up the human cargo were left to fend for themselves. Most were headed for the *Bonaventure* in Belfast. Other than a head, there were no other creature comforts. When we made a fueling stop at Goose Bay, we had to pay for our supper. I was nearly broke. Next morning we landed at Prestwick, and those of us heading for London were flown to Langar. By the time I collected my kit bag I was tired, sore and starved. I was given a travel warrant and told to catch the military bus to the railway station in Nottingham and take the next train to London.

I arrived at St. Pancras station that evening with three English pennies in my pocket and not a clue on how to get where I was going except that I'd been told to report to HMCS *Niobe*, home of CDLS.[42] I later learned I was supposed to have been travelling with three of the officers, but as ABs instinctively kept clear of officers of any kind, I never did make contact with them. A quick conversation with a sympathetic London bobby soon got me sorted out, into a taxi and off to an address in Ennismore Gardens. On arrival I was taken in tow by Petty Officer Bob Hamilton, who lived in an apartment there. After a much needed clean up, his missus sat me down to a very welcome cooked dinner. Afterward we watched television, a rare treat in those days. Meanwhile Bob Hamilton made a reservation for me at the UJC,[43] fixed me up with a casual,[44] educated me about my duty free allowances, fixed me up with a carton of

---

41 Submitted Request Forms
42 Canadian Defence Liaison Staff

43 Union Jack Club. A well known serviceman's hostelry near Waterloo Station.
44 Pay advance.

HMS *Dolphin*, much as it looked when the Canadians arrived in 1955. The walls of Fort Blockhouse are much in evidence. Petrol Pier and the training area are on the right. (E. G. Gigg)

Exports and sent me on my way. I felt really good about the way the Hamiltons looked after me.

When I reached *Dolphin II* the next day, I discovered I was a draft of one. No matter—I was given an in-routine, a bunk and a locker in 11 Mess,[45] a meal card and bed linen. It was going to be a couple of weeks before the next course started so I had time to get myself sorted out. I found the NAAFI wet canteen in *Dolphin II* that night.

Things were a bit different in the RN than what I was used to back home, but survival comes naturally to a nineteen-year-old. For starters, the food in *Dolphin II* was dreadful. Little wizened-up spuds that were hard as rocks, scraps of mostly boiled fatty meat, maybe beef, maybe pork, lots of mutton, marrow-fat peas, tiny portions—not what you'd call wholesome and delicious, even by RN standards. There were stories aplenty about how the Canadians had caused a few riots over this only the year before, but it took a while for the RN to react. Within a month of my arrival, a new civilian contractor had been installed. The food improved, but it was never as a good as *Stadacona*. In fact, in all the time I was over there RN victuals never reached Canadian standards.

That's where the NAAFI came in. The woman who ran that place served much better meals for a very modest price. Trouble was she only cooked for the noon-hour crowd. Finding out where to get good, cheap vittles became a priority.

RN heads, washplaces and bathrooms were ventilated by openings in the walls at ceiling height that led straight to the great outdoors.[46] That was interesting, especially in wintertime. The bathtubs were magnificent though, big enough to swim in. English toilet paper was curious stuff, a bit like thin waxed paper. I took to keeping a supply of suitable old magazines like those we used to keep in the out-houses on some of the farms I'd lived on. It wasn't long before I discovered that the British issue No. 8 working dress was a lot more comfortable than the Canadian No. 5s. Sailors are a very adaptable lot.

Most of the hands in my bunkroom were transients so I didn't get to know many at the time. Once training started a few weeks later, those on the course concentrated in one mess and we soon came to know one another.

After a few duty watches I discovered that the leading hands and POs were a reasonable bunch. They were a lot less concerned with the finer points of dress and deportment than what I had been used to in what I soon learned to refer to as "Gens."[47] The senior rates weren't always trying to impress us junior hands with their importance, as had been the case most of the time at home.

Duty watch in *Dolphin* was something of an adventure. When there was a fire drill, we grabbed a big two-wheel handcart full of fire extinguishers, axes and other firefighting gear and with two pullers and two pushers roared off as fast as we could to the mock fire. There were some spectacular crashes. We also had to patrol the long lonely sea wall. I'm still not sure why, but my imagination provided all kinds of possibilities, especially during the middle watches. For this, we were outfitted with a greatcoat, usually size much-too-large, a tin hat, a big steel-bodied "torch" and a wooden entrenching-tool handle as a weapon. We slept all-standing in a bunkroom in one of the small buildings near the old gate. I think we stood one night in six, which was pretty good in those days.

The Coxswain of *Dolphin* II felt a bit bad that I was the only Canadian in the place. Within days, he found me a job as permanent canteen sweeper. Had to keep me busy, didn't they. It was summer, I was in England and I was going to be in submarines. I had overnight leave and was allowed into pubs. I was doing all right.

A few days after my arrival at *Dolphin II* I turned nineteen and my duty-free rations started coming through. I had to go to the *Duchess of Kent* barracks to pick them up.[48] It was good to get in a supply of Canadian cigarettes, I didn't fancy surviving on the RN issue "blue-liners" which were pretty rough. The three 40-ouncers I was entitled to each month had really good bargaining possibilities. I couldn't take the stuff on board so I rented a locker in which to keep my duty-frees in the back room of the Cartoon Café, a greasy spoon in Squeeze-Gut Alley in Gosport.

---

45 Where the Submarine Museum administration offices are now located.
46 In fact, so were most sanitary conveniences, including those in many homes.
47 General Service—the surface navy.
48 The WREN's (Women's Royal Naval Service) barracks and administrative headquarters, the supreme "Wrennery."

HMS *Alliance*, 1960: shipmates. (Author's collection)

Pompey, as Portsmouth was known, was a great place to go ashore. The majority of men living in barracks and aboard ship, and there were a lot of them, still went ashore in uniform. It was not unusual to find yourself in a pub packed with navy blue and the odd Royal Marine.[49] Serious drinking was done in uniform, and we did a lot. Nevertheless, civilian attire was preferred for dates. Once my pay started reaching me regularly I opened an account at one of the naval tailors in Gosport and outfitted myself with some decent civvies. I soon found some good restaurants and the dance halls. The Brits were still dancing ballroom although jive was popular and rock and roll had started creeping in. Soon I was dating and life seemed very complete indeed.

Another facet of RN life that soon became apparent was a whole naval sub-culture that permeated the communities of Gosport and Portsmouth. Both towns had known the navy since its inception in the seventeenth century and the sailors, the bases and the dockyard were an integral, yet somehow separate part of the social fabric of the community.

For the outsiders like the Canadian submariners, awareness undoubtedly started with the pubs. There was an aura about some of those places that was as old as the navy itself. Augmenting the pubs were the naval clubs, the Sailor's Home Club and the Royal Sailor's Rest, establishments devoted entirely to the welfare of the sailor. Jack, as sailors were known in England, was never homeless in Portsmouth, or Plymouth or Chatham or in any port where the navy had roots. Once we got to know a few of the British sailors it wasn't long before we came to know the parts of town where navy blue was welcome and understood.

Life picked up when the course started in the middle of June. The Training Area was primitive compared to what I'd experienced in Slackers. Just a series of wooden huts spaced out along a roadway running between Petrol Pier and the tank, the then brand-new 100-foot high (deep?) submarine escape training tank.

I was one of about a dozen trainees on my Submarine Basic Training Course. Our instructor was CPO Kitson. So far as the course was concerned, as long as you were making the grade and behaving yourself he was the only person you had to concern yourself with. I would learn many years later that the USN worked much the same way. It was great as far as I was concerned. He knew his stuff too, and when something specialized came up he'd bring in one of the other instructors to elaborate. We soon settled down to a demanding, but easygoing couple of months.

Classroom heat was provided by a small, pot-bellied, coal-burning stove. Fortunately, it was summer, but there were occasions when we had to light the thing. It worked alright, but I didn't fancy having to do a course in the cold weather.

Petrol Pier, where the Submarine Museum is now, was quite a sight then. Paid off wartime T's and S's were tied up there and even the odd U-class boat. One or two of the laid-up boats were used as floating classrooms; the rest were awaiting disposal. HMS *Taurus* was our usual haunt for on-board familiarization training, despite the fact that most of our classroom instruction was on A-class and modernized T-class boats.

The submarine acquaint course ended with a run through the escape training tank and three days of familiarization aboard HMS/M *Sea Scout*. We went out to one of the Solent exercise areas and practised diving and surfacing for the first day to give us trainees experience in the compartments, on the helm and planes and on the main vent and blowing panels. At night, we secured to a buoy and the trainees were berthed aboard an MFV, a small wooden motorised fishing vessel with a hold fitted out as a mess. The next day was spent doing dived drills and exercises including snorting. The third day was more of the same and we were alongside at *Dolphin* just after secure that afternoon.

The captain of *Sea Scout* stuck in my memory. He wore jodhpurs, a submarine sweater, a beret, long woollen socks and brown shoes. The meals were the best pusser's food I'd tasted since joining boats and the cook was one of the seamen. RN boats didn't have proper cooks then, although they were being brought in. All in all I was very impressed.

49 Otherwise referred to as "Boot-necks" because of the high, stiff, leather collars of their dress uniforms.

SENIOR
SERVICE
Satisfy

An 'A' class submarine loading torpedoes alongside her depot-ship.

SENIOR SERVICE
The Perfection of Cigarette Luxury

20 CIGARETTES

A 1950s advertising poster showing submarines. (Author's collection)

We wrote our final submarine acquaint exams shortly after that. Most of us passed; those that didn't were long gone before the marks came out. A week later I began my Underwater Weapons acquaint course, which was mostly given aboard the boats at Petrol Pier. By the time that was over, I had been given my draft chit for spare crew at Portland. I passed my acquaint course without any real problems. A week later I did my out-routine, packed my kit, made my farewells, and took a train to Weymouth along with four or five others in the same draft. At Weymouth station we were met by a pusser lorry that took us to Portland. I was in spare crew for one day only.

The day after my arrival I was on a train bound for Falmouth where I joined HMS *Solent.* Within hours we had hoisted anchor and headed for sea. By then it was lunch time which was preceded by tot time. I was really pleasantly surprised when the other seamen, who didn't even know my name at that point, offered me wets of their tots. I was under age and couldn't draw a tot, but that didn't seem to matter. Even though I had to sleep in a camp cot on the deck I had the feeling that I somehow belonged aboard that boat.

We returned to Portland the following afternoon. That was the RN for you.

## MANNING PROBLEMS

Because of the apparent ease with which the first Canadians were integrated into the RN, the RCN believed that continuing to provide the necessary personnel would be simple. Unfortunately, this was not to be. By mid 1956, concerns arose over the low number of men volunteering for submarine duty. A comprehensive study of all submarine issues was undertaken. One of the main personnel problems concerned the need to recycle the 171 RCN officers and men then serving in RN submarines in early 1957 when their initial submarine engagement period ended. The agreed number was 10 officers and 168 men, but in July 1956, the commitment was short by three officers and four men. The original expectation was that replacement volunteers for those not extending would be easy to find and that one group could be largely replaced by anoth-

er. By the end of June 1956,[50] only 29 volunteers had been screened and found suitable for submarine duty and a backlog of 75 volunteers awaited processing. Moreover, there was no way of telling at that point just how many of the original submarine draft would revolunteer. It was going to be difficult to find the right mix of ranks and trades. Some of the reasons for the lack of volunteers (and thus probably the willingness of those serving in submarines to revolunteer), stated at the time were interesting. It was strongly felt by many that serving with the RN had little personal appeal to Canadian personnel generally, while doing so was seen as a career dead end that did not enhance promotion prospects. Compensation was also important as the rate of RCN Risk Allowance was significantly lower, by proportion of base pay, than the RN's and the USN's. Consequently, NSHQ was forced to admit that it might be necessary to draft non-volunteers for submarine duty. The officer situation, however, was not a problem.

The personnel staff, on the other hand, believed that much of the problem could be resolved by changing the existing Risk Allowance to a Submarine Allowance and establishing a rate comparable with both the USN and RN. At the time, the RCN Risk Allowance represented some 10–15 percent of an individual's base pay depending on his rank. For an able seaman that was about $1 a day. The USN rate varied between 39 and 45 percent (other than the most junior seamen who got 55 percent), and the RN rates ranged from 28 to 35 percent. This, it was argued, was unreasonable, especially as the rate had not been changed since 1946. In addition, they had reason to believe that Risk Allowance was a major incentive. They proposed new rates that averaged 35 percent of basic RCN pay. In 1961, after a great deal of discussion, an agreement was reached and the new allowance was approved and paid.

Although many of the RCN submariners served in the submarines of SM6, others spent their entire time in RN boats based in the UK and abroad. Canadian submariners served aboard the boats of SM7 at Singapore, SM4 in Australia and SM5 at Malta. Another base, considered an outpost by many, was the home of SM3 at Faslane in the Gareloch in Scotland (popularly known as "3rd Division North" after the Scottish

---

50 The author joined submarines as an Able Seaman Torpedo Detector (Torpedoman) in April 1956.

football league). Today this is the location of HMS *Neptune*, Britain's premier submarine base and home of SM1. However, in the 1950s and 1960s it consisted of a jetty, a depot ship and a converted tank landing craft, the tank space of which was used for overflow accommodation. A utilitarian cinder-block building on the hillside served as the NAAFI wet canteen.

At times, the hard running experienced in SM6 had an effect on morale and the Squadron Commander had to be ever watchful that his technically temperamental charges were not overworked. Judging by the various *Reports of Proceedings* that the squadron commander submitted to the Flag Officer Atlantic Coast (FOAC), the submarine crews worked and played hard. In fact, they developed a lifestyle of their own, with the few RCN personnel on board adopting the same standards of dress and behaviour as their RN shipmates.

One example of the running of the A-boats is that recorded for HMS *Aurochs* when she was on station with SM6 between July 1960 and January 1962. During that eighteen-month period she steamed approximately forty thousand miles and spent 325 days at sea. By no means a record, it does illustrate a typical utilization of the boats. As a good deal of the at-sea time was spent in transit, it also shows just how unrealistic the training planners were in expecting to achieve 190 training days per year.

Sports were very popular with both the RCN and RN personnel. At Halifax, SM6 fielded a championship soccer team, a rugger team and a cricket team that played in a four-team local league. At one point, they even mustered a hockey team despite the fact that most of the RN players had first to learn how to skate. Baseball gained in popularity the longer the squadron was in Canada and the Canadians in Britain managed to field ball teams whenever there was an opportunity.

Although many were critical of the way the Canadians of all ranks embraced RN standards, there could be little argument with the fact that an integrated squadron now existed. As long as the basic concept of the original *Heads of Agreement* prevailed, SM6 would remain an RN organization with a smattering of Canadians. In time, the squadron would become Canadian, but a great deal more had to happen before that.

## THE SIDON INCIDENT

On the morning of Thursday, 16 June 1955, HMS *Sidon,* an 840-ton modernized S-boat commanded by Lieutenant Commander H. T. Verry, RN, was preparing to sail from alongside the depot ship HMS *Maidstone,* home of SM2, in Portland harbour. In all, there were fifty-six men on board, including six Canadians. Earlier that morning she had embarked and loaded two experimental practice torpedoes in Nos. 3 and 4 tubes that were to be fired on the torpedo range.

At 0825, as *Sidon*'s crew was closing up at Harbour Stations,[51] the high-test peroxide fuel supply of the torpedo in No. 3 tube exploded, blowing open the bow cap and jamming six feet of shattered torpedo body in the muzzle. The blast also tore off the torpedo tube rear door. The explosion sprayed the fore-ends with torpedo components like a burst of shrapnel. The tube space and forward accommodation space watertight bulkheads were badly damaged. The interior of the accommodation space was devastated. Debris was rammed against the forward control-room bulkhead in a near-impenetrable barrier. The blast was accompanied by a sheet of searing-hot flame and followed by toxic gases and a huge volume of smoke. Everyone forward of the forward control room bulkhead was killed. Six men died instantly in the explosion and six more succumbed rapidly from their injuries and suffocation. Elsewhere in the boat seven men were injured, several others concussed and all were affected by the smoke, toxic gases and shock.

The submarine started to settle by the bows with a list to starboard. The CO ordered the after hatches to be opened and all hands off the ship. He also sent the engineer below to see what could be done to save the boat. With only emergency lighting to guide them the able-bodied assisted the injured out of the boat through the conning tower and after hatches. The engineer and chief ERA did what they could to keep the boat afloat and attempted to break into the forward compartments in the hope of rescuing survivors.

The Fire and Rescue Party mustered aboard *Maidstone* while other vessels in the harbour were summoned to assist. Other boats in the trot slipped and moved clear. HMS *Solent,* which

---

51  Really Stations for Entering and Leaving Harbour but abbreviated to Harbour Stations for obvious reasons.

had just cleared the harbour entrance, was recalled and instructed to prepare to receive possible submarine escape survivors and the SUBSMASH procedures were initiated.

The commanding officer of SM2 personally led his senior technical staff aboard *Sidon* to see what needed doing. On reaching the control room they set to work trying to clear away the wreckage and reach the forward compartments. Two would-be rescuers actually made it through but were forced back by the fumes. By this time, it was obvious, the boat could not be saved and a final evacuation was begun. At approximately 0850 *Sidon* slipped below the surface and sank to the bottom of the harbour. She took twelve of her crew and one rescuer with her.

Six Canadians were aboard *Sidon* that fateful morning. One died. PO2 TD Verne McLeod had joined *Sidon* only hours before the explosion. It was his first boat and he had been drafted aboard to complete the on-job portion of his training commonly known as Part Threes. PO1 Spud Gregory had been forward with McLeod but had gone aft to use the head leaving him in the mess having a cup of tea. PO ERA Sam Jennings and LS Stoker Frenchie Gourdeau were at their Harbour Stations in the engine room and AB TD Ralph Romans was on the casing. Stoker PO Ray Spencer appears to have been in the conning tower disconnecting a fresh-water hose. When the blast ripped through the accommodation space McLeod was struck by a piece of debris, suffered a fractured skull and died instantly.

A native of Goderich, Ontario, McLeod had joined the RCN in 1949 at HMCS *Prevost* in London, Ontario. He undertook his basic training at HMCS *Cornwallis* and on completion, was drafted to HMCS *Athabaskan*. He served in Korea aboard *Athabee* between July 1950 and May 1951, and aboard HMCS *Huron* after that.

He was a member of the second group of RCN volunteers to undergo submarine training at HMS *Dolphin* where he arrived early in January 1955. He left behind a wife and two daughters, one aged two years, the other, whom he had never seen, but six weeks old.

The thirteenth victim was Surgeon Lieutenant Rhodes, RNVR, who had gone aboard the stricken boat with Captain SM2. Using an unfamiliar breathing apparatus, he managed to assist several casualties out through the conning tower. Unnoticed, he ran out of air and collapsed on the control room deck after everyone else had been evacuated. He died of asphyxiation before the boat sank.

The wreck was finally raised on Wednesday 23 June and beached in Portland harbour. It took three attempts before all of the bodies could be recovered. Canadian submariners numbered among the volunteers in the recovery team. The Coroner's inquest ascribed the deaths to "misadventure." They were all buried on Monday, 27 June, with full military honours in the Portland Naval Cemetery on top of the cliffs overlooking the harbour.

In Halifax, the events of 16 June made little impression. Verne McLeod's wife, Charlotte, was informed that her husband was aboard the stricken submarine but seems to have been given little in the way of information or emotional support. The navy offered to fly her to the UK but her recent childbirth made that medically inadvisable. Having performed its obligatory duty, the navy then appears to have left the family to sort out its own problems. Other family members stepped in and did what they could to provide comfort and support. It was not until the wreck was raised and the bodies removed that Charlotte McLeod gave up her desperate vigil and returned to her family in Ontario.

It was government policy at the time that deceased service personnel be buried in the country of their death. There was never any consideration given to bringing McLeod's body home. The family had to be satisfied with a memorial service in McLeod's hometown.

A court of inquiry cleared everyone aboard *Sidon* of blame for the loss of the boat. The experimental torpedo program was terminated shortly afterwards. Two years later *Sidon* was scuttled as a sonar bottom target in West Bay.[52]

---

52  By way of tribute to the Canadian Submarine Volunteer, a memorial display was commissioned in the name of PO L. D. McLeod, by the Submarine Old Comrades Association, Canadian Branch, and unveiled in a ceremony attended by McLeod's daughters, sister and other relatives as the final event in HMCS *Okanagan*'s paying off celebrations on 27 September 1998. The display is permanently on view in CFB Halifax.

# MEMORIES OF SM6

*Accounts of life in SM6 are hard to come by. The squadron is long gone, though not forgotten, and the personnel are scattered to the proverbial winds. However, the author did manage to convince friend, shipmate, historian and fellow author Peter Haydon to provide a few highlights from his time in the squadron.*

In 1959, as a naive young Sub-Lieutenant RCN, I volunteered for submarine duty after a week at sea in USS *Sea Robin* in the Caribbean. I think I expected to be sent to *Grilse*, which was then beginning the crewing-up process. That was not to be, training in the US submarine school in New London was only for those with degrees. However, Grade 13 was enough for the RN program!

So, in June 1960, I was sent to HMS *Dolphin* to begin the basic submarine course. I passed, but not with great standing and so had to accept the sweepings of the postings. The system then was that selection was according to one's standing on the course. Rather than stay in *Dolphin* or go to Faslane, I chose HMS *Alderney*, then in refit in Portsmouth, which was due to join SM6 for the second time in January 1962. It made sense at the time!

I had worked with SM6 submarines while in the frigates in Halifax and was quite comfortable with that lifestyle. It was a veritable McHale's navy, working hard at sea and playing hard when in port. My new CO was Ralph Cudworth (he was killed in an accident in the submarine escape training tower in 1964). The first lieutenant was a delightful person—Alistair Bruce (with whom I still correspond). The Engineer was Phil Thoms, a commissioned CERA, and the third hand was Jeremy Daniels, a happy-go-lucky soul. I was the navigator. We got a fifth hand just before work-ups.

Work-ups were an unmitigated disaster. Jeremy Daniel and Phil Thoms were both fired and in their places we got George Newton as the EO and Richard Sharpe (today editor of *Jane's Fighting Ships*) as the torpedo officer. The second work-up went much better. That is apart from a midnight crisis off the west coast of Ireland when we lost trim, became far too heavy, and rounded out close to 750 feet before recovering. The moral of the story being that blowing main ballast at 400 feet is not a "quick" reaction to a problem.

All was then well (as well as it would ever get) and we sailed for Halifax on 4 January 1962. The plan was to do a submerged transit all the way and provide some training for SOSUS and the maritime air people. We ran into one of the worst storms on record, had to surface, and hove to for a few days. The submarine and the whole crew took a beating. It was probably more frightening than diving out of control. Anyway, we lost the 187 sonar dome from the bow and several hunks of casing and fin. (somewhere there is a photo of us coming into Halifax showing the damage). We resumed the snort transit eventually and made a landfall on Cape Race by dead reckoning, finally getting into Halifax at the end of January.

After nearly a month of repairs, *Alderney* went to work on the standard training cycle: Monday to Friday with the ships, the weekend with the Argus and Tracker aircraft, all done in a God-forsaken piece of ocean known as the "Julie Hole" (at 41 30 North. 62 20 West—coordinates which none of us will ever forget because we spent so much damn time there). There were some breaks. We got to go into Ireland Island and St. George's (Bermuda) once in a while.

We participated in SUBICEX II in March 1962. This was the first such exercise for an *A* class (I think one of the early *Oberons* did a trip up by Iceland in late 1961) and we had some extra gear fitted, like upward-looking echo sounder, and some fairing plates over the main vents to prevent ice from jamming in them. The 187 dome should have been given a protective cage, but was not. As Navigator I had done some extra training before leaving UK and I had also spent some time in and around Newfoundland in the winters when I was in the frigates and so had a little experience. This turned out to be useful.

The exercise was conducted in the Gulf of St. Lawrence and the Strait of Belle Isle with two US nuclear submarines: *Nautilus* and either *Sea Wolf* or *Sea Dragon* (can't remember which) and HMS *Astute*, also from SM6. We were ill prepared for what happened, but soon became quite competent. The operating concept was that we were simulating Soviet submarines trying to transit into the St. Lawrence River to launch missiles, which we would do from the surface. To get to the area around Anticosti Island, we stayed under the ice as long as possible and then either found a hole (polynya) in which to snort or broke through thin ice.

Our problem was that there was more ice than holes and the ice that was there was too thick to break through without doing

HMS *Alderney* in heavy weather, on her way to join SM6, 20 January 1962. Note the gaping hole in the fore deck where the 187 dome was ripped away. (MARCOM Museum)

serious damage to the fin. The Navigator earned his pay that trip and was blessed with good luck in finding places where the ice was shifting enough to leave a small patch of open water. We did have to break through one afternoon; the battery was getting uncomfortably low and we had a long night transit to make. Pushing an A-boat fin through three feet of ice is an interesting experience. Again, the power of blowing main ballast when dived was over-estimated, and we eventually had to use the fin like an inverted ice pick and create some cracks in the ice through which we could push ourselves. It worked, but not without some tense moments, standard Brit yelling, and some luck.

Once through the ice we had a breather and charged the battery on the surface while watching the ice close in all around us. The other problem we had to solve was getting rid of a huge block of ice that lodged itself over the upper lid. Fortunately, A-boats still had a gun tower hatch and it was clear of ice. The sonar dome and the bow took a bit of a beating but nothing sufficiently bad to impede operations. Petty Officer Bob Churcher, the electronics technician, who was also RCN (one of only four Canadians on board because every sensible Canadian tried to keep out of SM6 for financial reasons–only we unmarrieds broke even), had to constantly check the radar and communications masts but they survived. He nearly didn't though. Bob was a large person and wriggling in and out of the back end of the fin was difficult and he was stuck back there for a while. I don't think the CO would have left him there, but he put Bob

SM6 representatives for the presentation of a Queen's Colour at Fort Blockhouse, 8 June 1958. L-R: L/S R. G. Ross and AB EM1 G. C. Steen (RCN) of HMS *Ambush*; M(E)1 H. Harvey, HMS *Alderney*; M(E)1 P. C. Robinson, spare crew; and L/S D. A. B. Sullivan, HMS *Alderney*. (MARCOM Museum)

on a very strict diet once we got back to Halifax. After that, we finished the exercise and went back to Halifax.

The summer of 1962 was uneventful and typically boring playing clockwork mouse for the ships and aircraft. However, the fall of 1962 was something else.

During the third week of October, we were doing the usual ASW training when, out of the blue, we were ordered back up to the surface and told to standby for new orders. That evening, the 22nd, we heard President Kennedy give his now-famous speech on Cuba, and were then told to enter Halifax that night and go straight to the magazine to store for war. We were also told to be clear of the harbour by first light. There was a debate over whether the RCN people could stay on board. Eventually we did, mainly on Admiral Dyer's insistence. By dawn on the 23rd, *Alderney* was headed Northeast for the southern tip of Greenland to set up a barrier to catch the Soviet submarines. We never found them, and it was only years after that I discovered that the reason was that they were already on patrol off the Eastern Seaboard by the time we sailed. We stayed there until early November and finally returned to Halifax—not to a hero's welcome but to be treated poorly once again because after two months at sea, we did not have "regulation" haircuts and were thus asked to leave the *Stadacona* Wardroom bar. The Chiefs and POs fared better, and there was no problem in the A-Block wets where the focus was on bar profits rather than appearance.

From the two submarines, six of us lived in the *Stadacona* Wardroom when not at sea and had a constant battle with the Base Commander and his staff. Some of the trouble was self-induced. For instance, there wasn't really a good reason to add a periscope to the painting of the battle of Trafalgar, and perhaps we did not have to emulate Russians in throwing glasses into the fireplace, and perhaps we should have been more prudent in leaving the nurses' residence in the early hours of the morning. Generally, the RCN didn't really accept the officers of SM6 (RN and RCN) with open arms; we were a bit wild. The C&POs usually had a great time and integrated into the local community very easily. In fact, we would occasionally run[53] with the C&POs because they enjoyed themselves far more. The LS and ABs were also a thorn in the RCN administration's side. I cannot remember all the stories, but C-block, the hands' barrack block, was often a den of iniquity and the wet canteen in A-Block the scene of many notable parties that had to be closed down by the shore patrol. Being Submarine Squadron Duty Officer, (something we all had to do when in harbour) had its lighter moments.

The RN hands never understood parts of the Canadian system, yet were able to exploit other aspects shamelessly. The tool exchange policy was continually exploited for instance. A broken wrench, screwdriver, or pair of pliers could be exchanged for a brand new item on a one-for-one basis. Low-end tools from Canadian Tire could be turned in for the best quality equivalent anytime! Jeeps and staff cars were as abused as anything in the surface fleet. In one incident, the squadron duty driver backed the truck off Jetty 5 [Jetty NK] and it had to be recovered by floating crane. At the subsequent Captain's Table in *Stadacona* (the Base Commander was too incensed to let the Squadron Commander deal with it) the driver was apparently asked what he was thinking about as the truck went over the edge of the jetty. His reply, unintelligible to a non-submariner, was "I'd better shut off for going deep!"

The last *Alderney* story concerns our ignominious return to UK. In early February 1963 (I'd have to check the date), the main engine holding-down bolts started to crack. This could not be explained and we went through all the spares and many more shipped over from UK. Eventually the engines were condemned as other problems arose, and so we were sent back to UK with the head of each engine firmly held down with wooden shores wedged into the deckhead and deemed unfit to dive. The Admiralty's concern for this "black sheep" submarine was such that they sent a tug to escort it back to Portsmouth. The engines, obviously knowing that the time in Halifax was behind them, behaved perfectly all the way. We even made good speed, and at one time the tug had to ask us to slow down so that it could keep up and thus be an effective escort.

*Alderney* paid off in April 1963, after a short and not very glorious commission in SM6. I don't think the RCN got a very good return for its investment in us. Other A-boats in SM6 fared much better, but *Alderney* seemed plagued with problems from the day we left the Portsmouth yard until the day we got back.

---

53  Any group foray ashore was known as a run. It was usually a marathon pub-crawl.

A beautiful shot of HMS *Alderney* in mint condition, showing the hinged snort mast arrangement to advantage. (CDR E. G. Gigg)

## NEW SUBMARINES FOR THE RCN

From the very beginning, it had been obvious to naval planners that renting submarines was a relatively expensive proposition. It was a widely held conviction that the money could be better spent in providing a Canadian submarine branch. The A-boats supplied by the RN were past their prime and seldom in the best of condition. Under the *Heads of Agreement* the RCN was obligated to spend large sums on repairs that it was felt should have been the responsibility of the Admiralty. For instance, boats often arrived on station with worn-out batteries that were being nursed through a second commission. On one occasion, an entire battery section had to be replaced at considerable expense. Engine breakdowns were a constant and expensive problem, both in the training time lost to make repairs and in the actual material cost.

Experience with the A-boats soon showed that they were achieving far less than the anticipated 190 days of ASW training time per year. Nevertheless, SM6 often commented in his reports that his boats were the hardest run of any British submarines and that both morale and materiel would suffer if some relief were not forthcoming. The only way this could be achieved was at the expense of training time, which displeased the Canadians, or to cut back on pro-submarine time, which upset the Admiralty.

Another consideration was the fact that the Admiralty had the right to withdraw all of the submarines in times of crisis. Although the RN was committed to providing substitute training submarines, this would leave the RCN without submarines at the very time when they would probably be needed more than ever.[54]

NSHQ fully appreciated that submarines were useful for more than anti-submarine training. Operationally the modern submarine was becoming an acknowledged ASW platform in its own right. Long-range sonars and improved homing-torpedoes were revolutionizing the value of the submarine as a component of the anti-submarine force and particularly in the role of submarine hunter-killer. Various schemes for starting a submarine branch were once more put forward from within NSHQ, but none was successful.

The process of introducing and acquiring new equipment in the RCN then, and in the Canadian Armed Forces of today, is long and convoluted. The military need must first be identified and substantiated. This can only be done after many studies have been conducted and documented, usually over a number of years. Then, the most suitable piece of equipment to meet the need must be selected—this again only after a series of studies and possibly tests and trials have been carried out and the results summarized on paper. Selection is followed by a process of cost analysis to determine whether the equipment is worth what it will cost and if that expense can be justified in terms of the benefits and in light of other expenditures.

All of this is processed even before a formal proposal is made at senior military levels. In the case of the submarines, this was the Naval Board. Once the concept, equipment options and costs were approved at the senior military level, a Statement of Requirement (SOR) was drawn up and forwarded to the Cabinet Defence Committee for consideration. Once approved by the Cabinet Defence Committee, the SOR had to be approved by Cabinet, and that is where all decisions for major purchases are ultimately made.

The Cabinet is also where political considerations enter the picture in force. What benefits, other than meeting the military need, can Canada secure through the acquisition of this equipment? Whose riding would stand to benefit? What region? Which industries? How many man-hours of work were involved for Canadians? How much payroll will be generated? Where will it be spent? And so it goes.

By 1958, it had become obvious that there had to be a better way to provide submarine services. In the minutes of the Fifty-sixth Meeting of the Naval Board held on 2 April 1958, it was agreed that submarines, *particularly nuclear-powered submarines*, constituted a legitimate element of the Canadian navy. This caused a flurry of planning at headquarters but other than a series of studies and planning sessions; no further official action was taken for some time. At that particular juncture, the possibilities of nuclear power being the way of the future for marine propulsion generally were being seriously examined, and this was causing considerable consternation in the corridors and

---

54 As recounted in Peter Haydon's account, the two SM6 submarines were deployed under Canadian command as part of the Labrador-Greenland A/S barrier during the Cuban Missile Crisis in 1962.

back rooms at NSHQ. There is no doubt that on the face of it, nuclear-powered submarines seemed to provide a plausible answer to both the training submarine problem and to the need for an improved ASW platform. However, before any plans were laid, the concept had to gain political sanction. This was the same year in which the first American SSN, USS *Nautilus,* made her famous dived passage under the North Pole.

In the meantime, studies of existing and predicted ASW training needs for the RCN and the RCAF determined that, ideally, thirteen training submarines would be needed—three for use on the west coast and the remainder at Halifax. As well, it was noted that the *A* class lacked the speed and endurance needed to simulate the Soviet long-range fleet submarines then being encountered with increasing frequency. Again the suggestion was put forward from within DND that Canada should consider building nuclear submarines, preferably in the USA, but in Britain if necessary. The American option was favoured even though it would be more expensive.

In November 1959, the Chief of Naval Staff submitted a memorandum to the Chairman, Chiefs of Defence Staff, making the following recommendations:[55]

> That a submarine service be introduced into the RCN with the purpose of improving our A/S capability and at the same time augmenting, and eventually replacing, the present submarine training program (i.e. SM6); and

> That submarines should be nuclear propelled if funds can be made available. If no increase in the present budget is possible, it is recommended that conventional submarines of proven US or UK design be constructed on the basis of equal priority with surface vessels of the planned ship replacement program.

In January 1960, the Minister for National Defence made a submission to Cabinet in which he outlined the requirement to replace ageing ships in order to maintain an adequate peacetime fleet strength and to meet training requirements. At the same time, he provided an estimate of the costs of providing nuclear and conventional submarines, while suggesting:

> … that approval in principle be given to establishing our own submarine service to gradually replace the training submarines on loan from the RN with submarines capable of ASW in time of war.

In March 1960, a paper submitted to the Cabinet Defence Committee[56] reaffirmed the RCN's need for ten to twelve submarines for training, but added that even as few as six to eight would be a big improvement over the present arrangement. The same paper concluded that nuclear-powered submarines would be too costly without a significant increase in the budget. Once again, approval for a submarine service was requested. It was suggested that this could be done most effectively by replacing obsolete anti-submarine vessels with ASW-capable submarines.

In August 1960, a Chiefs of Staff paper prepared in conjunction with the Defence Treasury Board and the Department of Defence Production, was set before the MND recommending that approval be given for the procurement of six USN *Barbel* class submarines.[57] This paper recommended building the submarines in Canada at a cost of $171 million, which included spares, stores and shore-support facilities.

Discussions and delays followed. The Supreme Allied Commander, Atlantic (SACLANT) had to be consulted as to whether or not it would be acceptable to replace obsolete anti-submarine ships with ASW capable submarines. Concerns were also raised about public acceptability of having submarines in the RCN.

In the meantime, both Britain and the United States dispatched their sales teams to Canada to help NDHQ make the "right" choice. Both nations sensed a deal in the offing. One thing was certain; the Canadian shipbuilding industry was not in an advantageous position when it came to bidding on submarine contracts. Canadian yards had neither the experience nor the infrastructure in place to build submarines and Canadian labour rates were considerably higher than in Europe and the United States. Wherever the submarines were to be built, there would have to be significant, if not total, input from the successful bidder.

55  CSC 1242.1 (TD 17) 649th Meeting COS, 18 Nov 1959.
56  CDC document D3-60—DHH 73/1223 File 404, 10 Mar 1960.

57  An advanced type of diesel powered submarine based on contemporary SSN construction concepts.

A fine shot of *Grilse* at sea shortly after commissioning. (MARCOM Museum)

In October 1960, the Chief of Defence Staff presented a paper to the MND in which he compared the relative costs of American *Barbels* and British *Oberons* in a program costing about $160 million. It was concluded that:

> Six *Barbels* could be built in Canada for about $22 million[58] (sic) apiece and that, by 1965, they would make the most effective ASW contribution to NATO; or

> Six *Oberons* could be bought in the UK for $11 million each and four General Purpose frigates built in Canada for $22 million each, making the most valuable ASW contribution to the RCN for about the same money.

Nothing comes easily in National Defence, especially when there are choices. Planning, discussions and back-room struggles continued. In January 1962, the MND presented a ship replacement program to the Cabinet Defence Committee recommending:

> That Canada purchase three *Oberons* (Phase 1);

> That firm proposals be developed for building advanced-type submarines in Canada in the future (Phase 2);

> That construction of eight General Purpose Frigates, to be phased in at two per year, be commenced in Canada; and

> That no announcements be made regarding these decisions until discussions had been completed with the UK on "swap" arrangements that the purchase of the *Oberons* might make possible.

In the meantime, in order to meet urgent ASW training needs on the west coast, a surplus, unmodified USN fleet boat was acquired on a five-year lease. Refitted at Charleston, she commissioned in 1961 at New London, Connecticut, as HMCS *Grilse*. *Grilse* was the first submarine in the RCN since the CH-boats of 1919-1922. The bulk of the crew for *Grilse* was drawn from among the RN-trained Canadians, while additional officers and men were trained in the United States. At best, *Grilse* had a very limited operational capability. Nevertheless, she put in her time as training boat very effectively. During her first sixteen months of service, she steamed 51,740 miles, spent 374 days at sea, 34 percent of that time submerged, and 31 percent of the total time submerged, snorkelling.

Cabinet approval for the purchase of the first three *Oberons* was given in March 1962 under Phase 1 of the two-part submarine acquisition program. Phase 2 was to provide the RCN with nine additional submarines of an unspecified "advanced type" to be built in Canada. The purchase of the *Oberons* was confirmed by the succeeding government in October of 1963.[59]

Studies were initiated to determine what type of submarine should be produced under Phase 2. In a report presented to the

---

58 There appears to be a discrepancy here as elsewhere $22 million is given as the purchase price if built in the USA. Built in Canada the estimate was more like $26 million each.
59 Conservatives under Diefenbaker succeeded by Liberals under Lester B. Pearson.

Naval Board in 1962[60] the plan envisaged the acquisition of three modernized *A* class boats for training beginning in 1963, and the building of six SSNs of the *Thresher* type. These were to be built in Canada at an estimated cost of $65 million apiece. Support costs would have added a further $15 million to the tab for a grand total of just over $4 billion.

As the SSNs entered service between 1968 and 1972, they would displace the A-boats, which by that time would have reached the end of their usefulness. Once the scheme was completed, Canada would possess three *Oberons* and six SSNs. Altogether these would have been manned by nearly one thousand officers and men plus support staff.

However, because of failing Cabinet support and the fiscal constraints imposed with increasing severity during the late 1960s and early 1970s, these plans were arbitrarily terminated without any further proposals being put forward. This left the navy with the three *Oberons* only. At the same time, the eight-ship General Purpose Frigate and other naval shipbuilding programs were cancelled before any starts had been made.

## CANADIAN *OBERON* CLASS SUBMARINES

The *Oberons* were essentially advanced Second World War submarines. Their design dates back to the immediate post-war era and was the product of British wartime experience influenced by the innovative concepts found in the German Type XXI Electro-boats and experience gained in modernizing the *T* class boats. At the time of their purchase, the *Oberons* were considered to be among the quietest, most capable non-nuclear submarines in the world. The American *Barbel*s were materially superior in many respects, but the O-boats had the inestimable advantage of costing half as much as their American competitor. In addition, Canada would have had to wait for a building program to be started in the United States, whereas the British were prepared to transfer a boat already under construction to Canada and to begin a building program immediately the deal was concluded.

The three Canadian O-boats were, as far as was possible, built according to the particular requirements of the RCN. The first, HMCS *Ojibwa*, had originally been laid down as HMS *Onyx*, a standard RN *Oberon*. Because of her advanced state of

A classic photograph of an O-boat entering Halifax harbour. HMCS *Ojibwa*, 1966. (MARCOM Museum)

60  The Report of the 1962 Submarine Committee, July 1962.

HMCS *Okanagan*, ca 1976. Looking down the tower from the bridge. It's a long drop.
(K. Nesbit)

construction and the cost involved in making changes, it was not possible to incorporate a full range of modifications in her. The second boat, *Onondaga*, was one of the first of the "super O-boats" to be constructed. She received many changes including an open-concept control room, relocation of the radar office to the machinery space under the control room and the CO's cabin to the after end of the control room as well as an inboard battery-ventilation system, enhanced air-conditioning and Canadian communications equipment. However, as far as accommodations were concerned, she was still a standard *Oberon*. The third boat, *Okanagan*, received many additional improvements. To improve habitability, the galley was relocated to the accommodation space instead of in the after end of the control room. This eliminated the undesirable stream of traffic through the control room at mealtimes that was a thrice-daily feature in *Ojibwa* and *Onondaga*. A spacious cafeteria was provided adjacent to the galley while the traditional broadside messes became bunk spaces.

Curiously, the watertight door fitted in *Ojibwa*'s bulkhead 49 was a spare T-boat door. *Okanagan* was the last submarine constructed in HM Dockyard Chatham, a yard steeped in submarine construction history.

The RN was anxious to have a super-O and they transferred that project to a new *Onyx*, which became the only one of its kind in the RN. The Australian navy went on to have six super O-boats built by Scotts at Greenock. Three more were built by Vickers, Barrow, for Brazil and a further pair by Scott-Lithgow for Chile.

With the commissioning of *Ojibwa*, Canadian personnel were gradually withdrawn from the RN to man their own submarines. SM6 was first reduced to divisional status, and then, in March 1967, closed altogether. In 1966,

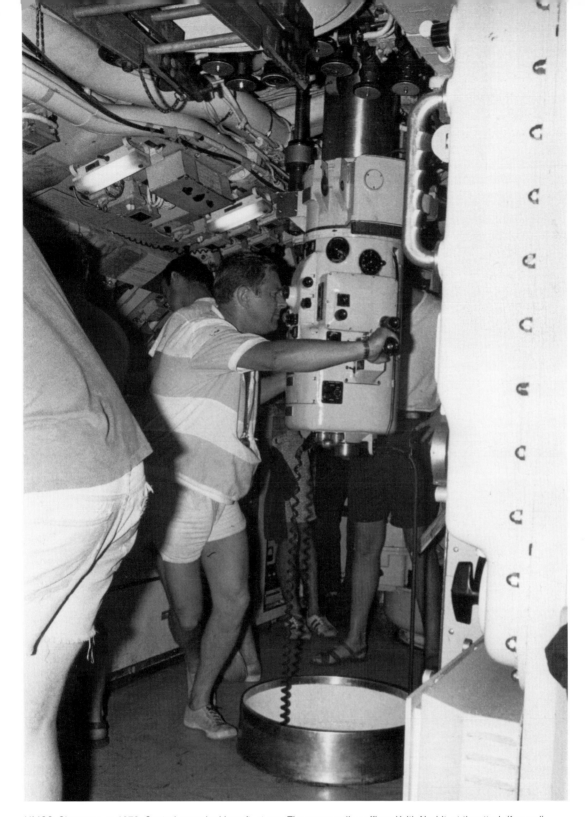

HMCS *Okanagan*, ca 1976. Control room looking aft, at sea. The commanding officer, Keith Nesbit, at the attack (forward) periscope. (K. Nesbit)

HMCS *Ojibwa*, WESTEX 77. Civilian technicians and crew preparing for a firing on the Nanoose Range. (Author's collection)

a submarine basic-training facility was opened at HMCS *Stadacona* in Halifax. At first an integral part of the submarine organization, it was soon absorbed into the Canadian Forces Fleet School organization. In 1989 a fourth hull, ex-HMS *Olympus*, was acquired for use as an alongside submarine training facility.[61] Later, when the RN began scrapping their *Oberons*, Canada purchased HMS *Osiris* and completely stripped her of useable components for spare parts.

When the First Canadian Submarine Squadron (CANSUBRON ONE) was created, the organization was allocated office, workshop and lay-apart space[62] in building D7 in the north end of the dockyard and the boats were berthed on Jetty 5 (now Jetty NK). Meanwhile, a dedicated facility was being planned for the south end of the yard. With the expansion of DND property southwards along the waterfront to what had originally been the Cunard Wharf, space was found for CANSUBRON ONE in the one-time warehouse on Jetty 8 (now Jetty NC).

The jetty face was expanded by sinking concrete caissons around the perimeter against the old jetty, filling them with rock-fill and laying a new top surface. A new mobile crane and rails were added a few years later. The old building was gutted and extensive submarine maintenance and administration facilities were built within the old steel shell. This included a battery maintenance shop; a submarine pipe shop and an electrical workshop, all run by the dockyard and staffed by the civilian workforce.

The naval facilities occupied the seaward end of the building. These housed the CANSUBRON ONE administrative offices, engineering offices and workshops, a lay-apart store for each of the three boats as well as a cafeteria, galley and refrigerated storage facilities. The submarine squadron moved into the new facility during the summer of 1968. At first, little in the way of creature comforts was provided for the sailors except for the cafeteria. However, within the first year a wardroom, messes for senior and junior ratings and a communal locker space for the men were installed. There was also a small sickbay and a bunk space for the inevitable duty watch.

Hauling an O-boat from the synchrolift into the submarine refit shelter. (DND)

Originally, the portable emergency submarine rescue equipment was held by the Fleet Diving Unit at HMCS *Granby*, as had been the case with SM6. This consisted primarily of a decompression chamber and the equipment necessary to operate it, all of which could easily be placed aboard a ship in an emergency. Eventually this too was moved into the building on Jetty NC.

At the same time, construction was begun on the synchrolift and submarine refit area. Originally intended for the short-lived hydrofoil program, the facility was easily expanded to accommodate submarines. The original concept provided for a lift, haul-out and traverse. This would have allowed a vessel to be lifted out of the water by the synchrolift with its keel (or cradle in the case of the hydrofoils) resting on a series of trolleys rigidly linked together. The trolleys and their load could be hauled ashore on rails and then traversed sideways into a "parking"

---

61  On delivery *Olympus* was a fully functional O-boat and was steamed to Canada by an RN passage crew.
62  When a submarine is alongside for any reason, and particularly during maintenance, kit, spare gear, stores and all kinds of loose equipment are landed in order to provide accessibility and to make room on board in which to work. As a consequence, whenever a submarine comes alongside she is allocated a lay-apart area for her gear.

area parallel to the haul-out, leaving the lift and haul-out areas free for additional ships. As there were only three submarines, and as these were considerably heavier than hydrofoils, the traverse idea, although successfully employed in many locations throughout the world, was discarded at an early stage.

Construction commenced in February 1967. By June 1968, the lift was finished and load-lifting trials were able to start. To test the lift, a water tank large enough to exert a loading of fifteen tons per linear foot was built on the platform. The tank was made of wood, lined with polyethylene sheet and filled with sea water to the requisite loading. The trials were carried out in six stages beginning at ten tons per linear foot.

As originally built, the synchrolift was 307 metres long with seventeen electric hoists a side each having a lifting capacity of 180 tons. The lift was rated at 4,600 tons capacity, sufficient to lift an *O* class submarine or a destroyer escort. However, only the submarines could be hauled ashore. Three years later a large shed was built completely enclosing the refit area allowing work to be carried out under cover regardless of the season. During the early 1980s, and at a cost of $13.5 million shared by the Canadian government and NATO, the synchrolift was strengthened, extended to 413 m in length and had an additional twenty, 280-ton hoists added. It can now lift the *Iroquois* and *Halifax* class ships and most NATO frigates as well. The enlarged synchrolift made its debut on 1 November 1986 when it lifted HMCS *Iroquois*.

For the first decade of their existence, the three Canadian O-boats were considered to be training submarines and were not expected to be fully up to operational standards. Although they were originally provided with a state-of-the-art sensor suite, little effort was made to keep the equipment up-to-date.

The O-boats were "defensively" armed with the Northrop Mk 37 electric torpedo only.[63] Introduced in 1956, these lightweight, 19-inch diameter, active/passive acoustic homing, anti-submarine torpedoes were designed for launching from submarines and surface ships. In USN submarines, they were carried as one of several types of torpedoes. The Mk 37 was supplied in both wire-guided and non-guided versions. The shorter, non-guided Mk 37 Mod 0 was carried aft and discharged through the coun-

termeasure torpedo tubes. The longer, wire-guided Mod 2 was carried forward. Both Mods were "swim-out" launched, that is, they propelled themselves out of the torpedo tube and did not need to be "fired" out using compressed air. The original electric Mk 37 lacked the speed and endurance to catch a determined nuclear-powered submarine and was prone to flooding at a depth well above that which any self-respecting SSN or SSBN was capable of reaching with ease. It also had a very limited anti-ship capability. This weapon was later upgraded with a new propulsion system, giving it another six knots and twelve nautical miles additional range. The weapon was also provided with deeper diving ability and marginally improved homing, although the control section retained the original vacuum tube technology. Nevertheless, its reliability was never very good and it always lacked the long-range, high-speed capabilities and "punch" of a heavyweight multi-purpose weapon.

Another serious drawback to all marks of the Mk 37 torpedo was its inability to withstand sustained immersion. Once the tube had been flooded, the weapon either had to be fired within a few hours or withdrawn and stored as it could no longer be relied upon. In RN practice it was an operational requirement for submarines on patrol to have warshot torpedoes loaded and the tubes flooded at all times. This provided for the eventuality of a "snap attack" in which a target of opportunity could be fired at with a minimum of delay. Flooding torpedo tubes was a noisy and time-consuming procedure. In an anti-submarine situation, flooding-up had to be carried out either well in advance, with the risk of rendering the weapons useless, or at the last moment, the worst possible time in an attack in which to be making a noise. All British torpedoes of that era could be carried in a flooded tube with complete reliability for the full duration of a patrol.

In the standard Admiralty design, power-loading gear was only provided for the bottom pair of bow torpedo tubes. This was not a serious problem as long as the submarines were not considered operational and were armed with only the Mk 37 torpedoes. It would become a significant disadvantage when the heavyweight Mk 48 was introduced and the status of the boats upgraded. Loading a six-meter-long 533 mm torpedo

---

63  Speed 24 kts, range 21.5 nm, warhead 150 kg.

weighing 1.6 tonnes is no laughing matter when trying to do it with a makeshift rig of portable sheaves, a wire rope and a check tackle.

One positive note to the carrying of the Mk 37 was that its short length allowed additional bunks to be fitted in the fore ends.[64] These were the infamous "bridal suites"—two sets of removable, side-by-side bunks that were shipped in the space at the rear end of the lower and middle torpedo stowage racks on each side of the compartment. Another single bunk was fitted in each top rack. This augmented accommodation allowed up to ten trainees to be carried per boat above the normal crew requirements. It was not unusual during the 1970s for there to be twenty or more men under training simultaneously aboard these submarines.

Commander E. G. Gigg, wartime RCNVR submariner with the RN, commissioning CO of HMCS *Grilse*, and first commander, CANSUBRON ONE, had his own ideas on how the squadron was to be run. His introduction of modified USN terminology and procedures was not popular although, in retrospect, there might have been a good case for it. Had any of the various schemes for acquiring USN *Barbel*s or *Thresher*s succeeded, Canada's submariners would have had to become totally Americanized.

Modified USN terminology and procedures were applied universally—in the submarine school, aboard the boats and in the dockyard. The British term snort became snorkel; the fore-planes and after-planes became bow planes and stern planes. Instead of turning-out the fore planes the crew rigged-out the bow planes. The quick-diving tank, which in RN parlance was Q-tank, became negative, the abbreviated form for negative buoyancy tank. One night in *Ojibwa* while making tortured preparations to snorkel, dead silence followed the order to "Light-off both," the USN equivalent of "Start both generators." To those trained in Britain, this tinkering with terminology for no apparent reason was regarded as somewhat farcical. Aboard the boats the men continued to use British terminology among themselves. The situation was complicated by the fact that all of the ship's drawings, equipment manuals, planned maintenance documentation and instructions used RN terminology and procedures.

HMCS *Ojibwa*, WESTEX 77. Embarking a Mk37. "Down the hatch she goes." (Author's collection)

*Ojibwa* WESTEX 77. Preparing for a firing on the Nanoose Range. A worried-looking Petty Officer Halvorson amidst the torpedoes. (Author's collection)

For a brief period a number of surplus USN-trained officers and men came east to help ease the chronic shortage of personnel and the full-scale use of American terminology came into vogue. Modified terminology was quickly re-instated when some potentially dangerous situations developed because

---

64 The stowages were about 6.5 metres in length, the Mk 37 Mod 1/2 only required 4.1 metres of space.

*Ojibwa's* interior, inside the engine room on the platform looking aft along the gleaming 16-cylinder ASR1 diesel engines. (Author's collection)

HMCS *Rainbow*, recently commissioned, early 1969. (MARCOM Museum)

HMCS *Ojibwa* passes under the Angus L. MacDonald Bridge during her paying off sail past, 21 May 1998. (DND)

neither the old guard nor the new really understood the other. Petty though it may seem to the layman, to many of the men in the crews it was confusing to say the least, and could be dangerous under stress when orders had to be clearly understood and instinctively obeyed. By the early 1970s it was obvious

Canada would not be buying any USN designs, at least in the near future, and a reversion was made to British terminology and procedures. This made life aboard the O-boats simpler and certainly safer.

In the 1980s, a shift was made towards a higher level of operational capability for the O-boats. It had finally been admitted at NDHQ that the ageing destroyer escort fleet was falling behind in ASW capability and no longer measured up to NATO requirements. Because of the cancellation of the General-Purpose Frigate program, there were no new ships entering service to take their place. As a stopgap measure, it was agreed that modernized O-boats would form a credible ASW contribution while Canada started a long-delayed ship-replacement program.

To make the O-boats battle-worthy, they were given a wide range of improvements in a program known as the Submarine Operational Update Project, or SOUP. Beginning with *Ojibwa* in 1980, as each boat entered its cyclical refit it was fitted with the Singer Librascope computerized Submarine Fire Control System (SFCS) Mk 1, Mod C, Gould Mk 48 Mod 4 dual-purpose, heavy-weight torpedoes[65] forward, upgraded navigational aides and other operational improvements. In 1989, the "Triton" sonar suite was purchased for fitting in all three boats. It was as part

---

65  Speed 40-55 kts, range 24.5 nm, warhead 267 kg.

Scanned from originals provided by Keith Nesbit who retired from the CAF in 1996 with the rank of Captain (N). Keith started in submarines in the late 1960s as weapons officer in *Ojibwa*. He was XO in *Ojibwa* and *Onondaga* and commanded *Okanagan*, *Onondaga* and CANSUBRON ONE. Most of these photographs were taken by Keith himself.

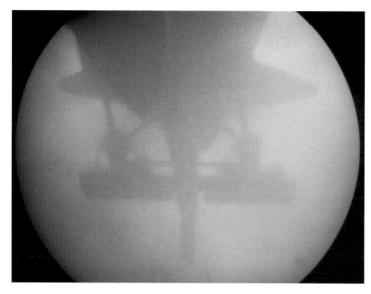

A 35 mm photo taken from the search periscope of the screws of another O-boat passing overhead, also dived.

HMCS *Okanagan*, ca 1976. Taken from the search periscope using a 35 mm still camera. This is a photo of a Canadian *Tribal* class destroyer launching a Sea Sparrow surface-to-air missile. The photo has been "doctored" with a fake torpedo track to make it look as if the ship had been torpedoed.

HMCS *Onondaga*, 1973. A USN P3 Orion ASW aircraft over-flies *Onondaga*. Photo taken using 35 mm still camera through the search periscope.

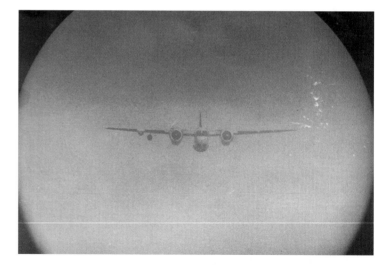

HMCS *Onondaga*, 1973. Periscope photo of a Tracker A/S aircraft. 35 mm still camera through the periscope. Caption could be "Here comes trouble."

HMCS *Onondaga* 1973. HMCS *Saguenay* taken through the search periscope using the 35 mm still camera.

HMCS *Okanagan*, 2 March 1977. HNLMS *Friesland* taken through the search periscope using the 35 mm still camera.

CDR Keith Nesbit, CO of *Okanagan* 1975-77, at the chart table, 1976.

HMCS *Okanagan* 1980. Sea Cadets admire *Okanagan*'s pink panther mascot logo from the fin-top maintenance platform. *Okanagan* had legal permission to use the mascot.

of this upgrade that the bulbous bow dome that characterized their external appearance during their last decade in service was fitted. At that time, the redundant stern countermeasure torpedo tubes were removed to make room in which to install equipment for a towed array passive sonar. This gave the O-boats an enhanced operational capability that could be supported well into the 1990s. However, unlike the Australian navy, Canada stopped short of incorporating weapon handling and fire control improvements that would enable them to employ the Harpoon submarine-launched SSMs.

In the meantime, a replacement had to be found for *Grilse*. A wartime-built, modernized USN fleet boat was purchased in late 1968 and commissioned as HMCS *Rainbow*. *Rainbow* enjoyed but a short career and was paid off at the end of 1975, having become too costly to support. No submarine has been based on the west coast since that time although HMCS *Ojibwa* made two operational visits to the west coast before being paid off. The first, in 1977, known as Operation WESTEX 77, was reasonably successful. However, her final trip to Esquimalt in 1997 was fraught with serious mechanical breakdowns and a myriad of other technical problems, all of which served to emphasize the inherent unreliability of an old submarine, no matter how well maintained. At the time of writing (1999), only one of the three Canadian *O* class submarines remains in operation.

During the late 1980s, it had become apparent that the training for commanding officers being given in Britain was no longer suited to Canadian requirements. The RN was phasing out their diesel boats, and although the *Upholder*s were commissioning, their future was already doubtful, so the training program was concentrating on producing COs for nuclear submarines. In 1992, a study team was convened to examine the feasibility of establishing a Canadian training course for submarine COs. As a result of their report, the first Canadian submarine commanding officer course was run in 1994 and since that time all submarine COs have been trained in Canada.

Always based at Halifax, the Canadian *Oberons* and their support services constituted the First Canadian Submarine Squadron from July 1966 until February 1996. In the budget-driven rationalization of military units that took place in the mid 1990s, the submarine service received a decisive blow to morale when it was decided to close the squadron. This plan called for the merging of the submarines, shore assets and personnel into Maritime Operations Group Five (MOG-5), then a collection of miscellaneous naval vessels most with a low operational value.

At the time, this move was viewed in one of two ways. Either MOG-5, in running the submarines, had acquired a truly operational component, or, the operational status of the submarines had been downgraded to something less than fully operational. Many observers, both in and out of the navy, leaned towards the latter and felt that it was the beginning of the end for submarines in the Canadian navy. However, Commander MOG-5 inclined to the optimistic viewpoint and always considered the submarines to be his organization's greatest asset. Now that the Maritime Coastal Defence Vessels (MCDVs) are also part of MOG-5, that organizaton has taken on a new vitality. Nevertheless, for the submariners, the change of status took some getting used to, and the initial decline in morale among the men was almost palpable.

Those who serve in submarines, be they volunteers or not, find themselves in a very different environment from their counterparts in the surface fleet. Their domestic, technical and professional problems are almost incomprehensible to the surface fleet sailor, and alienation at the local level is inevitable when the two groups have no option but to co-exist.

To provide for both the surface element and the submarines under the same umbrella organization, a compromise has been reached. The submarines, under the Commander, Submarine Division, will form an operational unit separate from MOG-5, but relying on MOG-5 for administrative and material support. It is also intended that the *Victoria* class boats will be provided with berthing and shore support facilities separate from but supported by MOG-5. This will give the submariners the professional autonomy they need while, at the same time, meeting the navy's whole-fleet concept.

## THE ROYAL NAVY *UPHOLDER* CLASS

IN the late 1970s, the UK Ministry of Defence proposed selecting a diesel-electric submarine design to replace the fleet of fourteen *Oberons* that were due to reach the end of their hull life in the mid 1990s. The new boats were intended to provide a cost-effective alternative to SSNs for Home waters defence and ASW training. Initially, five designs were put forward. The naval staff opted for a boat of about 1,960 tons submerged displacement. However, MoD considerations had to be tempered by the need for industry to produce a product that would have competitive export potential. This led to an increase in displacement to 2,400 tonnes in order to provide for more flexibility in the selection of alternative machinery and systems.

Ultimately the Vickers Shipbuilding and Engineering Limited's Type 2400 diesel-electric patrol submarine design was arrived at. A formal Naval Staff Requirement was approved in 1980 and Admiralty Board approval was forthcoming the following year. The original long-range plan called for the production of up to eighteen of the new boats, although by the time Admiralty approved the design, this number had been reduced to an initial program of nine. These were to be constructed in three stages. Stage One was the prototype boat. Stage Two would consist of three boats identical to the prototype. Stage Three was to provide a further five boats having an updated sensor suite. Long-lead ordering commenced shortly afterwards, and an invitation to tender for building the boats was sent out in 1982.

An order for the first Type 2400, SSK 01, was placed with VSEL on 2 November 1983 and construction began at the Barrow-in-Furness shipyard almost immediately. From

that point on a design freeze was imposed to ensure strict uniformity of the class. Construction of the three boats of stage two was awarded to VSEL-owned Cammel Laird and Company Limited, Birkenhead, on 2 January 1986. The cost for the four submarines was announced as being £620 million plus long-lead items, or a little over $2 billion Canadian (1987 values). Stage three was never put out to tender.

The scheme was soon in jeopardy. In the 1992 defence review that followed the collapse of the communist state and the disintegration of the Soviet Union, MoD made the decision to divert all expenditure exclusively to nuclear-powered submarines. No further orders were placed for conventional attack submarines. In 1994, the RN decided to abandon the Type 2400 program after the four completed boats had been commissioned as the *Upholder* class. The submarines were decommissioned, placed in reserve at Barrow and offered for sale.

## FAILED SUBMARINE REPLACEMENT PROGRAMS

At NDHQ during the early 1980s, an unofficial submarine replacement program office was created and a Statement of Requirement for a modern SSK replacement for the Canadian *O* class was prepared. Based on Cold War deployment projections the Department of National Defence (DND) was predicting a minimum requirement of twelve, and a desirable total of sixteen SSKs. In 1985, the project achieved official status as the Canadian Submarine Acquisition Project (CASAP SSK) but was limited to considering the acquisition of only four submarines, all to be built in Canada. In July 1986, a source qualification document was distributed to potential Canadian submarine builders. The objective of this document

## THE SUBMARINE REPLACEMENT PROGRAM

**HMS *Unicorn* launching at Birkenhead. (Author's collection)**

was to identify Canadian prime contractors who could build and support a suitable submarine and to identify acceptable designs. Submissions for the building of as many as twelve submarines in groups four, six, eight and twelve were invited.

Seven designs were proffered in the responses. Of these only four were considered acceptable, and all required modifications to meet Canadian requirements. The German, 2400-tonne Thyssen Nordseewerke TR1700 was the front runner, with the VSEL Type 2400 coming second. The Australian *Collins* class project, which was just beginning, was also considered. Although the technical concept fulfilled the CASAP SSK requirement, it was rejected as a contender on the grounds that it was an unproven design for which no support existed and would probably be too costly. The remaining designs lagged considerably behind the front runners.

The SSK replacement program was dramatically overtaken when, on 5 June 1987, the first White Paper on Defence in fifteen years, *Challenge and Commitment: A Defence Policy for Canada,* boldly called for the construction of a dozen SSNs. This was the death knell for the SSKs, as all CASAP efforts were then switched to SSNs.

Citing concern over the proliferation of Soviet SSBNs and SSNs in the northern areas of the Atlantic and Pacific and in the Arctic in particular, the White Paper proposed that Canada should acquire combat-worthy submarines that could counter the threat anywhere, including under the arctic ice. Canadian SSNs would be expected to play a significant role in the NATO concept of defence-in-depth aimed at preventing a Soviet breakout. This would include patrolling the transArctic routes under the polar ice cap and through the Canadian Arctic Archipelago and guarding the choke points in the Smith, Jones and Lancaster sounds and the Davis Strait.

The 2400-tonne French *Rubis* at $350 million apiece and the 4,730 ton British *Trafalgars* at $450 million each, were the primary contenders, and proposals for building the boats in Canadian yards were requested. Preliminary cost estimates published by DND predicted a price tag of $8.5 billion for the submarines and their support facilities. This amount was to be spread over the twenty-six-year life expectancy of the boats and was based on built-in-Canada prices. To reduce infrastructure costs, the SSNs were to be based at existing naval facilities.

Neither design met the Canadian requirements. The *Trafalgar* class came very close and, being a well-proven design would have incurred the least cost overrun. However, she required a large crew and used an American reactor. It would have taken an agreement from the American government before the technology could be used by Canada. Although the American president eventually indicated that this permission would be forthcoming, the matter was never put before Congress.

The French authorities made a particularly strong pitch for their submarine as a less complicated and cheaper alternative to the British offering. However, the *Amethyste* class, the second generation *Rubis* and the design ultimately put forward, left a lot to be desired. She was ten knots slower than *Trafalgar,* her torpedo tubes were too short for the Mk 48, she was known to be noisy and was unproven in service, all of which meant it would ultimately incur more cost to bring the design up to Canadian standards. The debate within DND and the government was intense. There was a strong feeling that the French design was likely to win out because it was cheaper, and there would be no problem with the transfer of technology.

In the fall of 1987, both the British and French governments were given an opportunity to demonstrate their submarines to Canadian authorities when visits to Halifax were arranged for HMS *Torbay* and the French submarine *Saphir.* This was probably the high point of the project: from then on it was all downhill.

Dissension from within DND, resistance from within government, lack of support from the United States, opposition from a very vocal anti-nuclear lobby and the general public and a huge increase in program cost estimates soon caused the government to have second thoughts. Figures, reported in the media as having been leaked from inside government, had reached a "guesstimated" $33 billion plus for the program.

By November 1988, support had almost evaporated. One public opinion poll revealed that 71 percent of Canadians were now opposed to the program. A lack of voter support, the inability to gain Cabinet confidence, the sudden onset of the democratization of eastern Europe and accelerating fiscal restraints all came to a head in the budget of April 1989. This document effectively relegated all proposals for new submarines of any kind to obscurity. The CASAP office lingered on with a low-level staff but was officially closed in August 1990.

## THE PUBLIC FORUM ON NUCLEAR-POWERED SUBMARINES

The quest for nuclear-powered submarines brought to light a whole new layer of organized opposition from within the national social fabric. The effect that these groups exerted took many observers by surprise. At the beginning of the nuclear submarine debate, it was apparent that most Canadians were either in favour of the nuclear power option or indifferent to it. It was known that a vocal anti-nuclear lobby, estimated by some to represent about 25 percent of public opinion, existed, but under the circumstances the prospects for gaining public support looked good.

The "legitimate" anti-war lobby was based mostly in religious groups such as the anti-war organization Project Ploughshares. These groups did not want to see an escalation of armaments anywhere and were utterly opposed to Canada acquiring weapons of significant strategic consequence for any reason. As a group dedicated to total disarmament their opposition to the nuclear option was entirely in keeping with their stated mandate.

Another prominent anti-nuclear lobby, headed by the Canadian Centre for Arms Control and Disarmament, vehemently espoused opposition to the proliferation of nuclear devices of any kind. To them, the use of nuclear-power plants in the Arctic, or anywhere else, was reprehensible. It was their contention that the intended use by Canada of weapons-grade uranium in the nuclear reactors in the submarines was contrary to the Nuclear Non-proliferation Treaty to which Canada was a signatory. Accidental nuclear pollution and nuclear-waste disposal were also matters of concern. The same group always figured prominently whenever costs were being quoted in newspaper columns. Their cost predictions were uncannily convincing and there is a lingering suspicion that these dissenters were being abetted from within the government itself.

A small but vocal proportion of those offering public opposition to the concept espoused an agenda that bordered on the subversive. Although their usually sensationalist outpourings received prominence in the popular tabloids and some more respectable newspapers, their arguments were largely rhetorical, often specious and seldom convincing to the discerning reader. Nevertheless, they had a significant impact on popular opinion and received extensive media coverage. The vehemence with which these groups pursued their objectives caused many Canadians to wonder whether they actually represented Canadian opinion or were espousing a foreign agenda.

Ultimately the SSN project was terminated. Public reaction included a strong, negative, response to the cost of the project, the lack of transparency in the costing process as well as a growing, vocal, organized resistance to the nuclear power option and to strategic armaments in general.

There remains, even today, considerable speculation as to whether the nuclear-powered submarine option was really a genuine bid for a more powerful navy or a political/diplomatic ploy designed to create some kind of advantage in the international political arena. Many observers agree that the Canadian navy of the day could never have manned or managed a fleet of twelve nuclear-powered submarines, even if industry could have produced them. The entire navy would have had to be restructured, including a substantial reduction of the surface fleet. There is also considerable doubt as to whether the government, then, or at any time, would have been willing to accept responsibility for the enormous strategic potential inherent in the possession of such powerful weapons systems. Significantly, the proposal never reached Cabinet.

Considering the world-shaking political events that were waiting just a few months down the road, it is perhaps fortunate that the project never reached fruition. However, the fact remains that today Canadian arctic waters remain totally unguarded by Canada, and, as far as Canadian military capability is concerned, are indefensible.

## THE LONG WAIT

The 1990 Report of the Standing Committee on National Defence again supported the need for replacement conventional submarines, but admitted that such a large capital expenditure would be hard to justify on the heels of the twelve-ship, $9-billion, Canadian Patrol Frigate Program. The 1994 White Paper on Defence reinforced this view but at the same time stated that the government intended to explore the purchase of the four redundant *Upholder* class boats recently decommissioned by the RN.

This recommendation was made despite repeated and vociferous attempts by members of Project Ploughshares to scuttle the submarine service altogether. When the Parliamentary Committee on Canada's Defence Policy made its cross-country fact-finding tour, Project Ploughshares made presentations against having any submarines at all in nine of the eleven cities visited. Their primary assertion appeared to be that surface ships could perform the same roles at less cost and that the people of Canada simply could not afford to buy useless, second-hand weapons systems. The arguments put forward by the Ploughshares proponents completely ignored the recognized and already accepted fundamental need for a balanced fleet capable of responding to threats in all three maritime elements.

However, even the modest one-billion-dollar price tag then being asked by MoD proved too rich for Cabinet, and the government backed off. MoD reacted by offering the *Upholders* to Portugal and Chile. A number of unsolicited proposals from within the Canadian shipbuilding industry to build Canadian-modified, European-designed submarines in Canada also failed, again due to fiscal restrictions and a lack of will on the part of the government.

In 1996, there was a flurry of announcements and denials when another scheme for acquiring the *Upholders* was aborted almost as soon as it was launched. According to media reports, the army's need for new, armoured, wheeled transports was more pressing.

HMS *Upholder* (now HMCS *Chicoutimi*) running her first of class trials in 1990. (DND)

## CANADIAN TYPE 2400 SUBMARINES

On 6 April 1998, after twelve years of uncertainty and a long trail of abandoned submarine replacement schemes, the Canadian government announced publicly that it was Canada's intention to acquire the surplus *Upholders*. The published cost was $750 million, or about one-third of what they actually cost to build. This was divided into two components: $610 million for the four submarines and $140 million for related expenses. All of the money was to be taken out of the defence budget and the public was assured that no "new" money would have to be found.

Three months later, on 3 July 1998, and only after a careful appraisal of public opinion—which appeared to be completely ambivalent—the deal was ratified. To all appearances, the submarines were acquired in response to pressure exerted on the government by DND and Canada's military allies and, of course, because the price was right. The navy was quietly delighted. There had been a real danger of losing its submarines altogether.

Two contracts were signed that day. The first, with the British government, was an eight-year, interest-free, lease-to-purchase agreement for the four submarines, five sophisticated training simulators and other training aides, as well as a computerized technical-data package. The lease payments will be made, at least in part, in a barter arrangement for the continued use of military training facilities at Canadian Forces Bases Wainright, Suffield and Goose Bay by British forces.

The second contract is with VSEL. This provides for reactivation refits, including Canadianization modifications and new batteries, all available spare parts, and a comprehensive training program for the commissioning crews. The reactivation refit will last about six months for each boat. The first boat to be taken in hand, HMCS *Victoria*, entered Devonshire Dock Hall, one of the big VSEL building sheds, in April 1999. The refits will include hull surveillance and underwater hull survey; re-preservation of tanks and free flooding structures; pressure testing of systems to full diving depth; HP air bottle re-validation; refurbishment of the weapons handling and discharge system; nickel alloy bronze casting re-validation and the testing and commissioning of all safety systems.

HMS *Unseen.* (Author's collection)

As part of the purchase deal, VSEL will provide upwards of $150 million in direct and indirect submarine related industrial benefits in Canada. An additional $100-million has been allocated in the form of waivers to provide offsets in the UK for Canadian companies bidding on submarine support contracts. It has been estimated that the acquisition of these submarines will create approximately six hundred person-years of work in Canada throughout the designed twenty-six-year life of the boats. This compares favourably with the workforce employed in support of the *O* class boats. Presumably, the bulk of the work will remain in the Halifax naval dockyard as at present. The incessant drive for greater economies would seem to dictate otherwise, but the skills and equipment already reside at Halifax and the dockyard has learned how to compete.

On 30 March 1999, in an announcement made in Victoria, BC, by the Minister for Fisheries, the submarines were given names. The new boats are to be known as the *Victoria* class, after the first to be commissioned, HMCS *Victoria*. The remaining three, in order of commissioning, are *Windsor, Chicoutimi* and *Corner Brook*. According to DND, these names follow the convention recently established with the *Halifax* class frigates and perpetuated in the *Kingston* class MCDVs of naming warships after Canadian communities. The *Victorias* are named after secondary seaport communities. All but *Chicoutimi,* which was a Second World War corvette, are new to the naval lexicon. The first of the slightly-used new-to-Canada submarines is now scheduled to enter service around September 2000, with the remainder following at six-monthly intervals.

## A QUICK LOOK AT THE *VICTORIA* CLASS

The *Victoria* class are single hull submarines having about the same internal space as the *Oberons*. (See diagrams, pp 164-5.) With a length-to-beam ratio in the neighbourhood of 9:1, the hull can be characterized as short and broad rather than long and narrow like the O-boats which have a length-to-beam ratio of about 16:1. The 47.55-metre-long pressure hull has a constant diameter of 7.6 metres except for a slight tapering in the after compartment. It is strengthened by internal frames and both ends are capped by unsupported dome bulkheads. The pressure hull is divided into three main compartments by two transverse watertight bulkheads—Bulkhead 35 forward and Bulkhead 56 aft. The three main compartments are about equal in size. The forward and middle compartments are divided into three levels by 1 Deck and 2 Deck while the after compartment has only two levels. The entire submarine is constructed using the techniques and standards developed by VSEL in building nuclear submarines.

The bow and stern are free-flooding extensions built onto the pressure hull. These are joined along the top by a fibreglass casing. The casing provides an upper deck workspace with reasonable freeboard and acts as a fairing around the hatchways and equipment mounted along the crown of the hull. The space inside the casing is utilized for the stowage of berthing lines, disappearing bollards and fairleads and pressure-proof containers for inflatable utility boats, outboard motors and other sea-manlike gear. A hollow ballast keel extends the full length of the pressure hull, enabling the submarine to be docked without a special cradle. The keel, like all other external features, is shaped and faired into the hull to minimize drag and prevent the creation of undesirable hydrodynamic effects.

The bow is a substantial steel structure about thirteen metres in length. It is composed of two semi-ellipsoids that give it a round-nosed bullet shape with a slight downward droop. This shape reduces drag and provides for optimum water flow over the bow sonar array. A cylindrical sonar array measuring approximately four metres in height by three metres in diameter occupies the entire lower forward third of the bow structure. The area in way of the sonar array is covered with fibreglass panels.

The upper bow section accommodates most of the length of the torpedo tubes, and associated equipment. The torpedo tubes are arranged in two groups of three, one above two on either side of the centre line. Only the breech ends penetrate beyond the dome bulkhead. Below each set of torpedo tubes is an air turbine pump (ATP) housing. These are connected by trunking to large, rectangular, grating-covered intakes in the side of each bow. The two ATPs are situated in the compartment immediately below the tube rear ends inside the dome bulkhead on 2 Deck. The pump impellers project beyond the dome bulkhead into the intake trunking. The space in front of the dome bulkhead around each group of torpedo tubes and the ATP discharge outlets is partitioned off to form the two water transfer tanks. These are used to transfer the pressurized water flow created by the ATPs to the torpedo tubes by way of inlet valves in the torpedo tubes.

The structure in way of the torpedo tube muzzles has fairings that guide the torpedoes through the bow. Shutters streamline the torpedo exit ports. The bowcaps and shutters work independently of each other. The bow cap and bow shutter operating gear is external to the pressure hull. A circular torpedo-loading hatch is located in the top centre of the dome bulkhead and is accessed from outside through a covered embarkation trough in the casing. With the exception of a short length in way of the hatch, the torpedo embarking rails that guide the torpedo into and out of the submarine are permanently rigged.

HMS *Unseen* under construction at Birkenhead. (Author's collection)

The anchor handling gear is located in the centre of the bow structure. The Admiralty standard anchor stows in a recess in the bottom of the bow in a fashion reminiscent of the arrangement in the CC- and H-boats. The cable locker occupies a space adjacent to the anchor stowage. A hawsepipe leads the cable upwards from the cable locker to a hydraulically powered cable holder located in the casing above the torpedo tubes. This is offset to starboard to clear the torpedo embarking trough. A continuation of the hawsepipe leads downward to the anchor in its stowage recess. Access to the cable holder, clutch, operating points and cable securing arrangements is provided through a hatch in the casing. Unlike in the old Electric Boat Company designs, the anchor cannot be worked from inside the boat.

A wire-rope towing pennant is permanently rigged between a slip secured to a strongpoint on the hull inside the fore casing, and the bridge. The pennant is carried in a channel along the starboard upper edge of the casing and the eye is led to the bridge in a channel in the side of the fin. The whole length of the pennant is cemented in place and smoothed over.

The forward hydroplanes are mounted in a rectangular, transverse recess directly below the ATP inlets about midway in the bow along the axis of the hull. They are situated so as to maximize their effectiveness, particularly at slow speed. The operating piston for the fore-planes extends through the dome bulkhead from inside the ATP compartment. The planes are rigidly linked and operate as a pair. These planes have no dynamic effect at speeds above five knots, and when not in use are retracted to streamline the bow and protect them from damage.

Much of the middle portion of the bow structure below the torpedo tubes is occupied by No.1 main ballast tank with No. 2 occupying the space below the hydroplane recess. Both main ballast tanks are open-bottomed, and the main vent pipes are led upwards inside the casing to the main vent valves and outlets. In conformance with modern submarine-building practices, the bottles for the HP air groups, the built-in breathing system (BIBS), which is used for escape, and the emergency blow bottle group, are all stowed inside the main ballast tanks. The bottles are divided almost equally between the bow and stern. Utilizing the ballast tanks in this way is a departure from previous con-

ventional classes and frees up a considerable amount of space inside the boat, most of which is taken up by fuel oil tanks.

Amidships, the steel-framed, fibreglass-clad fin rises about seven metres above the hull and provides a fairing around the masts and the bridge access trunk. The bridge access trunk, or tower as it is sure to be called, is fitted out as a five-man diver lockout chamber. Because the hatchway leads into the interior of the fin, it would not be suitable for use as an escape chamber under ordinary circumstances. There is a deck around the top of the hatchway leading to doors in either side of the fin. A ladder leads upwards to the small bridge in the top forward corner. Two sonars are mounted in the front of the fin and a buoyant radio aerial is housed inside the rear of the structure. Narrow walkways and handrails around the outside of the fin provide a means of access between the forward and after parts of the casing.

Inside the fin, the two periscopes, a fixed ventilator and five masts are arranged from aft to forward in the order: ventilator (which does not extend outside the fin), snort exhaust, snort induction, attack periscope, communications, radar, electronic support measures (ESM) masts and the search periscope. All masts and the periscopes are raised and lowered using twin hydraulic pistons which are mounted alongside their respective tubes and are external to the pressure hull. Only the two periscopes and the ESM mast penetrate the hull. The self-contained navigation radar mast is offset to starboard in order to maximize the available space. At the back of the bridge is a retractable mast on which is mounted the masthead-steaming light for use when on the surface. An overtaking light is positioned in the top after corner of the fin, and the usual port and starboard steaming lights are mounted on pivoting receptacles either side. In the back of the bridge there are brackets to accept a small flagstaff. In the front of the bridge, a retractable transparent windscreen has been provided for the benefit of the watchkeepers.

The top of the fin is roofed over except for the mast and bridge openings. All masts retract below the top of the fin while the "roof" is contoured to minimize drag and water noise.

The stern is a fourteen-metre-long cone-shaped extension of the pressure hull and continues the taper of the after compartment into a point at the single, seven-bladed propeller. The rud-

HMS *Unseen*, Birkenhead. (Author's collection)

ders and after hydroplanes are mounted in a cruciform arrangement immediately forward of the propeller. The pistons for the after planes and the rudder are located inside the dome bulkhead. Operating rods extend through hull glands in the dome bulkhead to the mechanical linkage arrangement in the after part of the cone. The after planes, like the upper and lower rudders, are rigidly linked and operate as a pair. Each hydroplane is hinged along the trailing edge of a triangular fairwater, which also acts as a hydroplane guard.

The widest part of the interior of the stern is partitioned into Nos. 3 and 4 main ballast tanks. The aftermost portion is free-flooding. The propeller shaft exits the centre of the dome bulkhead through a stern gland and passes through the centre of the ballast tanks in a stern-tube. There is a bearing assembly at the hub. Also contained within the after section are the bearing supports for the rudders and hydroplanes. Nos. 4 and 5 HP air bottle groups, part of the emergency blow air group and part of the BIBS bottle group are all located inside the after main ballast tanks.

The internal arrangements are illustrated in the following diagrams, "A Comparison Between the *Oberon* class and *Victoria* class Submarines." As can be seen in the drawing, the internal layout is a considerable departure from the O-boats and offers some real advantages. The weapons stowage and tube space is a dedicated magazine and is not used as a living space as it was in the O-boats. All accommodations and domestic spaces are arranged in two adjoining areas on 2 Deck. Machinery, though scattered throughout the ship of necessity, is concentrated in dedicated spaces. The control room itself is not a thoroughfare. End-to-end movement forward of Bulkhead 56 takes place on 2 Deck. Although the only access to the after compartment is through the after end of the control room, the hatchway and passage arrangements are well clear of the command area proper.

## OPERATIONAL CONSIDERATIONS

Considering the precedent set by the priority originally given the O-boats, it is refreshing to note that these submarines are being accepted as fully operational units of the fleet from the

163

A Comparison of the *Oberon* Class and *Victoria* Class boats.

(Author's collection)

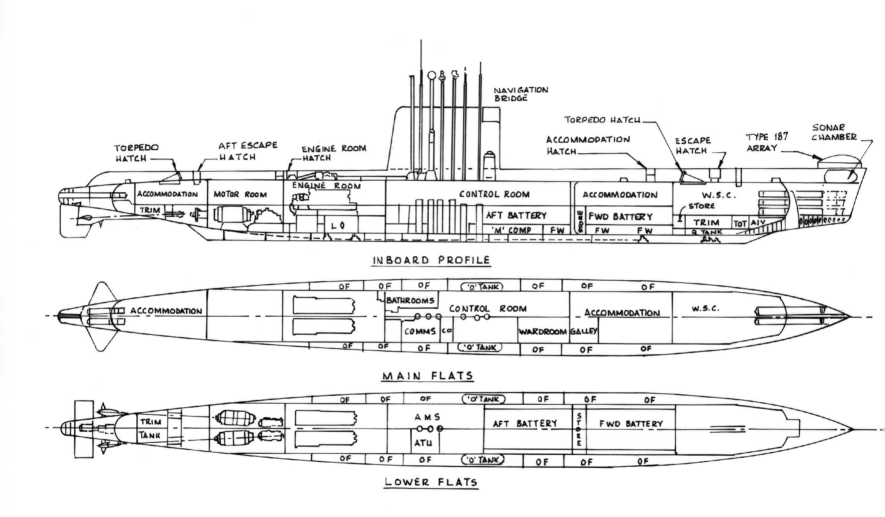

*Oberon* Class General Arrangement, as-built.

A Comparison of the *Oberon* Class and *Victoria* Class boats.
(Author's collection)

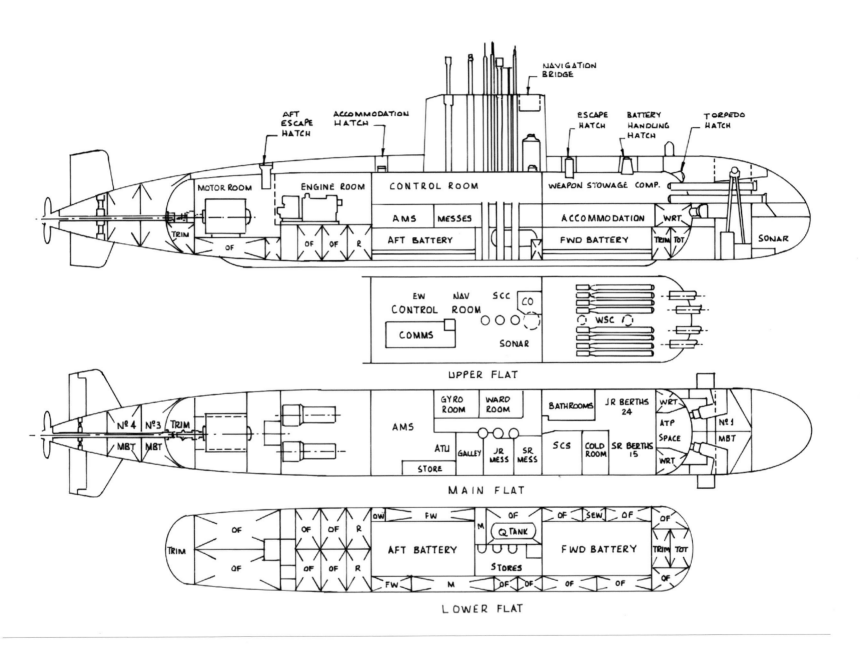

*Victoria* Class General Arrangement, as-built.

outset. Already technologically seventeen years old (the design was frozen in 1983), the *Victoria*s compare favourably on most points with conventional submarines entering service in other navies during the 1990s. However, there are some operational features worth considering.

The *Victoria*s were purchased without the British fire control system, missile weapon system and electronic support measures outfit. Whether this was a decision on the part of the Canadian authorities to bring down the cost, or because the equipment was never offered in the MoD package deal, is not known. These were always optional items of equipment in the VSEL commercial export promotions.

When asked about the removal of the UGM-84A Harpoon missile capability Canadian naval authorities offered a startling explanation. They stated that the likelihood of the Harpoon SSM ever being required or used in Canadian service was negligible.

This response can only lead to the conclusion that the Canadian government is prepared to accept the boats with less than full combat capabilities. Considering that all front-line NATO submarines, including SSKs, are routinely equipped with SSMs, the removal of the Harpoon equipment leads to the question of just what does the government mean by "operational unit"? What submarine CO is going to pass up a 1200 km/h anti-ship missile with excellent accuracy and a range in excess of 200 nautical miles?

However, as these submarines were built with these systems installed, it is conceivable that, should circumstances warrant, the Harpoon missile, or a similar system, could be restored. This would also mean modifying the fire control system, but that too is a proven add-on feature having been included in the very similar Australian O-boat fire control system. It is common practise for Canadian submarines to operate in exercises as if they were fitted with the capability so at least the tactics are familiar to the submarine officers, if not the actual handling and use.

The original fire control system is being replaced by the twenty-two-year-old Lockheed-Martin Librascope SFCS Mk 1 Mod C recovered from the paid off O-boats and the tactical trainer. A fifth system will be manufactured to provide for the additional unit. This equipment is being modernized with new plasma displays and software updates and will be installed when the submarines reach Halifax.

Considering that the British fire control system was not compatible with the Mk 48 torpedo, replacing it with the SFCS Mk 1 Mod C is probably the most cost efficient alternative available. Reconfiguring the British system would undoubtedly have been a very expensive undertaking.

The *Victoria*s will be armed with the Mk 48 torpedoes purchased in the 1980s as part of SOUP. It is anticipated that the entire Mk 48 Mod 4 torpedo inventory will be upgraded with the USN ADCAP Block III improvements. These upgrades will improve the performance of the weapon in both deep-sea and shallow-water environments.

No decision regarding a replacement for the ESM system has been made public. This too may have to be salvaged from the O-boats as another cost-cutting but combat-compromising, measure.

The *Upholder* class was intended for deployment in waters around the UK. Consequently, the patrol endurance of the *Victoria*s is only forty-nine days compared to fifty-six days for the Canadian *Oberon*s and seventy days for the custom-built, six-boat Australian *Collins* class. Originally, it was held that a seventy-day patrol endurance would serve the Canadian situation better too.

As currently configured, the fuel endurance range of the *Victoria*s is a modest 8,000 nm at 8 kts. This is considerably less than the 10,000 nm at 10 kts attributed to other contemporary submarines of the same tonnage. Presumably, the navy will have to be satisfied with both the patrol endurance and fuel range, as improvements in these areas would be expensive.

Power generation is inferior to that being provided in contemporary European designs. The twin Paxman Valenta generators in the *Victoria*s produce 2800 kW as compared to 4400 kW produced by four smaller generators in the German TR 1700 design of the same tonnage. During the reactivation refit, the *Victoria*s are being outfitted with a new battery which should make the existing power generation capability somewhat more tolerable, for a while at least. There has also been some discussion of improving the output of the existing generators, but this has not been substantiated. In one of its commercial export promotions, VSEL indicated it would be possible to install three smaller generators to provide for an increased power output. However, this would be an expensive option as the navy would have to bear the entire cost.

*Victoria* Class. The electronic equipment room, looking into the bunk space. (DND)

The engine room, looking aft through the soundproof bulkhead into the motor room. (DND)

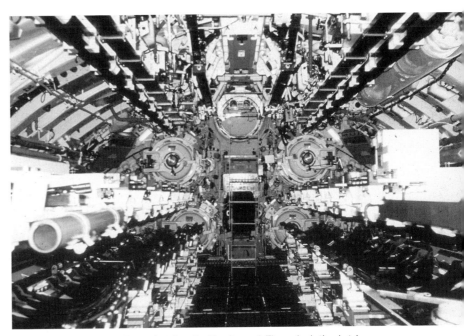

The weapons stowages and torpedo tubes, looking forward. The embarkation hatch is in the upper centre and the embarking rails are a permanent installation. (DND)

Although these considerations will probably have no appreciable impact on the navy's plans for the boats, cumulatively they relegate the *Victoria*s to second-line status according to NATO conventional submarine standards. Nevertheless, even this is a significant improvement on the *Oberons*. There are some imaginative solutions that could be applied, but how, or even if, these operational limitations are to be addressed will be a matter for future interest.

On the positive side, the Barr and Stroud state-of-the-art periscopes will give these boats a big advantage. Both periscopes can be used for optical viewing in the conventional way, as well as electronically using television cameras and other space-age enhancements. They are power-driven in all modes and the watchkeeper's seat automatically folds up when the periscope is lowered. The primary operating mode is by remote control from a dedicated tactical TV display and control console. All time, range, and bearing outputs are electronically channelled into the fire control system for analysis and integration into the attack plot while the image is monitored by the operator and captured on video tape.

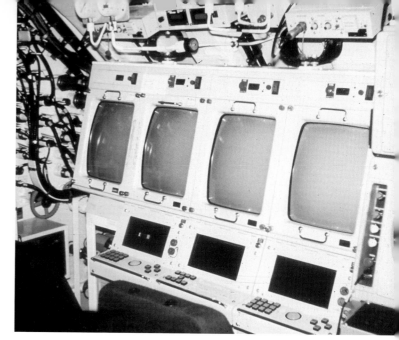

The control room, starboard side forward, showing the attack centre consoles. The (after) attack periscope is in the centre, the cover for the ESM mast is on the left. Mast control and fire control consoles are on the right, with the sonar consoles beyond. (DND)

The sonar consoles. (DND)

Exposure of the periscope during an attack or a sensitive surveillance operation can be a critical factor in remaining undetected. To minimize the exposure time, both the search and the attack periscopes are provided with a quick look round (QLR) capability. Using the QLR feature, the periscope is raised until it breaks surface then makes a rapid 360-degree sweep while the integral TV camera captures the image, after which the 'scope is lowered. The whole process takes only seconds. The recorded image can then be studied and analyzed in slow time.

The search periscope is fitted with an automated artificial horizon sextant. The attack periscope can be fitted with a variety of options such as laser range finding, thermal imaging, image intensification and a low-light television camera. Both periscopes can accept a 35 mm still camera.

Space-age "stealth" technology has been incorporated in the form of anechoic tiles that cover the exterior surface of the hull and fin. This material absorbs sonar-emitted sound waves, reducing, or even preventing, a return echo that would indicate the presence of a solid object in the water. The idea was first put into practical use by the Germans in the Second World War when they coated the external surfaces of some U-boats with a synthetic rubber-like material that was given the code name

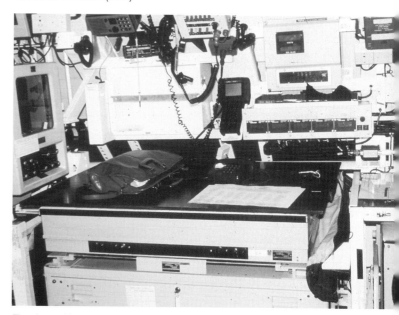

The chart table and navigating instruments, control room, port side. (DND)

*Alberich*. Although effective, it was costly to produce and proved difficult to maintain.

Noise-source reduction and shock protection has been carried to new heights in these submarines. All major machinery is secured to individual platforms or rafts using shock-absorbing, sound-attenuating mountings, and these in turn are anchored to the ship's structure on a second series of shock and sound mountings. All piping is connected to machinery and pumps

Part of the ratings' bunk space. Room for twelve here. (DND)

using flexible, sound-isolating, shockproof connections. Since the late 1950s it has been normal practise to provide for self-monitoring of noise sources.

One big advance incorporated into the *Victorias* is a considerably enhanced fresh-water making capability provided by an Admiralty two-stage, reverse-osmosis desalinator plant (ROD). The ROD plant produces four hundred litres of potable fresh water per hour. As a consequence of the efficiencies expected from this plant, on-board storage of fresh water has been limited to eighteen tonnes, which compares well with the seventeen tonnes of the *Oberons*.

Habitability is Spartan, as befits a submarine. About the same living area per person has been provided as was available in the O-boats, and no major improvements to the domestic facilities are being undertaken during the reactivation refits. This is significant in view of the anticipated mixed-gender manning. Given the compact layout of the accommodations, it

will be interesting to see how the problem is handled. Any changes in this respect will have to be "made in Canada" after arrival.

With the exception of the captain's cabin, which is in the control room, the living spaces are conveniently concentrated on 2 Deck in two dedicated areas either side of Bulkhead 35. The wardroom, senior rates' and junior rates' messes and the galley are all located in the forward half of the middle compartment while the main storeroom is in the space below. All bunk spaces, except that for the officers which is contiguous with the wardroom, are in the forward compartment. As is usual for a submarine, the sanitary facilities are minimal. The heads and washplaces are grouped together in the accommodation space forward of Bulkhead 35 and adjacent to the bunk spaces. The cold-room and an electronic equipment room are also located in this space.

Fire detection and suppression has received some serious attention in these boats. All spaces are fitted with smoke and ion detectors. The status of the detectors is monitored on the machinery control console (MCC) in the motor room, and warnings are displayed and enunciated on the ship control console (SCC) in the control room. Automated fire-suppression systems are fitted in many spaces and these can be initiated automatically, locally and from remote locations. The usual selection of portable fire extinguishers are situated at key points throughout the boat. Critical operator stations have been provided with emergency breathing masks and connections to the emergency breathing system (EBS) while back-pack style breathing equipment is carried for firefighting. Two dozen individual smoke masks, similar to those recommended for personal use aboard airliners, are sited in fire-prone spaces for use by personnel forced to escape from a smoke-filled space.

The motor room, engine room, auxiliary machinery space and sonar and radio equipment spaces are provided with Halon drenching. When this system is activated, Halon gas completely fills the affected space to deprive the fire of oxygen. The big advantages of Halon are the speed of application, fire suppression effectiveness and, unlike most other suppressants, it does no further damage to equipment. Brief exposure to Halon does not pose a risk to human life and anyone caught in a Halon-flooded space has time to evacuate.

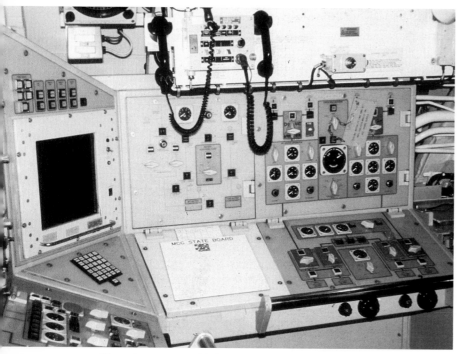

The motor room, port side forward, showing the machinery control console. (DND)

The control room, starboard side, showing the ship control console. (DND)

When a fire is detected in the engine room, "crash-stop" shut-down of the engines and related hull valves can be initiated from the MCC or the SCC. At the same time, the Halon drench system would be activated.

A water-borne foam spray system has been built into the weapons stowage compartment while lockers containing ammunition and explosives are provided with remotely activated flooding.

The galley has been provided with heat and smoke detection as well as a fire-suppression system of its own. Initiation is from outside the galley and all galley power is shut off, the ventilation and exhaust system is shut down and isolated and steel lids are released to cover the deep-fat fryers.

As so many spaces are unmanned, an extensive system of bilge and flooding alarms has been built in. Like the fire-detection system, warnings are enunciated and displayed on the SCC.

## AVAILABILITY

An interesting concept built into these submarines is the so-called seven-year maintenance life cycle. The entire submarine has been designed and constructed to provide for this extended operational availability. The Type 2400 life-cycle philosophy or Whole Ship Profile, is predicated on a 25-year, 45-week ship life expectancy. This is subdivided into three, 385-week (7-year, 21-week) operational commissions, with two 95-week, full scale refits.

Each 7-year, 21-week, commission is divided into four "running cycles" each varying in length between 85 and 98 weeks duration. Interposed between these cycles are three maintenance periods, a two-week docking after the first and third cycles and a 15-week docking in the middle.

A typical 85-week running cycle consists of five operations periods in succession. A typical operations period is seventeen weeks in duration and comprises 2 weeks of training at the outset, 11 weeks of actual operations and a 4-week, assisted, alongside maintenance period at the completion.

The outcome of the Type 2400 life-cycle philosophy is an operational availability prediction of 64 percent. This compares well with the proven 54 percent for the *Oberons* which was considered high in its day. By comparison, the *Halifax* class frigates were built to achieve 70 percent availability. However, in order to

In the galley—lots of stainless steel! (DND)

meet this standard, every important platform system in the ship has been provided with 100 percent redundancy, something that could never be done within the confines of a submarine.

The four *Victoria* class submarines are the only ones of their kind in existence. Sufficient spare gear was manufactured and stored to provide for the first operational commission of each submarine. Beyond that, Canada will have to find ways to supply spares for the remainder of the life cycle. This will be helped to a certain degree by private industry, as VSEL, in concert with MoD, designed the Type 2400 to utilize as much commercial off-the-shelf equipment as possible. Also, this class has many features in common with the *Churchill* class SSNs and so, to a limited extent, will continue to be supported by British manufacturers.

Other considerations aside, these boats are a vast improvement over the obsolete Canadian *Oberons*. With its sophisticated suite of sensors and advanced performance capabilities, the *Victoria* class will serve to introduce Canadian submariners to nuclear-age submarine technologies at a very reasonable cost and without the nuclear headaches. They will also provide a much more suitable platform on which to base future developments, such as the addition of the air independent propulsion system that would give the *Victoria* class boats prolonged patrol endurance and a limited under-ice ability.

## AUSTRALIAN TEETHING TROUBLES

In the early stages of CASAP, the Canadian authorities considered the possibilities of tying into the Australian submarine-building program. The original Australian submarine design criteria seemed to be what Canada was looking for, but as the scheme developed and the costs began to add up, doubts were raised concerning affordability. Another complicating factor was concern over the formation of the Australian Submarine

Corporation and a certain uneasiness over some of the industrial alliances being proposed. Before even considering what would be involved in the transfer of the work and technologies to a Canadian yard, Canada decided against participation.

Rumours of problems with the six-ship *Collins* class began circulating from the time the lead submarine began trials in 1996. In June 1999, these were confirmed in a formal report solicited by the Australian Minister for Defence. The *Collins* class program is in deep, and expensive trouble.

Even considering that it is a brand new class of submarine for which there is no proven prototype, and that it is being built by a new company formed specifically for the purpose, these boats are experiencing far more than mere first-of-class "teething" problems.

The litany of problems is extensive. The propeller shaft gland seals leaked excessively, but this was resolved through the acquisition and installation of a different seal assembly. Water contamination of the diesel fuel is an unresolved problem that has been partly to blame for constant diesel engine breakdowns. Both the design and the quality of the engines themselves have been severely criticised. An excessive number of internal noise shorts have been experienced which are indicative of a poor standard of workmanship and inspection. Cavitation is being caused by the shape of the superstructure. Fatigue failures have developed in the high-tech propeller and the resulting cracks cause cavitation. Severe vibration of the periscopes, even at moderate speeds, has resulted in an impairment of the optics, giving rise to a dispute with the manufacturers. The communications mast has been the site of problems severely compromising long-range communications. Last, and probably most expensively, there has been a total condemnation of the entire combat system while the contract under which it was designed, manufactured and installed has been strongly criticised.

At the time of these revelations, five of the six boats were in the water and three had been delivered to the RAN. The navy, however, had grave misgivings about accepting the submarines under the circumstances and none of them was considered to be in operational condition. This means that Australia is left with one operational submarine, the twenty-one-year-old *O* class boat HMAS *Otama*. The remaining five O-boats have already been paid off in order to release the personnel and resources to the new submarines, and two of these are beyond recovery.

The report outlines a long list of corrective recommendations. These include several senior personnel changes, both in the Ministry for Defence and in the Australian Submarine Corporation hierarchy, as well as significant changes to the way in which equipment contracts are handled. A sweeping series of technical recommendations were also outlined for implementation. Whatever is done, it will be many years and many millions of unbudgeted dollars before the new Australian submarines can be considered operational.

The Australian problems will eventually have a negative impact on Canada's submarine force. Any time in the future when the possibility of Canada building its own submarines is under discussion, opponents to the concept will be certain to cite the unfortunate Australian program as an example of just how wrong such a scheme can go. Any group proposing the building of our own submarines, and we should be planning the replacement class now, will be well advised to examine the Australian experience in intimate detail and prepare their proposal accordingly.

At the same time, the four Canadian *Victoria* class boats were being stripped of their British fire control, missile and electronic warfare systems, docked and opened up for examination in Barrow. Almost immediately rumours began circulating. The alloy used in the hull valves was breaking down, the main vents would have to be replaced and most of the hard sea-water piping was badly corroded and would also have to be replaced. All of this when only the first boat had been opened up. Whether or not these rumours are based on fact, and what, if any, cost it will be to Canada, remains to be seen. In any case, the boats had been laid-up for over four years and something of the sort was anticipated and budgeted for in the reactivation refits.

One serious problem affecting the three Cammel Laird-built submarines is the failure of the welded joints in the HP air system piping. The problem was first identified in *Victoria* in October 1999, when it was discovered that many of the joins exhibited cracks indicating widespread failure of the welding process. Subsequent investigation revealed similar defects in two of the other boats. In December 1999, the

Canadian news media grossly overstated the problem describing it as being capable of causing a submarine to lose the ability to surface. It was also stated that correcting the defect would add six months to *Victoria*'s reactivation refit. Naval authorities were quick to point out that the problem was a warranty matter and that the cost of making repairs would be borne by VSEL. Better to have caught the problem during the reactivation refits than when the boats were in service.

It is well known that the *Upholders* had problems. Canadian authorities will no doubt be wondering whether or not these were properly rectified, as VSEL claims, or if they were just patched up to get the boats sold.

One problem experienced in 1991–92 during the first-of-class trials was a catastrophic power failure that happened during dived propulsion trials. As a result of an otherwise normal combination of propulsion control movements, all power except emergency circuits was lost and could not be restored by ordinary means. In effect, the boat was dead in the water and remained that way for some time. The only corrective action taken at the time was to place temporary restrictions on the operation of the propulsion system to reduce the chance of it happening again while a permanent solution was being engineered.

Other known failures occurred during torpedo firings when it was discovered that the bow caps would not remain shut after firing and that the hydraulically operated firing valves were creeping open. These problems were directly associated with the design of the torpedo tube hydraulic operating system. VSEL claims that these problems have been corrected.

Also, some mechanical problems were experienced with the Paxman Valenta diesel engines during these trials. Despite being a proven commercial design, the engines were adapted for use in submarines and have yet to be proved by performance in that demanding environment. With only two diesel generators providing a barely acceptable power output, the engines must be absolutely reliable if the operational capability of these boats is not to be degraded even further. As the unfortunate Australian experience is demonstrating, getting the new boats into the water can be a long way from making them operational.

## AIR INDEPENDENT PROPULSION— A FUTURE POSSIBILITY

The time a submarine spends in charging batteries is known as indiscretion time—for good reason. While snorting, the submarine is relatively vulnerable. Any masts that have been raised are not only visible, but can be detected by radar. Engine noise can be detected by ship-borne and air-dropped sonars while at the same time degrading the submarine's own sonars. The diesels release a cloud of hot exhaust gas into the atmosphere and the wake of the boat is marked by a trail of relatively hot cooling-water discharged from the engines via the heat exchangers. These "hot-spots" can be detected by ship- and airborne sensors.

Fortunately, modern batteries and generators allow for a much shorter charging time than in the older diesel boats, but even so, the art of detection has kept pace. Ideally, indiscretion time should be kept to an absolute minimum.

In order to reduce the need to run the diesels and to extend the dived range of the submarine without depleting the battery, alternative methods of generating electrical energy that do not require the use of external air and internal combustion engines have been devised. There are three air independent propulsion (AIP) methods currently available; the Stirling closed cycle system, the Ballard fuel cell system and a miniature nuclear reactor developed by the Energy Conversion Systems Group.

In the Stirling system, heat produced by the combustion of pressurized, super-cooled, liquid oxygen (LOX) and diesel fuel in a special burner is used to heat a gas (e.g. helium) in a closed cycle system that drives a special, double-acting, piston engine coupled to a generator. The output of the generator is fed directly to the electrical distribution system. A small quantity of gas and hot water are exhausted from the burner. The exhaust gas is collected and recirculated in the burner while the water is cooled and either stored for treatment and domestic use or discharged overboard.

Stirling systems are already widely used in offshore underwater vehicle and habitat applications and are currently installed aboard some Swedish and German submarines.

Ballard Power Systems Inc. is a Canadian company based at Burnaby, British Columbia, and they have been world leaders in the development of proton exchange membrane (PEM) fuel cell power systems for over a decade. The heart of the proprietary Ballard fuel cell consists of an anode and a cathode, separated by a polymer membrane electrolyte. One side of each of the electrodes is coated with a thin layer of platinum catalyst. Hydrogen is introduced at the anode where it catalytically disassociates into free electrons and protons (positive hydrogen ions). The free electrons are conducted through the external circuit in the form of useable electric current that is fed into the main battery. The protons migrate through the membrane electrolyte to the cathode where they combine with oxygen and electrons from the external circuit to form pure water and heat, which is led off as exhaust.

In a submarine application, where air is at a premium, the oxygen is stored in a container as LOX while hydrogen is supplied from either methanol or natural gas or it can be stored in a special hydride alloy. The process is very quiet and the only exhaust product is hot water, which can either be discharged overboard or stored and treated to make it potable. The big advantage of the PEM fuel cell is that there is no detectable exhaust and little excess heat. Fuel cell technology is developing very rapidly and becoming more efficient and less bulky all the time.

In addition to their already successful automotive power cell installations, Ballard has completed a 40 kW submarine methanol power plant demonstrator for the Canadian Department of National Defence. They have also developed fuel cell power plants for the German shipbuilder, Howaldtswerke-Deutsche Werft, who are interested in Ballard Fuel Cell power plants to provide auxiliary power aboard merchant vessels while in harbour.

The Autonomous Marine Power Source (AMPS) was developed by the ECS Group of Companies in Canada. AMPS is built around a Canadian designed miniature, light-water-cooled, nuclear reactor. It produces steam to drive a conventional turbogenerator. The only exhaust product is hot water. There are several significant drawbacks to this system. It is nuclear, therefore expensive, and will eventually create "dirty" waste products in the form of spent fuel and radioactive reactor components. Another is that its operation depends on a number of potentially noisy pumps. Some advanced development has taken place, but no commercial models have been produced.

The installation of any of these AIP systems would be accomplished through the insertion of a short hull section,

about five metres long, between the middle and after pressure hull compartments. All three systems can produce enough electricity to supply normal "hotel" requirements and to propel the SSK at a moderate speed. The Stirling and Ballard fuel cell systems depend on a finite fuel supply, but even at current developmental levels could provide the total power requirements of a *Victoria* class boat for about a week while propelling continuously at 5-6 kts. The AMPS could provide all "hotel" power requirements indefinitely while propelling at 8 kts. Where high speed was required, the battery would have to be used and charged later using the diesel generators.

Canada is a world leader in both AMPS and PEM fuel cell development. The latter appears to hold the edge as far as submarine application is concerned because it is much less expensive and non-nuclear. Whether or not the government will undertake to install one of these systems in the *Victoria* class boats remains to be seen, but the possibilities are exciting.

## THE NEW MANNING POLICY

Until recent times, all personnel in Canadian submarines were volunteers. With the manning reductions brought about by government funding cutbacks, and the resultant streamlining of naval trades that took place during the late 1980s, it was found expedient to dispense with the volunteer-only rule. This allows the navy to post non-volunteer hard sea trade personnel into submarines as necessary in order to maintain the right mix of skills and experience levels. As far as postings are concerned, submarines are now considered to be one of the four main combatant units of the fleet. These include *Halifax* class general-purpose frigates, *Iroquois* class command and control ships, *Victoria* class SSK submarines and *Kingston* class MCDVs, the last mentioned being almost the exclusive preserve of the naval reserve.

The four *Victoria* class boats will be based in Halifax, with one boat on permanent west coast deployment. Initially these will be manned by five east coast-based crews. Two crews will rotate on the west coast boat while the remaining three will man the east coast submarines. Most of the training, major maintenance and administration will continue to be located in Halifax. Eventually it is hoped to man the submarine on west-coast deployment with personnel permanently living on that coast.

It is claimed that in the long run the Submarine Division can only benefit through being brought into the mainstream of the fleet. This is undoubtedly so in the areas of support and materiel. A more efficient operation should be the result, but there may well be problems on the manning side. Supporters of the policy point out that it will be much easier to keep the boats manned with qualified personnel now that non-volunteer personnel are being posted into submarines. However, this bright spot has its dark side. The Submarine Division relies on maintaining a dedicated, long-term cadre of experienced personnel in order to sustain the high level of technical expertise essential to the efficient running of the submarines. This cadre is composed largely of volunteers or of non-volunteers who have found their niche in submarines. These may be considered the "professional" submariners.

However, consider the effect on the professional submariner, who has worked his way up in position and rank aboard submarines, and who now finds himself blocked from advancing to a higher position by a senior but totally inexperienced man posted in from the surface fleet. This can only have a depressing effect on the dedicated submariner who may well be forced back to surface ships in order to accept a promotion in rank or to advance in his trade standing.

This has always been the case with some trades and it is made clear at the time of entry into submarines that an eventual return to the surface fleet or original branch of the service must be anticipated. This kind of turnover is almost entirely predictable and is easily accommodated through advanced planning. However, the unnecessary loss of the experienced senior rate means the permanent loss of his expertise and the lowering of the overall technical standard.

It would be impractical for NDHQ to institute a total non-volunteer policy. If submarines were to experience the same rate of personnel turnover as surface ships, it would cause an unacceptable dilution of expertise aboard the submarines and overwhelm the training facilities. Keeping the balance between the career aspirations of the professional submariner, who wants to serve in boats, and maintaining the overall manning requirements will demand considerable understanding on the part of the career managers at NDHQ.

At present, submarines are exempt from the mixed-gender manning policy. The exemption is based on the standard of accommodations and the working conditions found aboard the *O* class submarines. Already it has been indicated that NDHQ is considering the introduction of a female component into the crew of the *Victoria* class boats. Having almost the same internal volume as the *O* class and almost the same allocation of accommodation space per crew member, the *Victoria*s are not going to be much more hospitable than their predecessors. Although the layout has improved considerably, there has been little real change in the standard of accommodations.

The possibility of mixed-gender crews is being explored nonetheless. The whole procedure appears to be a managerial exercise conducted as a matter of principle, rather than a practical and necessary application of leadership dedicated to meeting the real needs of submarine manning requirements. Part of the reasoning put forth by NDHQ is that, as service in submarines is no longer voluntary, the exclusion of hard sea trade female personnel from this duty would be unfair to male members. This would seem to suggest that NDHQ is preparing to accept female volunteers or even to draft women into submarines.

Setting aside the psychological and physiological dilemmas as being far too complex for this book, the manning and accommodations arrangements alone seem to compound the problem enormously.[66]

These boats are manned by a minimum crew. Every crew member must be on board to run the submarine efficiently and safely at sea. All crew bunks are arranged in vertical stacks of three and there are no spares, nor is there space for spares. For obvious reasons, the very minimum of privacy can only be obtained by assigning one or more sets of three bunks to the use of female members. The initial problem will be to find sufficient women of suitable trade levels to fill the bunks in groups of three simultaneously. The crux comes when one or two female crew members cannot make it to sea. In order to make up for the missing women, other female members of the same trade, experience level and qualifications will have to be found to replace them. If this is not possible, then men will have to be

66  For those who would advocate male-female equality in all things, I suggest they consider the ramifications of introducing half a dozen men into an all-female crew and sending them to sea for six weeks.

substituted. As it would be unthinkable to allow male members to bunk in close proximity with the remaining females, the men will be forced to hot-bunk—two men in opposite watches taking turns using the same bunk. What this will do for male-female relationships is best left to speculation. The only other option will be to temporarily replace all of the women with men until their numbers can be restored.

The situation vis-à-vis female officers is a little different only because they would have to "bunk-in" with the rest of the officers without any particular privacy except that afforded by the officers having a separate head and washplace. If a female officer was unable to sail, a male officer could easily be sent in lieu.

In the writer's opinion, the introduction of female personnel into the crew can only impose an irreconcilable stress factor out of all proportion to the gains to be made.

## TRAINING

The Canadian navy is now faced with manning four submarines of a type very different from the familiar *Oberons*. This must be accomplished in such a way as to bring the *Victoria*s into commission as safe, ready-to-run, fully effective components of the fleet. No more the heady days of 1915 when the nineteen-man crew could go aboard and sail the submarine on their own after only a week of hands-on experience and almost no instructions. The modern submarine is far too complex a machine for that, and, as ever, there is precious little allowance for error.

All four boats are being refitted in the VSEL shipyard at Barrow-in-Furness on the northwest coast of England. They are being taken in hand for reactivation refits one at a time at six-monthly intervals beginning with HMCS *Victoria*, (ex-*Unseen*). The training schedule is timed to coincide with the refits and crews will join their boats as the work nears completion. In this way, they will be aboard for the post-refit trials and acceptance program which will be carried out with VSEL personnel in attendance. At the same time, crew members will be able to familiarize themselves with the boat and complete a Type 2400 certification program. They will also be able to undertake watchkeeping qualification boards and team training as necessary. This phase will culminate in acceptance of each submarine by Canada and its journey home to Halifax.

The entrance and exterior of the ship control simulator dynamic module. (DND)

The main motor control panel trainer. (DND)

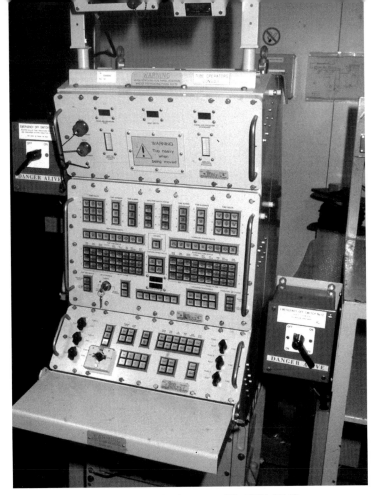

The torpedo operator's (TOP) panel trainer, part of the TWS. (DND)

The ship control trainer (SCT) which includes the SCC and OMC. This is a fully dynamic trainer.(DND)

The machinery control trainer (MCT). (DND)

Personnel attending this program must first be qualified submariners. Although the paying off of two of the O-boats has released a significant number of trained personnel, additional submariners will be needed to make up the necessary total while the changeover takes place. The first source will be the trained submariners already serving in the fleet. Many of these will be posted in to provide immediate support for *Onondaga's* crew and for disposing of *Ojibwa* and *Okanagan*. In addition, basic submarine training will continue as at present at the Fleet School and aboard the alongside trainer *Olympus*. *Onondaga* will be used as an advanced, sea-going submarine trainer for the on-job portion of the course which is completed at sea.

In all, 340 officers and men will receive the Type 2400 training in the UK. These personnel are scheduled to leave for England in four "waves" of around eighty-six trainees each.

The first wave arrived in the UK at the end of February 1999 while the second started arriving in November. Those requiring the longest training—engineering officers, weapons officers, senior technical personnel and instructors—will be in the first group, along with the crew for HMCS *Victoria* and the men who will relieve *Onondaga's* crew for their Type 2400 training.

Training is divided into classroom, dry and wet phases. It is being given under contract to VSEL by Flagship Training Limited (FTL), a partner with the RN training organization. Classroom instruction is being conducted at HMS *Collingwood* in Fareham, a suburb of Portsmouth, and takes anywhere from four to twenty-seven weeks depending on trade or specialty classification.

The dry phase utilizes the five purpose-built, Type 2400 trainers which are still set up in what was HMS *Dolphin*. They are now owned by the Canadian navy. This equipment consists of the weapons handling trainer (WHT), the ship control trainer (SCT), a machinery control trainer (MCT), the tactical weapon system trainer (TWS), and a complete propulsion control switchboard.

The WHT is a working duplication of the starboard half of the torpedo stowage compartment where all aspects of torpedo handling can be demonstrated and practised. The WHT incorporates a simulation of the upper part of the bow including the torpedo-loading hatch and embarkation rails. The simulated bow also contains one torpedo tube complete with all fittings. The other two tubes are represented by dummy rear ends only. As well as torpedo-handling, maintainers will also be given a complete range of equipment familiarization, something that would be impossible to do aboard the submarines except when in dock.

The SCT is mounted on a full-motion base manufactured by Link, the same company that makes aircraft cockpit simulators. The interior contains a complete mock-up of the port forward part of the control room. This consists of the one-man control console (OMC), the ship control console (SCC) and an integral instructor's console which is divided from the control room area by a bulkhead and one-way glass observation window.

The SCC provides remote, one-man operation of many of the features that were manually controlled by operators in the control room and compartments aboard the *Oberons*. These include the operation of all hard and soft compensating tanks, the valves and pumps on the main line and trim line, main ballast tank blows, main vents, the LP blower and distribution system. The ship's ventilation system, battery ventilation system, hydraulic pumps and hydraulically operated equipment are also controlled

and monitored from the SCC. This console also monitors all fire and bilge alarms and can initiate fire suppression systems.

Every feature of ship control including steering, depth-keeping, surfacing and diving, depth changing, speed changes, trimming and compensating and the starting, running and stopping of secondary machinery can be experienced in this dynamic trainer-simulator.

The instructor has full control over all aspects of the trainer. From his console, he can simulate the sea state in order to exercise planing and steering, alter the trim and cause system faults forcing the OMC and SCC operators to respond accordingly. The instructor can also simulate emergencies including smoke, the effects of flooding and catastrophic system breakdowns.

The MCT is a stationary mock-up of the port forward corner of the motor room containing the machinery control console. This is complemented by an instructor's enclosure with full control over the MCT. The three-unit machinery control console (MCC) controls the operation of the generators, the propulsion motor and battery charging. It also monitors fire and bilge alarms and can activate fire suppression systems. From his console the instructor can simulate a wide range of environmental conditions as well as system faults and failures in order to exercise the students in all aspects of machinery and systems control including emergency and breakdown procedures.

The most complex of the trainers is the TWS. For instructional ease of use, the units are much more spread out than they are aboard the submarine. This allows more students to be present at each location and provides more room for the instructors during training sessions. This trainer roughly equates to the Submarine Command Team Trainer currently in use at Halifax.

Most of the combat system is represented in the TWS. This includes the data control consoles (currently with British fire-control equipment but this will be replaced in Canada), sonar consoles, remote periscope operating station, plot table and echo sounders. The TWS is not fully integrated as presently configured and functions as a set of linked trainers. It will be used both for operator procedural training as well as for maintainer familiarization and training. This equipment is capable of being integrated into a submarine command team trainer at some future date.

For the electricians, a full working mock-up of the main propulsion switchboard provides realistic hands-on operating procedure and maintenance training.

All of these trainers will be shipped to Canada for installation and customization at Halifax once the initial training program is complete. All training will then be concentrated at Halifax, ultimately using Canadian personnel. At that time, it is anticipated that the *Olympus* alongside training facility will be shut down and offered for disposal.

## INTO THE 21ST CENTURY

In matters of international politics, trade and defensive alliances, it is said that the Canada of the new millennium will be much more on its own than ever before in history. Gone is the buttress of the British Empire. Gone too are the strategic certainties of the Cold War era. In the UN, Canada is but another small nation among many. Canada has withdrawn most of its combative military stake in NATO and has chosen instead to employ its meagre land forces in the peacekeeper role, parcelled out in small, lightly equipped units in a variety of global hot spots.

Geographically, Canada is a maritime nation and has the longest coastline of any country. Canada is linked by sea to trading partners and allies around the globe and its economy is heavily reliant on seaborne trade and offshore marine resources. The North America Free Trade Agreement has made Canada more dependent than ever on a free flow of trade, and the advent of the European Economic Community will only increase this dependency. Because of this, belligerent submarines represent one of the greatest security threats the country could face. Even without an immediate direct military threat, such as that once posed by the Warsaw Pact navies at the height of Soviet sea power, the proliferation of submarines in the navies of the worldwide community means that the maintenance of an ASW capability continues to be of critical importance. To be effective, Canada's navy must maintain a high level of general readiness in all three maritime elements. This cannot be done without the continued inclusion of submarines as an integral part of the navy. Submarines have a vital role to play as a component of Canada's balanced fleet concept from both the operational and the training perspectives.

The forward end of the WHT. The bottom inboard torpedo tube and the torpedo operator panel are fully functional. (DND)

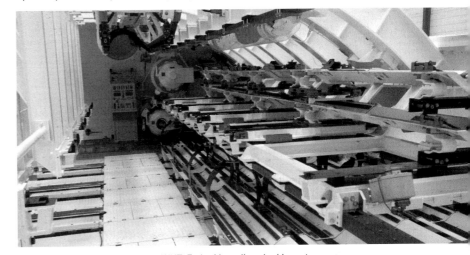

The weapons stowage part of the WHT. Embarking, disembarking, stowage, loading and weapons preparation can all be practised here. (DND)

The exterior of the weapons stowage compartment and the torpedo tube trainer showing the complete torpedo tube and the embarking rails and hatch above. (DND)

179

As a training vehicle, the Canadian navy's *Victoria* class submarines will provide the means to ensure that all aspects of ASW are thoroughly exercised by Canada's air and surface forces. Frequent, well-planned ASW exercises are beneficial to all participants—honing the skills of intruder and defender—the hunter and the hunted alike. There will also be opportunities for Canada to repay its allies for the services rendered during the Cold War. Neither the USN nor the RN have conventional submarines and if their ASW assets require training time with conventional submarines, Canada will be able, indeed beholden, to oblige.

In addition to its training and combat roles, the submarine is ideally suited to conducting covert surveillance and interdiction. Already the O-boats have demonstrated that a submarine is capable of monitoring a very large area of sea for extended periods without exposing its presence or requiring any sort of material support. This is particularly useful from a diplomatic as well as a practical sovereignty-policing viewpoint, as a number of boundary violation charges and smuggling interception successes have shown. The value of the submarine lies in its ability to track and report *without* making its presence known. Having knowledge of what is happening in Canada's waters is often enough—when necessary, diplomacy will ensure the rest.

The problem of sovereignty over the Canadian Arctic Archipelago still requires resolution. Regardless of whether Canada agrees or not, the nuclear-powered submarines of other nations continue to use and develop routes through Arctic waters claimed by Canada. At present, Canada has no way of effectively monitoring this traffic or of exercising any kind of control over it. The government and the nation abrogated that capability when the nuclear-powered submarine programs were terminated.

In times of East-West tensions, Canadian SSKs will still be able to monitor the approaches to the ice-free choke points and provide at least a minimum presence in those areas. In other areas, they can be used as an effective part of the overall sea frontier surveillance and defence in co-operation with air and surface assets. Simply being in possession of accurate and timely marine intelligence would give Canada an incalculable advantage. With the future possibilities presented by the utilization of air independent propulsion, these roles would be considerably enhanced.

The same holds true for the Grand Banks and other sensitive marine areas, although it is possible to exercise more direct action in these cases. As worldwide fish stocks decline, foreign deep-sea trawler fleets can be expected to employ more and more sophisticated methods to avoid surface ship and airborne surveillance while making incursions into fishing grounds over which Canada claims jurisdiction. Long term surveillance by a combination of submarines, ships and aircraft may well become necessary if these valuable resources are to be policed effectively.

The submarine has a vital and important role to play as part of the balanced fleet concept. As the nation has declined the adoption of nuclear-powered submarines, then it must make do with the most up-to-date conventional ones. The *Victoria* class boats will fulfil that role.

Exciting times lie ahead for Canada's submariners. As they have done in the past, the men—and perhaps the women too—of Canada's navy will meet that challenge resolutely and with the high level of professionalism the nation has come to expect of them.

# THE SUBMARINER'S BADGE

THE WEARING of a distinctive badge to denote a specialty qualification is an old naval tradition. Some navies have been awarding a unique insignia to submariners since a very early date. As the dolphin is featured in many of the designs, including those of the RCN and CAF, the device is commonly referred to as the submariners' dolphins. The award of the insignia marks the submariner as having successfully completed his on-board qualifications, the final step in becoming a submariner.

The RN did not have a submarine badge until April 1958. Previously the only distinguishing piece of uniform kit was the cap ribbon of ratings in "square rig" (bell bottom trousers, jumper top, striped collar and round cap) which was embroidered with HM SUBMARINES in place of the usual ship's name. Officers and ratings dressed in the "fore-and-aft rig" (straight trousers, jacket and tie, peaked cap outfit) bore no outward symbol denoting their special service.

The original RN badge, which could be worn by Canadian personnel who qualified aboard RN submarines, was for ratings only. It was supposed to represent the silhouette of one of the early classes of submarine, but it looked most peculiar and the men quickly dubbed it "the sausage on a stick." It was not popular. The typical embroidered cloth badge was produced in gold wire or red thread on a navy background and blue thread on a white ground for tropical kit. This badge was worn on the right sleeve, just above the cuff, or directly above a chief petty officer's centre button. Wearing this badge was optional. It was never officially issued and had to be purchased from slops by the individual. It was

officially withdrawn in 1964. The present-day RN submariners' badge made its first appearance in July 1971.

The first Canadian submariners' badge was introduced on the west coast in 1961. It was the invention of then Lieutenant Commander E. G. Gigg, RCN, a wartime submariner and commissioning CO of HMCS *Grilse*. He engaged a graphic artist to create the design (which bears a striking resemblance to the device featured on the badge of HMS *Dolphin*), and submitted it to the authorities in Ottawa for approval. Originally authorized for ratings only it was extended to officers within a few months of its adoption.

The badge consisted of a single diving bottlenose dolphin and was worn on the left sleeve. It was mounted on a navy blue rectangular backing and was embroidered in gold wire for officers and ratings' best uniforms, red for everyday ratings' uniforms and royal blue on a white ground for white rigs. It was worn three inches above the cuff or directly above a CPO's centre button, or crown, and above the loop of an officer's upper rank stripe. An unofficial, full size, brass pin-on brooch was also produced. Originally intended as a ladies' keepsake it was soon adopted for wear on the left breast of officers' tropical whites.

At the same time, the cap ribbons of ratings in seaman's square rig bore the names of the individual submarines. These were produced for all of the boats including *Rainbow*, which must have been the last HMC ship to receive them. When she commissioned the navy was already becoming part of the unified CAF. Round sailor caps and cap ribbons were not part of the new green kit.

When the CAF green uniform was adopted in 1968 it was determined that the single dolphin badge would be worn centred over the left

# PART 3
# STATISTICS AND INFORMATION TABLES

breast pocket leaving a space below it for ribbons or medal mounting bars if these were worn. An embroidered single dolphin badge, deep yellow on dark green cloth, was produced for wear on the CAF greens. The backing for this badge was contoured to the shape of the dolphin device. The brooch-type badge became particularly popular for wear with the short-sleeved CAF green summer shirts and optional tropical whites.

In order to provide a badge in keeping with the CAF range of specialty badges, a new submariners' badge was designed. This received Royal approval in April 1972. The device is described as "… a crimson garnet wreath of laurel between two swimming dolphins in gold, above the wreath a crown, within the centre of the wreath a gold coloured maple leaf." This badge superseded the single Dolphin for wear by all ranks and was worn in the same position as the single Dolphin badge.

A full-colour embroidered badge on a black cloth background was provided for dress uniform. A badge of old-gold thread on a dark green background was produced for operational orders of dress and working dress. By 1975 a contoured,

full-colour, enamelled metal badge secured by clutch pins was produced for wear on launderable items such as the CAF green short-sleeved summer shirt, which was worn without a jacket, and the optional tropical whites.

With the adoption of navy blue (really black) cloth for full dress naval uniforms and dark blue for working dress in 1986, the positioning of the badge reverted to the pre-unification location on the left sleeve. Black backing is now also available as well as dark green. The badges with green backing have been retained for wear by qualified members of the land element.

In 1994, the badge was moved to a position on the left chest midway between the top of the pocket and the shoulder seam. This was unsatisfactory as the badge was easily covered by the jacket lapel. It was soon re-sited to a position centred directly above and parallel to the top of the pocket, leaving a space for medal ribbons and mounting bars to be mounted between it and the top pocket seam.

## HMCS *CC1*

Electric Boat Company design 19E. Ex-Chilean *Iquique*. Built in the Moran Bros. shipyard at Seattle, Washington, by the Seattle Construction and Drydock Company. Laid down 1912, launched 3 June 1913 and completed for trials in July 1914. Failed to meet Chilean contract specifications.

Purchased by the premier of British Columbia on behalf of the Naval Service of Canada and arrived Esquimalt, BC, on 5 August 1914. Commissioned into the RCN on 7 August 1914.

Paid off for disposal at Halifax on 13 December 1918.

## HMCS *CC2*

Electric Boat Company design 19B. Ex-Chilean *Antofagasta*. Built in the Moran Bros. shipyard at Seattle, Washington by the Seattle Construction and Drydock Company. Laid down 1912, launched 31 December 1913 and completed for trials in July 1914. Failed to meet Chilean contract specifications.

Purchased by the premier of British Columbia on behalf of the Naval Service of Canada and arrived at Esquimalt, BC, on 5 August 1914. Commissioned into the RCN on 7 August 1914.

Paid off for disposal at Halifax on 13 December 1918.

## THE SUBMARINES 1914—1923

*CC1* in diving exercises off Esquimalt, 1914. (RNSM)

## NOTES:

*For commanding officers see Table 1*

*CC1* and *CC2* were identical except that *CC1* had four 18-inch bow torpedo tubes and *CC2* only two. The finer lines in the bows of *CC2* gave her about a half-knot better speed. Both boats had a single 18-inch torpedo tube in the stern.

## CHARACTERISTICS

| FEATURE | *CC1* | *CC2* |
|---|---|---|
| Displacement | Surface 313 tons | Surface 313 tons |
| | Dived 421 tons | Dived 421 tons |
| Length | 144 ft 6 in | 151 ft 6 in |
| Beam | 15 ft 6 in | 15 ft 6 in |
| Internal dia | 15 ft | 15 ft |
| Draught | 11 ft | 11 ft |
| Torpedo tubes | Bow 4 x 18-inch | 2 x 18-inch bow |
| | Stern 1 x 18-inch | 1 x 18-inch stern |
| Reloads | 2 forward | 2 forward |

### BOTH *CC1* AND *CC2*

| | |
|---|---|
| Drive | Twin screw, direct diesel drive & electric motor |
| Engines | 6 cyl MAN reversible 300 bhp @ 300 Revs |
| Main motors | Electro-dynamic 19c 130 hp each @ 370 revs |
| Battery | 120 cells in 2 tanks, 3,800 Amp hrs |
| Periscopes | Main periscope in central operating compartment |
| | Navigating periscope in the conning tower |
| Speed | Surface 13 kts |
| | Dived 10 kts |
| Fuel | Normal 5,356 US gal |
| | Max 8,448 US gal |
| Crew | 3 officers, 17 men |
| Max depth | 200 ft |

# HMC SUBMARINES *CH14* AND *CH15*

Electric Boat Company contract 602E. Ex-Royal Navy *H1* class submarines *H14* and *H15*. Laid down during December 1914 at the Fore River shipyard, Quincy, Massachusetts. Completed in December 1915 and placed in reserve. Delivery was delayed by American neutrality. *H14* accidentally flooded and sank alongside. Raised and refitted. Both vessels used as a source for parts for British *H21* class. Completion refits were given following the entry of the USA into the war. Completed trials in August 1918 and commissioned in the RN in October 1918.

They were paid off into reserve during December 1918 at Bermuda while en route to the UK.

*H14* and *H15* were ceded to Canada in February 1919 to replace the worn out CC-boats and they arrived at Halifax later that year. They were refitted at Halifax and commissioned into the RCN as *CH14* and *CH15* on 3 March 1921.

Paid off for disposal at Halifax on 30 June 1922.

*CH14* and *CH15* in drydock, Halifax 1920. (Author's collection)

## COMMANDING OFFICERS

▶ *CH14*

| NAME | FROM | TO |
|---|---|---|
| Lt R.C. Watson | 1 April 1921 | June 1922 |

▶ *CH15*

| NAME | FROM | TO |
|---|---|---|
| Lt R.W. Wood | 1 April 1921 | June 1922 |

## CHARACTERISTICS: *H1* CLASS

| FEATURE | DETAILS | |
|---|---|---|
| Displacement | Surfaced | 364 tons |
| | Dived | 434 tons |
| Length | 150 ft 3.5 in | |
| Beam | 15 ft 9 in | |
| Internal dia | 15 ft | |
| Draught | 12 ft 4 in | |
| Drive | Twin screw, direct diesel drive and electric motors | |
| Engines | 8 cyl, 4 cycle NLSECO 480 bhp @ 350 rpm | |
| Main motors | Electro dynamic 640 hp | |
| Periscopes | Main periscope in control room | |
| | Navigating periscope in conning tower | |
| Crew | 3 officers, 16-20 men | |
| Diving depth | 200 ft | |
| Battery | 120 cells in 2 tanks Gould or Exide | |
| Speed | Surface | 13 kts |
| | Dived | 10 kts |
| Range | Surface | 2,800 nm @ 11 kts |
| | Dived | 130 nm @ 2 kts |
| Torpedo tube | Bow 4 x 18-inch | |
| Reloads | 4 x bow | |
| Guns | *H1–H4* carried a 6-pdr gun | |

# HMCS *U889*

Type IXC/40 German U-boat built by AG Weser, Bremen. Commissioned 4 August 1944.

Member of the 33rd Flotilla, Flensburg, based at Lorient. Made one patrol only.

CO was Kptlt Freidrich Brauecker

*U889* had been conducting a weather patrol. On 10 May 1945 in accordance with instructions, *U889* surfaced approximately 250 nm SE of Flemish Cap off Newfoundland. She hoisted the black flag of surrender to a patrolling RCAF Liberator later that day. Escorted to harbour by Canadian escort vessels, a formal surrender was held on board off Shelburne Whistle buoy on 13 May and the boat was taken over at Shelburne. Manned by a mixed RN/RCN crew. HMCS *U889* was commissioned in the RCN on 14 May.

*U889* carried out a Victory cruise of the Maritimes and St. Lawrence ports. Never operational.

Being one of 10 U-boats allocated to the USN for technical appraisal, she was paid off for disposal at Portsmouth, New Hampshire, 12 January 1946.

## HMCS *U889* COMMANDING OFFICERS

| NAME | FROM | | | TO | | |
|---|---|---|---|---|---|---|
| Lt E.A.D. Holmes, RNVR | 14 | May | 45 | 5 | October | 45 |
| Lt J.A. Cross, RCNVR | 6 | October | 45 | 27 | October | 45 |
| Lt J.R. Johnston, RCNVR | 28 | October | 45 | 31 | December | 45 |
| Lt J.R. Johnston, RCN(R) | 1 | January | 46 | 12 | January | 46 |

HMCS *U 889* running at speed. (F. Deadman)

**THE SUBMARINES 1945—1998**

**HMCS *U190* and *U889*, Halifax 1945-46. (Author's collection)**

# HMCS *U190*

Type IXC/40 German U-boat built by AG Weser, Bremen. Commissioned on 29 September 1942.

CO was Oblt Hans-Edwin Reith.

Member of the 33rd Flotilla, Flensburg, based at Lorient. Was on sixth war patrol when war ended.

*U190* had a later style "cut-away" forward casing, unlike *U889* which had a conventional full-width casing. The fore casing was reduced in width and volume in an attempt to accelerate the diving time of these boats and to reduce the planing area of the deck when running at slow speed near the surface, such as when snorkelling.

Surrendered to RCN ships at sea about seven hundred miles east of Newfoundland early on 12 May 1945 and was taken over at Bay Bulls, Newfoundland. The surrender was signed aboard HMCS *Victoriaville* at sea. *U190* was the submarine that sank HMCS *Esquimalt* off Halifax on 16 April 1945, the RCN's last wartime casualty.

Commissioned into the RCN on 19 May 1945. Made Victory cruise of Maritime and St. Lawrence ports. Carried out surfaced and dived trials and technical evaluation. Never operational.

Paid off at Halifax on 24 July 1947. Deliberately sunk near the position of her last victim in "Operation Scuppered" on Trafalgar Day, 21 October 1947.

## HMCS *U190* COMMANDING OFFICERS

| NAME | FROM | | TO | |
|---|---|---|---|---|
| Lt M. Wood, RNVR | 14 May | 5 | 24 June | 45 |
| Lt M. Pope, RNR | 25 June | 45 | 27 September | 45 |
| Lt C. Larose, RCNVR | 28 September | 45 | 5 October | 45 |
| Lt E.A.D. Holmes, RNVR | 6 October | 45 | 17 January | 46 |
| Lt J.R. Johnston, RCN(R) | 18 January | 46 | 24 July | 47 |

## CHARACTERISTICS: TYPE IXC/40

| FEATURE | DETAILS | |
|---|---|---|
| Displacement | Surface | 1144 tonnes |
| | Dived | 1257 tonnes |
| Length | 76.8 m | |
| Beam | 6.8 m | |
| Draught | 4.7 m | |
| Propulsion | Direct diesel drive and main motors | |
| Engines | 2 x MAN 2,200 hp (1.6 MW) | |
| Main motors | 2 x 500 hp (372.85 kW) | |
| Crew | 48 | |
| Max dive | 150 m | |
| Fuel capacity | 208 tonnes | |
| Speed | Surface | 18.2 kts |
| | Dived | 7.3 kts |
| Snorting | 3 to 5 kts | |
| Torpedo tubes | Bow | 4 x 54-cm |
| | Stern | 2 x 54-cm |
| Torpedoes | 22 total, 12 internal, 10 in deck stowages | |
| Range | Surface 12 400 nm @ 10 kts. Dived 64 nm @ 4 kts | |
| Gun armament | One twin 37 mm, two twin 20 mm | |
| Periscopes | One attack, one navigating, both in control room | |

*U190*, St. Lawrence River, during her victory cruise, 1945. (Frank Deadman)

# HMCS *GRILSE* S71

USN *Balao* class fleet submarine. Laid down at Portsmouth Navy Yard as hull SS *312*, USS *Burrfish.* Launched on 18 June 1943, commissioned 14 September 1943. Made six war patrols.

Postwar (1949) was converted to radar picket (Migraine I), becoming SSR *312*, and fitted with snorkel. Placed in reserve 17 December 1956.

Taken on a five-year lease from the USN and commissioned into the RCN at New London, Connecticut, on 11 May 1961.

Transfer papers signed by Mr. J.P. Sévigny, Associate MND. In attendance were HMC ships *Terra Nova* and *Chaudière.* Acceptance speech given by Vice Admiral Rayner RCN, Chief of Naval Staff.

Ship's motto: *Sauriter in modo, fortiter in re* (Suavely in manner, stronger in matter)

International radio call sign:     CGKZ

Used exclusively for ASW training duties on the west coast.

Received a $1.2 million refit at Esquimalt in 1967.

Ceased operation upon arrival of *Rainbow* in December 1968. Cannibalized for parts for *Rainbow.*

Paid off for return to the USN on 2 October 1969. Sunk off San Clemente, California, as a torpedo target on 19 November 1969.

*Grilse* entering harbour, 1961. (DND)

## COMMANDING OFFICERS

| NAME | FROM | | TO | |
|------|------|---|-----|---|
| Lt Cdr E.G. Gigg | 11 May | 61 | 2 December | 63 |
| Lt Cdr G.C. McMorris | 3 December | 63 | 27 September | 64 |
| Lt Cdr J. Rodocanachi | 28 September | 64 | 8 September | 66 |
| Lt Cdr M. Tate | 9 September | 66 | 19 August | 68 |
| MAJ(N) C.E. Falstrem | 20 August | 68 | 2 December | 68 |

## CHARACTERISTICS: HMCS *GRILSE*

| FEATURE | DETAILS | |
|---------|---------|---|
| Displacement | Surface | 1800 tons |
| | Dived | 2,425 tons |
| Length | 311 ft 6 in | |
| Beam | 27 ft 3 in | |
| Draught | 16 ft 10 in | |
| Drive | Diesel electric | |
| Main motors | 2 x 2,700 bhp GE | |
| Main Gens | 4 x 9 cyl 1,600 hp Fairbanks-Morse diesel + 1,100 kW Elliot Gens | |
| Aux Gen | 450 hp diesel + Elliot 300 kW Gen | |
| Crew | 72 | |
| Max dive | 400 ft as-built | |
| Battery | 252 cells Gould | |
| Speed | Surface | 20.25 kts |
| | Dived | 8.75 kts |
| | Snorting | 10 kts |
| Torpedo tubes | Bow | 6 x 21-inch |
| | Stern | 4 x 21-inch |
| | Reloads | 14 |
| Range | Surface 12,000 nm/10 kts | |
| | Dived 96 nm/2 kts | |
| Gun armament | None | |

HMCS *Ojibwa* during workups, Gareloch, Scotland, 1975. (Author's collection)

# HMCS *OJIBWA* S72

| | |
|---|---|
| Ship's motto: | *Ne ke che dah* (Let us be prepared) |
| International radio call-sign: | CZFQ |
| Voice call-sign: | Mountain home |
| Sponsor: | Lady Patricia Miers |

W.B. Christie in his account "Building Carriers and Subs" published in *Salty Dips* Vol.5 Chapter 11, explains why Lady Miers was sponsor of HMCS *Ojibwa* in 1965:

> "...the sponsor of the first ship was an RN lady—Lady Patricia Miers, wife of the very famous submariner "Crap" or "Gamp" Miers—because the ship had been laid down as HMS *Onyx,* and she had already been selected. I guess it is the only occasion in modern times where a British lady had been sponsor of an HMC ship."

Rear Admiral A.C.C. Miers, VC, KBE, CB, DSO*, RN, was one of Britain's most famous surviving wartime submariners and won his VC in 1942 as captain of HMS *Torbay,* another Chatham Dockyard-built submarine.

Standard Admiralty *Oberon* class. Laid down at Chatham Dockyard as HMS *Onyx* on 27 September 1962. Transferred to the RCN and renamed 15 February 1964. Launched 29 February 1964.

Commissioned into the RCN on 23 September 1965.

Commissioning CO—Lieutenant Commander S. G. Tomlinson

Received SOUP improvements during 1980–82 refit.

In her 1993–94 refit, *Ojibwa* was successfully re-engined by separating the hull aft of the engine-room bulkhead using a high-pressure water stream to cut the hull without metal loss or heat. The engines were withdrawn, rebuilt engines from HMS *Osiris* were inserted and the hull welded back together using conventional pressure-hull welding techniques.

Paid off into reserve at Halifax on 21 May 1998. Retained temporarily for alongside training. Scheduled for disposal.

## HMCS *OJIBWA* COMMANDING OFFICERS

| NAME | FROM | | TO | |
|---|---|---|---|---|
| Lt Cdr S.G. Tomlinson | 23 September | 65 | 14 November | 66 |
| Lt Cdr J. Rodocanachi | 15 November | 66 | 30 June | 67 |
| Lt Cdr J. Rodocanachi | 1 July | 67 | 25 August | 67 |
| Lt Cdr J. Wood | 26 August | 67 | 17 August | 69 |
| MAJ(N) J.E.D. Bell | 18 August | 69 | 17 July | 71 |
| MAJ(N) C.E. Falstrem | 17 July | 71 | 1 June | 72 |
| MAJ(N) R.C. Perks | 1 June | 72 | 3 July | 74 |
| MAJ(N) J.E.D. Bell | 23 September | 74 | 15 January | 75 |
| MAJ(N) L.W. Barnes | 15 January | 75 | 8 March | 76 |
| MAJ(N) W.J. Sloan | 8 March | 76 | 1 August | 77 |
| MAJ(N) J.T.O. Jones | 1 August | 77 | 9 July | 79 |
| MAJ(N) K.F. Macmillan | 9 July | 79 | 1 December | 79 |
| MAJ(N) J.M. Ewan | 1 December | 79 | 24 June | 80 |
| LCDR N.P. Nicolson | 24 June | 80 | 6 January | 84 |
| LCDR E.P. Webster | 6 January | 84 | 9 April | 85 |
| LCDR W.C. Irvine | 9 April | 85 | 22 September | 86 |
| LCDR J.A.Y. Plante | 22 September | 86 | 3 August | 87 |
| LCDR C.D. Soule | 3 August | 87 | 30 April | 88 |
| LCDR A.L. Macdonald | 30 April | 88 | 2 February | 89 |
| LCDR R.E. Bush | 2 February | 89 | 5 August | 89 |
| LCDR R.A. Davidson | 5 August | 89 | 5 December | 90 |
| LCDR D.C. Marsaw | 5 December | 90 | 29 October | 93 |
| LCDR P.T. Kavanagh | 29 November | 93 | 20 July | 94 |
| LCDR J.G.M. Dussault | 20 July | 94 | 27 May | 97 |
| LCDR J.R.L. Pelletier | 27 May | 97 | 21 May | 98 |

HMCS *Onondaga* diving. (MARCOM Museum)

## HMCS *ONONDAGA* S73

| | |
|---|---|
| Ship's motto: | *Invicta* (Unconquered) |
| International radio call-sign: | CGNQ |
| Voice call-sign: | Voyage Pride |
| Sponsor: | Mrs Paul T. Hellyer, wife of the Minister of National Defence |

First of the S22 Super *O* class to be laid down but second to be commissioned being preceded by the Australian *Oxley*. Built from the keel up for the RCN. Laid down at Chatham Dockyard 18 June 1964 and launched on 25 September 1965.

Commissioned into the RCN on 22 June 1967.

Commissioning CO—Lieutenant Commander Geoffrey R. Meek

Super *O* class features included:

Modified snort induction system, inboard battery ventilation system, open concept conrol room, radar office in the AMS, all washplaces aft and a Canadian communications suite.

Received SOUP improvements during her 1982–84 refit.

In 1996–97, *Onondaga* was re-engined in the same way as *Ojibwa* and received *Ojibwa's* rebuilt engines.

Completed final refit in late 1998. Currently performing limited operational ASW and submarine crew training duties at Halifax.

Scheduled to be paid off for disposal in 2001. Rumoured to be a candidate for removal to the Canadian War Museum.

# HMCS *ONONDAGA* COMMANDING OFFICERS

| NAME | FROM | | TO | | NAME | FROM | | TO | |
|------|------|---|-----|---|------|------|---|-----|---|
| Lt Cdr G.R. Meek | 22 June | 67 | 23 August | 68 | MAJ(N) K.F. Macmillan | 3 December | 79 | 17 March | 81 |
| MAJ(N) L.G. Temple | 23 August | 68 | 4 November | 69 | LCDR A.B. Dunlop | 17 March | 81 | 20 December | 81 |
| MAJ(N) G.R. Meek | 4 November | 69 | 23 December | 69 | LCDR P. Webster | 14 January | 82 | 1 July | 82 |
| MAJ(N) L.G. Temple | 23 December | 69 | 29 January | 70 | LCDR R. A. Perks | 1 July | 82 | 6 June | 83 |
| MAJ(N) G.R. Meek | 29 January | 70 | 21 July | 70 | LCDR P. Webster | 6 June | 83 | 15 August | 83 |
| MAJ(N) C.E. Falstrem | 21 July | 70 | 21 December | 70 | LT(N) L.M. Hickey | 15 August | 83 | 12 December | 83 |
| MAJ(N) C.J. Crow | 21 December | 70 | 1 September | 71 | LCDR J.A.Y. Plante | 12 December | 83 | 31 July | 86 |
| MAJ(N) H.R. Waddell | 15 October | 71 | 16 June | 72 | LCDR L.M. Hickey | 31 July | 86 | 13 May | 87 |
| MAJ(N) P.W. Cairns | 16 June | 72 | 1 July | 74 | LCDR R.D. Carter, RAN | 13 May | 87 | 29 December | 87 |
| MAJ(N) R.C. Perks | 1 July | 74 | 14 July | 75 | LCDR J. Deirks, RAN | 29 December | 87 | 17 July | 88 |
| MAJ(N) K.G. Nesbit | 14 July | 75 | 1 November | 75 | LCDR R.E. Bush | 17 July | 88 | 2 February | 89 |
| MAJ(N) C.R. Hunt | 1 November | 75 | 4 December | 75 | LCDR A.L. Macdonald | 2 February | 89 | 1 January | 90 |
| MAJ(N) W.J. Sloan | 4 December | 75 | 15 March | 76 | LCDR R.M. Truscott | 1 January | 90 | 20 July | 92 |
| MAJ(N) R.C. Hunt | 15 March | 76 | 23 July | 76 | LCDR W.A. Woodburn | 20 July | 92 | 5 August | 94 |
| MAJ(N) L.W. Barnes | 23 July | 76 | 26 July | 76 | LCDR P.T. Kavanagh | 5 August | 94 | 15 December | 97 |
| MAJ(N) W.G. Lund | 26 July | 76 | 19 July | 78 | LCDR A.R. Wamback | 15 December | 97 | Present | |
| MAJ(N) J.M. Ewan | 19 July | 78 | 3 December | 79 | | | | | |

## HMCS *OKANAGAN* S74

| Ship's motto: | *Ex imo mari ad victorium* (From the depth of the sea to victory) |
| --- | --- |
| International radio call-sign: | CGLM |
| Voice call-sign: | Coral Tree |
| Sponsor: | Mme Monique Cadieux, wife of the Associate Minister of National Defence |

S22 Super *O* class with RCN modifications. Last submarine to be built at Chatham Dockyard. Laid down on 25 March 1965 and launched 17 September 1966.

Some of the special features incorporated into *Okanagan* were:

Modified snort induction system, inboard battery ventilation system, galley forward, ratings' cafeteria, bunk spaces vice messes, all washplaces aft, open concept sound room and a Canadian communications suite.

Commissioned into the CAF on 22 June 1968.

Commissioning CO—Major(N) Nigel H. M. Frawley, CAF

Received SOUP improvements during her 1984–86 refit.

As a last act, *Okanagan* participated in the search for the black boxes from the wreck of Swissair Flight 111 which crashed in Saint Margaret's Bay off Peggy's Cove late on the evening of 2 September 1998. Both the flight data recorder and cockpit voice recorder were recovered.

Paid off for disposal at Halifax 12 September 1998.

## HMCS *OKANAGAN* COMMANDING OFFICERS

| NAME | FROM | | TO | |
| --- | --- | --- | --- | --- |
| MAJ(N) N.H. Frawley | 22 June | 68 | 18 August | 69 |
| MAJ(N) G.R. Meek | 19 August | 69 | 6 November | 69 |
| MAJ(N) L.G. Temple | 7 November | 69 | 21 December | 69 |
| MAJ(N) C.J. Crow | 22 December | 69 | 20 December | 70 |
| MAJ(N) H.R. Waddell | 21 December | 70 | 15 October | 71 |
| MAJ(N) C.E. Falstrem | 16 October | 71 | 6 May | 73 |
| MAJ(N) J.E.D. Bell | 7 May | 73 | 1 August | 74 |
| MAJ(N) R.C. Hunt | 2 August | 74 | 28 October | 75 |
| MAJ(N) K.G. Nesbit | 29 October | 75 | 21 July | 77 |
| MAJ(N) J.M. Ewan | 22 uly | 77 | 6 July | 78 |
| LT(N) J.S. Ferguson | 7 July | 78 | 13 July | 78 |
| MAJ(N) J.S. Ferguson | 14 July | 78 | 14 July | 80 |
| LCDR F. Sherber | 14 July | 80 | 20 December | 81 |
| LCDR A.B. Dunlop | 20 December | 81 | 3 May | 82 |
| LCDR M.B. Maclean | 3 May | 82 | 10 August | 83 |
| LCDR E.P. Webster | 10 August | 83 | 6 January | 84 |
| LCDR J.A.Y. Plante | 6 January | 84 | 12 March | 84 |
| LCDR D.F. Webb, RAN | 12 March | 84 | 14 April | 85 |
| LCDR E.P. Webster | 14 April | 85 | 30 July | 85 |
| LT A.L. Macdonald | 30 July | 85 | 1 April | 86 |
| LCDR A.L. Macdonald | 1 April | 85 | 8 February | 88 |
| LCDR N.P. Nicolson | 8 February | 88 | 24 July | 89 |
| LCDR W.C. Irvine | 24 July | 89 | 22 July | 90 |
| LCDR L.B. Mosher | 22 July | 90 | 3 June | 91 |
| LCDR R.E. Bush | 3 June | 91 | 15 June | 92 |
| LCDR L.M. Hickey | 15 June | 92 | | |

Details of commanding officers and their appointment dates between June 1992 and July 1997 are not available.

| LCDR D. Mullholland | July | 97 | 12 September | 98 |
| --- | --- | --- | --- | --- |

A brand-new HMCS *Okanagan* enters Halifax harbour, fall 1968. (DND)

First Canadian Submarine Squadron, Halifax, 1972. (Author's collection)

## CHARACTERISTICS: CANADIAN *O* CLASS

| FEATURE | DETAILS | |
|---|---|---|
| Displacement | Surface | 2,007 tons |
| | Dived | 2,406 tons |
| Length | 295 ft 3 in (90 m) | |
| External beam | 26 ft 6 in (8.1 m) | |
| Internal Dia. | 17 ft 9 in (5.4 m) | |
| Draught | 18 ft (5.5 m) | |
| Drive | Diesel electric | |
| Generators | 2 ASR1 V16 each 3,680 bhp, (2.74 MW) | |
| Electric motors | 2 shafts, each 3,000 hp (2.24 MW) | |
| Crew | 7 officers, 58 ship's company, up to 10 trainers | |
| Max dive depth | 600 ft | |
| Battery | 448 cells in two sections; 7420 Ah | |
| Speed | Surface | 12 kts |
| | Dived | 17 kts |
| | Snorting | 10 kts |
| Torpedo tubes | Bow | 6 x 21-inch, |
| | Stern | 2 x 21-inch countermeasure (removed in all as part of SOUP) |
| Reloads | 16 full-size forward, 2 short aft, power loading on bottom tubes only | |
| Range | Surface 9000 nm @ 12 kts | |

| FEATURE | DETAILS | |
|---|---|---|
| Sonars (final fit) | Type 2051 Plessey Triton passive-active search and attack | |
| | SUBTASS combined towed array and flank array; long-range passive search | |
| | AN/BQG-502 "Ranger" Sperry Micro-puffs; passive ranging provides target course, speed and range data | |
| | Type 773 deep echo sounder | |
| | Type 776 shallow echo sounder | |
| | VELOX active sonar intercept and analysis | |
| | AN/WQQ 501 underwater telephone | |
| | Type 183 emergency underwater telephone | |
| | Type 189 cavitation monitor for self noise monitoring and analysis | |
| | Type 2004 bathythermograph | |
| | Mk 8 expendable bathythermograph | |
| Radar | Type 1006 Kelvin-Hughes navigational radar | |
| Fire control | Singer Librascope SFCS Mk 1 Mod C | |
| Periscopes | Attack | Barr & Stroud CH 74 |
| | Search | Barr & Stroud CK 24 |

## CLASS NOTE:

Each of the Canadian O-boats originally had the CANAVSUB-REP (Canadian Naval Submarine Representative [Chatham]) badge painted in their attack periscope wells. The device included two, opposed, vertical dolphins on a sky-blue background with a diagonal red slash across the cypher. At the top centre of the badge was inlaid a "Churchill Crown," a British coin commemorating Winston Churchill's death and symbolizing the close affiliation between Canada and Britain. The coins vanished in the first refits at Halifax. The badges also disappeared in the course of time, probably through ignorance of their significance.

## HMCS *RAINBOW* S75

USN *Tench* class fleet submarine. Laid down at Portsmouth Navy Yard, New Hampshire, 28 June 1944, as hull SS 475, USS *Argonaut* (second of the name). Launched 1 October 1944, commissioned 15 January 1945. Completed one war patrol.

Post WW2 operated out of New London, Connecticut, from 1946 to 1955. In 1952 underwent "Guppy II" modification and was fitted with snorkel. In 1958 was converted to a "Regulus I" guided missile submarine. In 1962 she reverted to a normal configuration and served in various Atlantic commands until transferred to the Canadian navy in 1968. Decommissioned and stricken from the US Navy list 2 December 1968.

Purchased from the USN for $153,000. Commissioned into the CAF at New London, Connecticut, on 2 December 1968.

Commissioning CO—Major (N) C. E. Falstrem, CAF

Canadian voice call-sign:          Headmaster

International radio call-sign:      CGNE

Used exclusively for ASW training duties on the west coast.

Had to be refitted at Esquimalt by the RCN in 1972 before assuming operations, for a cost of $2.5 million.

Paid off for disposal on 31 December 1974. Sold for scrap.

Towed to the scrapyard at Zidell Ship Dismantlers in Portland, Oregon, on 24 March 1977 for breaking-up.

## CHARACTERISTICS: HMCS *RAINBOW*

| FEATURE | DETAILS | |
|---|---|---|
| Displacement | Surface | 1,526 tons |
| | Dived | 2,391 tons |
| Length | 3ll ft 6 in | |
| External Beam | 27 ft 4 in | |
| Draught | 16 ft 10 in | |
| Drive | Diesel electric | |
| Main motors | 2 x 2,700 bhp Elliot | |
| Main Gens | 4 x 9 cyl 1,600 hp Fairbanks-Morse diesel + 1,100 kW Gens | |
| Aux Gen | None | |
| Battery | 252 cells, Gould | |
| Speed | Surface | 20.25 kts |
| | Dived | 10 kts |
| | Snorting | 10 kts |
| Torpedo tubes | Bow | 6 x 21-inch |
| | Stern | 4 x 21-inch |
| | Reloads | 14 |
| Range | Surface 8000 nm/ 12 kts Dived 96 nm/2 kts | |
| Max dive depth | 400 feet as-built | |
| Crew | 75 | |
| Gun Armament | None | |

### HMCS *RAINBOW* COMMANDING OFFICERS

| NAME | FROM | | TO | |
|---|---|---|---|---|
| MAJ(N). C.E. Falstrem | 2 December | 68 | 1 April | 70 |
| MAJ(N). R.C Hunt | 1 April | 70 | 1 July | 72 |
| MAJ(N). C.J. Crow | 1 July | 72 | 1 August | 73 |
| MAJ(N). L.W. Barnes | 1 August | 73 | 31 December | 75 |

# *VICTORIA* CLASS SUBMARINES

## BUILDING AND COMMISSIONING HISTORY

| | | | |
|---|---|---|---|
| Canadian Name & No. | HMCS *Victoria* S876 (First of name) | Canadian Name & No. | HMCS *Corner Brook* S878 (First of name) |
| Commissioned in Canadian navy | Autumn 2000 | Commissioned in Canadian navy | Spring 2001 |
| Commissioning CO | CDR W. A. Woodburn, CAF | Commissioning CO | (To be announced) |
| Sponsor | Mrs Jill Garnett | Sponsor | (To be announced) |
| RN Name & No. | HMS *Unseen* S42 | RN Name & No. | HMS *Ursula* S43 |
| Where built | Cammel Laird, Birkenhead | Where built | Cammel Laird, Birkenhead |
| Start/launch | January 86/14 November 89 | Start/launch | August 87/28 February 91 |
| Commissioned in RN | 7 June 1991 | Commissioned in RN | May 1992 |
| | | | |
| Canadian Name & No. | HMCS *Windsor* S877 (First of name) | Canadian Name & No. | HMCS *Chicoutimi* S879 (Second of name) |
| Commissioned in Canadian navy | Winter 2000 | Commissioned in Canadian navy | Autumn 2001 |
| Commissioning CO | CDR S. A. Virgin, CAF | Commissioning CO | (To be announced) |
| Sponsor | (To be announced) | Sponsor | (To be announced) |
| RN Name & No. | HMS *Unicorn* S44 | RN Name & No. | HMS *Upholder* S40 |
| Where built | Cammel Laird, Birkenhead | Where built | Vickers, Barrow-in-Furness |
| Start/launch | February 89/16 April 92 | Start/launch | November 83/2 December 86 |
| Commissioned in RN | 25 June 1993 | Commissioned in RN | April 1990 |

HMS *Unseen* at Birkenhead. (Author's Collection)

## CHARACTERISTICS: *VICTORIA* CLASS

| FEATURE | DETAILS | |
|---|---|---|
| Displacement | Surfaced | 2,221 tonnes |
| | Dived | 2,475 tonnes |
| Dimensions | Length over all | 70.3 m |
| | Length of pressure hull | 47.55 m |
| | Hull dia. | 7.6 m |
| | Draught | 5.5 m |
| Pressure hull | NQ1 high tensile steel hull, NQ1 rolled or HY80 extruded frames | |
| Main ballast tanks | Four MBT's, all external. Nos. 1 & 2 in bow, 3 & 4 in stern | |
| Drive | Diesel electric | |
| Diesel generators | Two, Paxman Valenta 1600 RPA SZ diesels each driving a 1.4 MW GEC alternator | |
| Main battery | 480 NATO B-size cells divided equally between two battery compartments. 8800 Ah at 5 hour discharge rate. | |
| Battery endurance | 90 hours at 3 knots dived | |
| Propulsion | One 86.36 tonne GEC 4.028 MW (5,400 hp) dual armature electric motor driving a single shaft with a 7-blade, fixed pitch propeller | |
| Diving depth | In excess of 200 m | |
| Speed | Surfaced | 12 kts |
| | Dived | 20 kts |
| | Snorting | 12 kts |
| Range | 8000 nm @ 8 kts | |
| Patrol endurance | 49 days | |
| Crew | 7 officers, 17 senior rates, 24 junior rates | |
| Torpedo tubes | Six, 533 mm (21-inch) bow torpedo tubes with positive discharge provided by port and starboard air-turbine driven pumps capable of discharging all weapons down to full diving depth | |
| Signal launchers | Two Mk 9, 101 mm (4-inch) submerged signal and decoy ejectors | |
| Weapons | A total of 18 full-size weapons can be carried including one in each torpedo tube plus 12 reloads in full-size hydraulically operated, shock mounted stowage bays | |
| Torpedo | Mk 48 Mod 4 | |
| Navigation radar | Kelvin-Hughes Type 1007 | |
| Sonar (as-built) | Type 2040 Thompson Sintra ARGONAUTE bow mounted array | |
| | Type 2026 GEC Avionics passive towed array | |
| | Type 2019 Thompson Sintra PARIS passive - active & intercept | |
| | Type 2041 passive ranging (Micropuffs) | |
| | Type 2039 expendable bathythermograph | |
| | Type 2004 bathythermograph | |
| | Type 2008 Underwater telephone | |
| | Type189 cavitation monitor | |
| | Type 778 and 780 echo sounders | |
| Fire control | Lockheed - Martin (Singer Librascope) SFCS Mk 1 Mod C | |
| Periscopes | Search | Barr & Stroud Type CK 35 |
| | Attack | Barr & Stroud Type CH 85 |

HMS *Upholder*. (Author's collection)

# TABLE 1 WARTIME COMMAND

## CANADIAN SUBMARINES

### ▸ *CC1*

| CO | FROM | | TO | |
|---|---|---|---|---|
| Lt A. St. V. Keyes, RCN | 7 August | 14 | 1 October | 14 |
| Lt Francis B. Hanson, RN | 1 October | 14 | 1 November | 17 |
| Lt F.B. Hanson, RN (Refit) | 1 September | 17 | 26 September | 18 |
| Lt F.B. Hanson, RN | 26 September | 18 | 4 December | 18 |

### ▸ *CC2*

| Lt Bertram E. Jones, RCN | 3 August | 14 | 17 April | 16 |
|---|---|---|---|---|
| Lt Geoffrey Lake, RNCVR | 17 April | 17 | 1 November | 17 |
| Lt F.B. Hanson, RN (Refit) | 1 November | 17 | 6 September | 18 |
| Lt Arthur C.S. Pitts, RNCVR | 26 September | 18 | 14 December | 18 |

## ROYAL NAVY SUBMARINES

### ▸ 1915-1920

Cdr B.L. "Cap" Johnson, DSO, RNR, Vancouver, British Columbia

| HMS *H8* | 15 May | 15 | March | 16 |
|---|---|---|---|---|
| HMS *D3* | 19 April | 16 | 21 November | 17 |
| HMS *E54* | 11 December | 17 | 21 May | 18 |
| HMS *H15* | June | 18 | 12 November | 18 |

Lt William McKinstry Maitland-Dougall, RCN, Duncan, Vancouver Island, BC.

| HMS *D1* | 6 September | 17 | 22 November | 17 |
|---|---|---|---|---|
| HMS *D3* | 22 November | 17 | Lost 12 March | 18 |

Lt Ronald C. Watson, RCN, Edmonton, Alberta.

| HMS *V3* | 10 September | 18 | 28 December | 18 |
|---|---|---|---|---|
| HMS *R8* | 28 December | 18 | 27 May | 19 |
| HMS *R2* | 1 June | 19 | 1 November | 19 |
| HMS *H44* | 18 February | 20 | May | 20 |

Lt John Grant "Jock" Edwards, RCN, Liverpool, England and Toronto, Ontario.

| HMS *C18* | 25 November | 18 | 21 December | 18 |
|---|---|---|---|---|
| HMS *R1* | 1 June | 19 | 7 November | 19 |

### ▸ 1943-1946

Lt Cdr F.H. "Fredd;y" Sherwood, DSC and Bar, RCNVR, Ottawa, Ontario.

| HMS *P556* | | | | |
|---|---|---|---|---|
| (Reluctant Dragon) | 15 March | 43 | 15 June | 43 |
| HMS *Spiteful (P227)* | 21 July | 43 | November | 45 |

Lt J.A. "Jack" Cross, RCNVR, Montreal, Quebec

| HMS *Unseen* | 12 February | 45 | August | 45 |
|---|---|---|---|---|

# TABLE 2 WORLD WAR ONE SUBMARINE OFFICERS

| OFFICER | S/M | POS'N | FROM | TO | BASE & OPS AREA |
|---|---|---|---|---|---|
| W.J.R. Beech | *H9* | 1stLt | 01 02 17 | 01 03 18 | 8TH Flotilla, North Sea |
| | *L8* | 1stLt | 01 03 18 | 01 03 19 | HMS *Dolphin*, Atlantic |
| | *L1* | 1stLt | 23 06 19 | 26 09 20 | HMS *Titania*, China Stn |
| | *L1* | A/CO | 26 09 20 | 31 12 21 | HMS *Titania*, China Stn |
| C.D. Donald | *K22* | NO | 28 07 20 | 18 08 21 | HMS *Inconstant*, Rosyth |
| | *K6* | NO | 04 10 22 | 31 08 23 | HMS *Inconstant*, Rosyth |
| J.G. Edwards | *E55* | 1stLt | 01 11 17 | 12 10 18 | HMS *Maidstone*, North Sea |
| | *C18* | CO | 01 12 18 | 01 01 19 | HMS *Thames*, Perisher |
| | *L7* | 1stLt | 01 01 19 | 01 06 19 | HMS *Ambrose*, Portsmouth |
| | *R1* | CO | 01 06 19 | 07 11 19 | HMS *Dolphin* |
| V.S. Godfrey | *K9* | NO | 01 02 19 | 01 07 19 | HMS *Inconstant*, Rosyth |
| | *H27* | 1stLt | 01 11 19 | 18 05 20 | HMS *Dolphin* |
| | *M2* | Add'l | 18 05 20 | 17 08 20 | HMS *Inconstant*, Rosyth |
| | *M1* | Add'l | 17 08 20 | 17 08 20 | HMS *Inconstant*, Rosyth |
| B.L. Johnson | *H8* | CO | 07 05 15 | 26 03 16 | 8TH Flotilla, North Sea |
| | *D3* | CO | 12 04 16 | 11 11 17 | East Coast & Ireland |
| | *E54* | CO | 22 11 17 | 27 05 18 | HMS *Ambrose*, Ireland |
| | *H15* | CO | 07 07 18 | 09 12 18 | USA, To Bermuda Only |
| R.F. Lawson | *H10* | 1stLt | 05 06 16 | 01 08 17 | 8TH Flotilla, North Sea |
| W.M. Maitland-Dougall | *H10* | NO | 24 06 15 | 04 05 16 | 8TH Flotilla, North Sea |
| | *D3* | 1stLt | 05 05 16 | 11 09 17 | East Coast & Ireland |
| | *D1* | CO | 12 09 17 | 10 11 18 | Ireland & HMS *Thames* |
| | *D3* | CO | 12 11 17 | 12 03 18 | 6TH Flotilla, Channel (lost) |
| R.H. Oland | *R8* | 1stLt | 01 04 19 | 01 09 19 | HMS *Dolphin* |
| | *H30* | 1stLt | 01 09 19 | 18 06 20 | HMS *Vulcan* |
| | *H51* | 1stLt | 18 06 20 | 08 08 20 | HMS *Vulcan* |
| | *H34* | 1stLt | 18 08 20 | 15 09 22 | HMS *Maidstone* |
| R.C. Watson | *H2* | 1stLt | 01 10 16 | 01 01 17 | At Venice for Adriatic |
| | *E11* | 1stLt | 11 05 17 | 25 09 17 | HMS *Adamant*, Adriatic |
| | *E2* | 1stLt | 25 09 17 | 28 01 18 | HMS *Adamant*, Adriatic |
| | *E11* | 1stLt | 13 06 18 | 10 09 18 | HMS *Adamant*, Aegean |
| | *V3* | CO | 12 10 18 | 01 01 19 | HMS *Thames*, Perisher |
| | *R8* | 1stLt | 01 01 19 | 01 04 19 | HMS *Dolphin* |
| | *R2* | CO | 01 06 19 | 01 11 19 | HMS *Dolphin* |
| | *H44* | CO | 18 02 20 | 12 05 20 | Rosyth |
| R.W. Wood | *D4* | NO | 01 02 17 | 01 01 18 | East Coast & Ireland |
| | *E38* | 1stLt | 01 04 18 | 01 10 19 | HMS *Platypus*, Irish & N Sea |
| | *H27* | 1stLt | 24 09 19 | 01 11 19 | HMS *Dolphin* |

# TABLE 3 WORLD WAR TWO SUBMARINE OFFICERS

| OFFICER | S/M | POS'N | FROM | TO | OPS NOTES |
|---|---|---|---|---|---|
| R.C. Blake | *Truant* | WO | 21 12 43 | 16 11 44 | UK & Malta, Defects |
| | *Truculent* | NO 1stLt | 16 11 44 | 18 06 45 | USA Refit |
| F.M. Bunbury | *H32* | NO | 01 08 43 | 01 11 43 | AST Clyde, HMS *Cyclops* |
| | *Strongbow* | NO | 01 11 43 | 24 02 44 | UK, Comm & WUPS |
| E.C. Cayley | *Trespasser* | NO | 10 07 44 | 30 04 45 | UK Ops |
| J.A. Cross | *P512* | WO 1stLt | 28 04 42 | 07 11 43 | AST Halifax & Bermuda |
| | *Vigorous* | 1stLt | 29 11 43 | 19 11 44 | Med, Agean Patrols |
| | *Unseen* | CO | 12 02 45 | 07 08 45 | AST Fundy |
| R.B. Fahrig | *Trespasser* | NO | 05 12 43 | 27 07 44 | Far East |
| | *Sportsman* | NO | 27 07 44 | 30 06 45 | Phila. refit, UK WUPS |
| | *U2326* | 1stLt | 30 06 45 | 03 08 45 | UK experimental |
| | *Saga* | 1stLt | 03 08 45 | 24 09 45 | UK, WUPS & AST |
| R.G. Fennell | *Thorough* | 1stLt | 07 07 44 | 24 08 44 | Far East operations |
| | *Sea Rover* | NO | 11 09 44 | 28 10 44 | Australia, operations |
| | *Spiteful* | Add'l | 14 11 44 | 15 03 45 | Australia, Operations |
| | *Voracious* | WO | 12 06 45 | 03 10 45 | AST Australia |
| E.K. Forbes | *H44* | Add'l | 16 01 41 | 23 06 41 | AST 'Derry & operations |
| | *P34* | NO 1stLt | 23 06 41 | 07 11 42 | Med operations (Malta) |
| | *Stoic* | 1stLt | 26 04 43 | 02 07 43 | Building & WUPS |
| | *Seanymph* | 1stLt | 07 07 43 | 11 11 43 | UK operations |
| E.K. Fowler | *Truculent* | NO | 25 11 44 | 20 02 45 | USA refit |
| | *Scepter* | NO | 17 01 44 | 25 11 44 | UK, 6th-11th patrols |
| | *United* | 1stLt | 20 02 45 | 09 09 45 | AST Bermuda |
| J.M. Gardener | *Unswerving* | NO | 06 04 44 | 21 05 45 | Malta for Med operations |
| | *Upright* | 1stLt | 09 07 45 | 10 09 45 | AST Bermuda |
| E.G. Gigg | *Oberon* | WO | 15 20 44 | 22 03 44 | Barrow, defects |
| | *Uther* | NO | 22 03 44 | 03 07 44 | AST Clyde |
| | *Tradewind* | NO | 29 08 44 | 05 08 45 | Far East & Australia |
| W.A. Gilmour | *H33* | NO 1stLt | 04 01 43 | 24 03 43 | AST Clyde, HMS *Cyclops* |
| | *P241, Syrtis* | WO | 25 03 43 | 13 10 43 | UK operations |
| | *Truculent* | WO | 14 10 43 | 05 05 44 | Far East operations |
| | *Tantalus* | Add'l | 06 05 44 | 25 12 44 | Far East operations |
| W.H. Holmes | *Unrivalled* | NO | 03 07 44 | 13 07 44 | AST Clyde |
| | *United* | NO | 13 07 44 | 20 12 44 | AST Bermuda |
| | *U861* | NO | 01 06 45 | 20 08 45 | UK experimental |
| | *Unseen* | NO | 20 08 45 | 01 10 45 | AST Fundy |
| A.R.Y. Hunter | *P58, Untamed* | NO | 16 02 43 | 24 04 43 | AST Clyde |
| | *Torbay* | NO | 14 09 43 | 13 11 43 | UK operations |
| | *Tribune* | 1stLt | 15 01 44 | 09 08 44 | AST Clyde & Blyth |
| | *Thrasher* | 1stLt | 09 08 44 | 18 09 44 | UK operations |
| | *H34* | WO | 14 12 42 | 16 02 43 | AST Clyde, HMS *Cyclops* |
| | *Truculent* | 1stLt | 25 11 44 | 02 02 45 | USA refit |
| J.R. Johnson | *Una* | NO | 17 04 44 | 18 08 44 | AST Clyde, *Cyclops* |
| | *Upright* | NO | 14 08 44 | 20 02 45 | AST Bermuda |
| | *Truculent* | NO | 20 02 45 | 24 09 45 | USA UK & WUPS |
| | *Proteous* | Add'l | 15 02 44 | 17 04 44 | Clyde, COQC & AST |
| A.W. Jorgenson | *Otus* | NO | 27 03 44 | 01 02 45 | AST South Africa |
| | *Shakespeare* | WO | 01 05 45 | 12 07 45 | Ceylon, defects |
| E.P. Love | *Visigoth* | Add'l | 30 01 45 | 29 10 45 | AST Ceylon |
| G.L. McPhee | *Proteous* | Add'l | 15 02 44 | 08 06 44 | Clyde, COQC & AST |
| | *Varangian* | NO | 08 06 44 | 03 07 44 | UK operations |
| | *Tantalus* | Add'l | 24 08 44 | 10 10 44 | Far East operations |
| | *Sea Rover* | Add'l | 27 12 44 | 12 08 45 | AustraliaUK, refit |
| | *Unseen* | 1stLt | 12 08 45 | 01 10 45 | AST Fundy |
| C.W. Perry | *P553* | NO | 20 04 43 | 19 11 43 | AST Halifax |
| | *L23* | 1stLt | 02 02 44 | 01 12 44 | AST Bermuda |
| | *Unseen* | 1stLt | 31 05 45 | 30 08 45 | AST Fundy |
| H.D.S. Russel | *Traveller* | WO | 29 09 42 | 19 12 42 | Med, sunk |
| J.P. Saunders | *P58, Vitality* | NO | 23 04 44 | 25 11 44 | Refit & AST Clyde |
| | *Seanymph* | NO | 25 11 44 | 06 06 45 | UK operations |
| F.H. Sherwood | *Sealion* | WO | 22 12 40 | 22 08 41 | UK operations, (Bryant CO) |
| | *L23* | 1stLt | 22 08 41 | 07 01 42 | AST Clyde, HMS *Cyclops* |
| | *P211, Safari* | 1stLt | 07 01 42 | 25 11 42 | Med, Malta (Bryant CO) operations |
| | *P556* | CO | 15 03 43 | 15 06 43 | AST Clyde |
| | *Spiteful* | CO | 21 07 43 | 24 07 46 | Far East & Australia |
| A.H. Walkley | *L26* | NO | 31 07 43 | 04 10 43 | Philadelphia, refit |
| | *Seawolf* | NO | 04 10 43 | 15 07 44 | AST Fundy |

AST = anti-submarine training

WUPS = work-ups

COQC = Commanding Officer Qualifying Course

## SUBMARINE MANNING TERMINOLOGY

| | |
|---|---|
| CO | Commanding Officer, Captain |
| 1stLt | First Lieutenant (present day Executive Officer) |
| NO | Navigating Officer (in WWI frequently an RNR officer) |
| WO | Weapons Officer |
| Add'l | Additional to normal manning requirements, often under training |

These positions are listed in the order of their usual seniority although in some submarines the WO could be senior to the Navigating Officer.

In a typical WWI submarine, the First Lieutenant assumed the duties of Weapons Officer and Engineer Officer.

In WWII boats, the First Lieutenant often assumed the additional duties of Engineer Officer.

Some of the large, specialized, submarines in both periods carried an Engineer Officer, frequently a Warrant Officer or Commissioned Engineer.

## TABLE 4 DECORATIONS

Canadian officers have been decorated for their services in submarines during both World Wars. The recipients and their awards are:

LIEUTENANT COMMANDER
  B.L. JOHNSON, RNR.
  November 1917. The DSO for
  "Gallantry aboard *H8* and for
  continued service in sub-
  marines."

(RNSM)

LIEUTENANT E.K. FORBES,
  RCNVR.
  December 1942. The DSC for
  "Distinguished services in suc-
  cessful patrols in HM
  Submarines."
  (1stLt, HMS *P34*).

(Author's collection)

LIEUTENANT F.H. SHERWOOD,
  RCNVR.
  March, 1943. The DSC for
  "Bravery in successful subma-
  rine patrols." (1stLt, HMS
  *Safari*).
  July, 1945. Bar to DSC for
  "Gallant services in Far East
  war patrol." (CO, HMS
  *Spiteful*).        (Author's collection)

## TABLE 5 CASUALTIES

### FIRST WORLD WAR

12 March 1918. Lt Wm. McK. Maitland-Dougall, RCN, CO of HMS *D3,* which was sunk with all hands in error by a French airship in the English Channel off Fécamp.

### SECOND WORLD WAR

21 June 1942. Ty Lt (E) J.F. Magill, RCNR, was a passenger aboard HMS *P514* when she was sunk with all hands having been mistaken for a U-boat by HMCS *Georgian* when off the southern tip of Newfoundland.

12 December 1942. Lt H.D.S. Russel, RCNVR, was fourth officer aboard HMS *Traveller* which hit a mine while conducting a reconnaissance of the Gulf of Taranto as part of Operation Principal.

3 January 1943. Lt C. E. "Chuck" Bonnell, DSC, RCNVR, a Special Services Charioteer, was killed when HMS *P311* was lost after hitting a mine in the Straits of Bonifacio while on Operation Principal, a chariot raid on Maddalena in northern Sardinia.

Two of the Newfoundlanders were lost while serving aboard submarines:

21 June 1942. OSST Albert Edward Lidstone from St. John's, was a crewman aboard HMS *P514* which was sunk off the southern tip of Newfoundland by HMCS *Georgian* in error.

12 December 1942. ABST Colin Walter Forward from Little Bay Islands, was a crewman aboard HMS *P512* when he fell overboard and was drowned off Pictou, Nova Scotia. His remains are interred in a Pictou cemetery.

### POST-WAR

16 June 1955. PO2 TD L.D. McLeod was one of thirteen fatalities aboard HMS *Sidon,* which sank alongside the depot ship HMS *Maidstone* in Portland harbour after the explosion of an experimental torpedo. His remains are buried in the Portland Naval Cemetery high on the bluff overlooking the harbour at Portland, Dorset. Five other RCN personnel in the crew survived.

HMS *Astute* coming alongside HMS *Auriga*, SM6, August 1961.

(MARCOM Museum)

# TABLE 6 SQUADRON COMMANDERS 1914–1996

## THE *SHEARWATER* FLOTILLA

**Officer in Command of Submarines**

| | | |
|---|---|---|
| Lt A.St.V. Keyes, RCN | 6 August | 14 |

**Officer in Command of HMCS *Shearwater* I and Submarine Flotilla**

| | | |
|---|---|---|
| Lt A.St.V. Keyes, RCN | 1 October | 14 |

**Officer in Command , Flotilla**

| | | |
|---|---|---|
| Lt B.E. Jones, RCN | January | 15 |
| Lt Cdr B.E. Jones, RCN | 30 August | 15 |

**Commander Submarines**

| | | |
|---|---|---|
| Cdr B.E. Jones, RCN | 1 November | 17 |

**Senior Officer Submarines (*CH14* and *CH15*)**

| | | |
|---|---|---|
| Lt R.C. Watson, RCN | April | 21 |

## SIXTH SUBMARINE SQUADRON/DIVISION

| | | | |
|---|---|---|---|
| SM6 Sqdn. | Cdr W.T.J. Fox | 14 March | 55 |
| SM6 Sqdn. | Cdr J.S. Stevens, DSO, DSC | 19 June | 57 |
| SM6 Sqdn. | Cdr H.K. Gowan | January | 58 |
| SM6 Sqdn. | Cdr S. Jenner | 14 June | 60 |
| SM6 Div. | Cdr K. Vause | 1 October | 62 |
| SM6 Div. | Cdr J.V. Hervey | 21 September | 64 |

HMS *Ambrose* closed 22 April 1967

## FIRST CANADIAN SUBMARINE SQUADRON

| | | |
|---|---|---|
| Cdr E.C. Gigg, RCN | July | 66 |
| Lt Col (N) M. Tate, CAF | July | 69 |
| Lt Col (N) J.C. Wood, CAF | August | 72 |
| Lt Col (N) P.W. Cairns, CAF | July | 74 |
| Lt Col (N) J.E.D. Bell, CAF | July | 75 |
| Lt Col (N) R.C. Hunt, CAF | January | 78 |
| Cdr R.C. Perks, CAF | August | 81 |
| Cdr K.C. Nesbitt, CAF | July | 83 |
| Cdr W.J. Sloan, CAF | December | 84 |
| Cdr F.C. Macmillan, CAF | August | 87 |
| Capt. (N) A.B. Dunlop, CAF | July | 89 |
| Capt. (N) J.A.Y. Plante, CAF | December | 90 |
| Cdr F. Sherber, CAF | April | 92 |
| Cdr N.P. Nicolson, CAF | July | 94 |

On 9 February 1996 the First Canadian Submarine Squadron ceased to be an independent command and was absorbed into Maritime Operations Group 5.

# TABLE 7 ROYAL NAVY SUBMARINES AT HALIFAX 1947–1967

| YEAR | SUBMARINE | ARRIVE | DEPART | CO |
|---|---|---|---|---|
| 1946 | *Token* | July | September | |
| 1947 | *Artemis* | September | December | Lt Cdr J.B.De B. Kershaw, DSO |
| 1948 | | | | |
| 1949 | *Tudor* | February | June | Lt Cdr D. Swanston, DSO, DSC |
| | *Tally Ho!* | 12 July | 23 November | Lt J. A.R. Troup, DSO, DSC |
| 1950 | *Astute* | 8 April | 7 July | Lt .P.H. Jackson-Sytner, DSC |
| | *Andrew* | 30 August | 1 December | Lt Cdr E.R. Stone |
| 1951 | *Thule* | 1 April | 1 August | Lt D.R. Johnston, DSC |
| | *Artful* | 9 August | 12 December | Lt Cdr R.T. Smith |
| 1952 | *Alcide* | 30 January | 31 May | Lt Cdr J.S. Launders, DSO, DSC |
| | *Alderney* | 31 July | 15 September | Lt Cdr M.J.H. Bonner, DSC |
| | *Artemis* | 10 September | 30 November | Lt Cdr F.E. Ashmead-Bartlett |
| 1953 | *Andrew* | 5 February | 31 May | Lt Cdr W.D.S. Scott |
| | *Auriga* | 27 August | 5 December | Lt Cdr J.A.L. Wilkinson, DSC |
| 1954 | *Tally Ho!* | 31 January | 16 June | Lt Cdr B.D. Rowe, DSC |
| | *Alcide* | 6 August | 7 December | Lt Cdr P.T. Miles |

HMS *L23* approaching Digby Gut, 1944. (R.C. Foster)

# SIXTH SUBMARINE SQUADRON FORMED AT HALIFAX— 14 MARCH 1955

| YEAR | SUBMARINE | ARRIVE | DEPART | CO |
|---|---|---|---|---|
| 1955 | *Astute* | 4 April | 1956 | Lt Cdr T.B. Dowling |
| | *Ambush* | 15 May | 1956 | Lt Cdr A.J. Boyall, DSC |
| | *Alderney* | 19 July | 1956 | Lt Cdr D.E. Teare |
| 1956 | *Ambush* | 15 June | | |
| | *Alliance* | 11 September | 1958 | Lt Cdr H.R. Clutterbuck, DSC |
| | *Alderney* | | 10 October | |
| | *Astute* | | 10 December | |
| 1957 | *Alliance* | | | SM6 all of 1957 |
| | *Amphion* | 14 January | 1958 | Lt Cdr K. Vause |
| | *Alcide* | 19 October | 1958 | Lt Cdr J.H. Blacklock |
| 1958 | *Alliance* | | 22 February | |
| | *Amphion* | | 24 June | |
| | *Ambush** | 29 June | 1959 | Lt Cdr P.F.B. Roe |
| | *Alderney** | 26 September | 1960 | Lt Cdr R.A. Hedgecock |
| | *Alcide* | | 1 December | |
| 1959 | *Alderney** | | | SM6 all of 1959 |
| | *Ambush** | | 11 September | |
| | *Auriga** | 12 November | 1961 | Lt Cdr H.J. Bickford-Smith |
| 1960 | *Auriga** | | | SM6 all of 1960 |
| | *Alderney** | | 7 March | |
| | *Aurochs* | 27 July | 1962 | Lt Cdr O.B. Sharp |
| 1961 | *Aurochs* | | | SM6 all of 1961 |
| | *Auriga** | | 25 April | |
| | *Astute** | 19 August | 1963 | Lt Cdr C.J. Ringrose-Voase |
| 1962 | *Astute** | | | SM6 all of 1962 |
| | *Aurochs* | | 5 January | |
| | *Alderney** | 22 January | 1963 | Lt Cdr R.Cudworth |
| 1963 | *Auriga** | 1 February | 1964 | Lt Cdr M.R. Wilson<br>Nov–Lt Cdr K.A. Bromback |
| | *Astute** | | 4 February | |
| | *Alderney** | | 11 April | |
| | *Onslaught* | 31 August | 17 October | Lt Cdr C.A.W. Russell |
| 1964 | *Alcide** | January | 1966 | Lt Cdr S.R. Conway |
| | *Auriga** | | October | |
| 1965 | *Alcide** | | | SM6 all of 1965 |
| 1966 | *Alcide** | | March | |
| | *Acheron* | 19 March | 1967 | Lt Cdr Kennedy |

22 April - *Acheron* transferred to CANSUBRON ONE. Last A class at Halifax

| 1967 | *Acheron* | | 3 May | |

* Denotes submarine modernized

# TABLE 8 ROYAL NAVY AND ALLIED SUBMARINES IN CANADIAN WATERS 1939-1945

| SUBMARINE | OPERATIONS | BASE | ARRIVAL | DEPART |
|---|---|---|---|---|
| **Anglo-French Escort Force** | | | | |
| HMS *Cachalot* | Convoy escort duties | Halifax | 23 11 39 | 2 12 39 with convoy |
| HMS *Seal* | Convoy escort duties | Halifax | 23 11 39 | 2 12 39 with convoy |
| FS *Casabianca* | Convoy escort duties | Halifax | 25 11 39 | HX11, 4 11 39 |
| FS *Sfax* | Convoy escort duties | Halifax | 25 11 39 | HX11, 4 11 39 |
| FS *Achille* | Convoy escort duties | Halifax | 25 11 39 | HFX12, 10 12 39 |
| FS *Pasteur* | Convoy escort duties | Halifax | 25 11 39 | HX12, 12 12 39 |
| HMS *Narwhal* | Convoy escort duties | Halifax | 27 11 39 | HX14, 29 12 39 |
| FS *Beveziers* | Convoy escort duties | Halifax | 09 03 40 | HX29, 21 3 40 |
| | | | 23 03 40 | HX33, 6 4 40 |
| FS *Sidi Ferruch* | Convoy escort duties | Halifax | 09 03 40 | HX27, 13 3 40 |
| FS *Archimede* | Convoy escort duties | Halifax | Mid April | HX39, 30 4 40 |
| FS *Ajax* | Convoy escort duties | Halifax | Mid April | HX41, 8 5 40 |
| **Anti-Submarine Training** | | | | |
| DS *O-15* | AST | Halifax | 09 40 | 09 42 |
| **North Atlantic Escort Force** | | | | |
| HMS *Porpoise* | Patrols & escort duties | Halifax | 11 40 | HX105, 26 1 41 |
| | | | 15 03 41 | SC26, 20 3 41 |
| | | | 03 04 41 | SC29, 19 4 41 & UK for refit |
| HMS *Severn* | Anti-U-boat patrols | Halifax | 02 41 | 11 3 41 to Freetown SA |
| **2nd Flotilla** | | | | |
| HMS *Forth* | Depot ship | Halifax | 03 03 41 | |
| | | Saint John | 06 41 | 06 41 docking |
| | | St. John's | 06 41 | 09 41 to USA for refit |
| HMS *Thunderbolt* | Convoy escort | Halifax | 05 03 41 | SC25, 10 3 41 |
| | | | 04 41 | SC convoy, 29 4 41 |
| | Patrol | St. John's | 31 05 41 | 12 6 41, attacked *U-557* |
| | | Halifax | 28 06 41 | 8 7 41 to Mediterranean |
| HMS *Tribune* | Convoy escort | Halifax | 11 03 41 | HX117, 27 3 41 |
| | | | 15 04 41 | HX126, 10 5 41 & to UK |
| HMS *Talisman* | Convoy escort | Halifax | 26 03 41 | SC28, 9 4 41 |
| | | | 26 04 41 | SC32, 19 5 41 |
| | | | | 25 5 41 Grand Banks patrol |
| | | Halifax | 09 06 41 | 06 41 to St. John's |
| | | St. John's | End-June | 7 7 41 to Mediterranean |
| FS *Surcouf* | Repairs & escort duties | Halifax | Early March 41 | SC27, 1 4 41 & to UK |
| | Anti-raider patrols | Bermuda | 05 41 | 11 41 to USA for refit |
| | Invasion of St. Pierre | Halifax | 12 41 | |
| | Repairs | Halifax | 01 42 | To Panama Canal, Lost 19 2 42 |

Note on convoys: HX convoys – Halifax to UK, fast convoy
SC convoys – Sydney to UK, slow convoy

| SUBMARINE | OPERATIONS | BASE | ARRIVAL | DEPART |
|---|---|---|---|---|
| **ANTI-SUBMARINE TRAINING** | | | | |
| HMS *L27* | AST | Harbour Grace | 12 41 | 02 42 & to USA for refit |
| HMS *P512* (USS R17) | AST | Halifax/Pictou | 03 42 | |
| | | Bermuda | 06 43 | |
| | | Philadelphia | 06 09 43 | Returned to USN |
| HMS *P514* (USS R19) | AST | Halifax | 03 42 | |
| | | Argentia | 03 42 | Lost 21 06 42 |
| HMS *P553* (USS S21) | AST | Halifax | 01 10 42 | |
| | | Philadelphia | 11 07 44 | Returned to USN |
| HMS *P554* (USS S22) | AST | Argentia | 07 42 | |
| | | Halifax | 01 44 | |
| | | Philadelphia | 11 07 44 | Returned to USN |
| HMS *Seawolf* | AST | Halifax | 29 01 43 | |
| | | Bermuda | 11 11 43 | |
| | | Halifax | 18 03 44 | |
| | | Digby | 01 07 44 | |
| | Refit | Philadelphia | 17 07 44 | |
| | AST | Digby | 06 12 44 | 23 06 45 paid off To Scrap 11 45 |
| HMS *L23* | Passage | St. John's | 28 02 43 | |
| | Refit | Philadelphia | 22 02 43 | |
| | AAST | Halifax | 11 43 | |
| | | Digby | 06 44 | 21 06 45 paid off To scrap 05 46 |
| HMS *L27* | AST | Sydney | 10 43 | Repairs |
| | | Halifax | 12 43 | |
| | Refit | Philadelphia | 01 44 | |
| | | Bermuda | 06 44 | |
| | AST | Digby | 11 44 | |
| | | Halifax | 11 44 | 23 11 44 paid off To scrap 07 46 |
| HMS *L26* | AST | Halifax | 02 44 | |
| | | Bermuda | 06 44 | |
| | | Halifax | 12 44 | 21 12 44 paid off |
| | | | 24 09 45 | scuttled HFX approaches |
| HMS *Unseen* | AST | Digby | 27 07 44 | 03 10 45, to UK |
| HMS *Unruffled* | AST | Bermuda | 26 07 44 | |
| | | Digby | 01 08 45 | 03 10 45, to UK |
| HMS *United* | AST | Bermuda | 08 44 | |
| | | Digby | 23 08 45 | |
| | | Bermuda | 01 09 45 | 09 09 45, to UK |
| HMS *Upright* | AST | Bermuda | 08 44 | |
| | | Digby | 09 45 | 09 09 45, to UK |
| HMS *Una* | Submarine Training | Halifax | 09 45 | |
| | | Digby | 09 45 | 09 11 45, to UK |

# BIBLIOGRAPHY

UNPUBLISHED SOURCES

Haydon, Peter T. Canadian Naval Submarine Requirements 1945-1968. Centre for Foreign Policy Studies, Dalhousie University, Halifax, NS 1997.

Lt S. A. Brooks, RN. Letters telling the story of the fetching and bringing home of HM Submarine H9. Royal Navy Submarine Museum Collection, Gosport, Hants, UK.

Johnson, B. L. Naval Events, 1914-1918. Vancouver City Archives, Add. MS 581.

Moth, Oscar. Diary of a Submarine Coxswain. Royal Navy Submarine Museum, Gosport Hants, UK.

ADMIRALTY PUBLICATIONS

London. Ministry of Defence. *The Development of HM Submarines 1901-1930.* BR 3043. 1979.

London. Admiralty. *Naval Staff History, Second World War, Submarines. 3* Vols. BR 1736 (Previously CB 3306 (3). 1953.

London. Admiralty. *Naval Staff Monographs (Historical).* OU 5528 (Previously CB 917).

London. HM Stationery Office. *The Navy List.*

PUBLISHED SOURCES (A SELECTION)

Akerman, Paul. *Encyclopedia of British Submarines 1905-1955.* London: Maritime Books, 1989.

Compton-Hall, Commander Richard. *Submarine Boats.* London: Conway Maritime Press, 1983.

Compton-Hall, Commander Richard. *The Underwater War, 1939-1945.* Poole, UK: Blandford Press, 1982.

Ferguson, Julie H. *Through a Canadian Periscope.* Toronto, ON: Dundurn Press Limited, 1995.

Haydon, Commander Peter T. *The 1962 Cuban Missile Crisis: Canadian Involvement Reconsidered.* Toronto, ON: The Canadian Institute of Strategic Studies, 1993.

Lambert, John and David Hill. *The Submarine Alliance.* Annapolis: Naval Institute Press, 1986.

Macpherson, Ken and John Burgess. *The Ships of Canada's Naval Forces 1910-1981.* Don Mills, ON: Collins Publishers, 1981.

Perkins, Dave. *Canada's Submariners 1914-1923.* Erin, ON: The Boston Mills Press, 1989.

Rössler, Eberhard. *The U-boat. The evolution and technical history of German submarines.* English edition. London: Arms and Armour Press, 1981.

Smith, Gaddis. *Britain's Clandestine Submarines, 1914-1915.* Yale University Press, 1964.

Tarrant, V.E. *The U-boat Offensive 1914-1945.* Annapolis: Naval Institute Press, 1989.

Tucker, Gilbert. *The Naval Service of Canada.* Ottawa: King's Printer, 1952.

# GLOSSARY

| | |
|---|---|
| Admiralstab | The German Naval Staff |
| AMC | Armed Merchant Cruiser (heavily armed, fast, merchant ships) |
| Asdic | An acronym derived from "Allied Submarine Detection Investigation Committee." Anti-sub-marine sonar |
| A/S | Anti-submarine (the prosecution of attacks against individual submarines) |
| AST | Anti-submarine training |
| ASW | Anti-submarine Warfare (the broad concept of coping with hostile submarines) |
| ATP | Air turbine pump—part of the torpedo discharge system |
| boat | Derived from "Submarine Torpedo Boat," the original description of a submarine |
| boffin | Slang term for a member of the scientific community |
| CAF | Canadian Armed Forces. Since 1 February 1968 unified navy, army and air force, "the military" |
| CANSUBRON ONE | First Canadian Submarine Squadron |
| CASAP | Canadian Submarine Acquisition Project (SSK) conventional and (SSN) nuclear |
| CF | Canadian Forces (politically correct alternative to CAF) |
| CO | Commanding Officer |
| COMS | Chief of Maritime Staff (Canada–head of the Navy) |
| COQC | Commanding Officer Qualifying Course. RN. Conventional submarine captain qualification |
| DND | Department of National Defence (Canada) |
| DS | Dutch Ship |
| DSRV | Deep submergence rescue vehicle |
| FS | French Ship |
| HMCS | (His) Her Majesty's Canadian Ship |
| HMS | (His) Her Majesty's Ship |
| HP | High pressure (air and hydraulics) or high power (periscopes and electrical systems) |
| ICBM | Intercontinental Ballistic Missile. Long-range nuclear missile deployed by both sides in the Cold War |
| IJN | Imperial Japanese Navy |
| Kriegsmarine | the German Navy |
| kts | knots (per hour, ship's speed) One kt = 1.15 mph or 1.85 km/h |
| LP | Low pressure (air and hydraulics) or low power (periscopes and electrical systems) |
| MND | Minister of National Defence (Canada) |
| MoD | Ministry of Defence (Britain) |
| NAAFI | Navy, Army, Air Force Institute (British) |
| NATO | North Atlantic Treaty Organization |
| NDHQ | National Defence Headquarters (Canada, post-1948) |
| nm | nautical mile. In nautical terms, 10 cables or approx. 2,000 yds. 1 nm = 1825 m |
| NSHQ | Naval Service Headquarters (Canada, 1910-1948) |
| OMC | One man control - automated submarine depth and course keeping system |
| perisher | The COQC, "pass or perish" |
| RAN | Royal Australian Navy |
| rating | Old terminology for non-commissioned member |
| RCAF | Royal Canadian Air Force. Pre-unification professional air force 1923-1968 |
| RCN | Royal Canadian Navy. Pre-unification professional navy, 1910-1968 |
| RCNR | Royal Canadian Naval Reserve. Merchant navy qualified naval reserve personnel, 1922-1946 |
| RCN(R) | Royal Canadian Navy (Reserves) All naval reserve forces, 1946-1968 |
| RCNVR | Royal Canadian Naval Volunteer Reserve. Citizen volunteers for naval service, 1922-1946 |
| Reichsmarine | German navy during the Third Reich, 1933-1945 |
| RN | Royal Navy. British professional navy |

| | | | |
|------|------|------|------|
| RNCVR | Royal Naval Canadian Volunteer Reserve. Citizen volunteers for naval service, 1914-1920 only | | |
| RNR | Royal Naval Reserve. Merchant navy qualified naval reserve force (British) | | |
| RNVR | Royal Naval Volunteer Reserve. Citizen volunteers (British) | | |
| SACLANT | Supreme Allied Commander, Atlantic | | |
| S/M OTC | Submarine Officer Training Course | | |
| S/M | Submarine | | |
| SM(#) | Submarine squadron (with number) or the commander of the squadron | | |
| SOR | Statement of Requirements—a detailed description of a military equipment requirement | | |
| SOUP | Submarine Operational Update Project. Canadian *O* class S/Ms weapons-system modernization | | |
| SSBN | Nuclear-powered ballistic-missile-carrying submarine | | |
| SSK | Conventional attack submarine | | |
| SSM | Surface-to-surface missile | | |
| SSN | Nuclear-powered attack submarine | | |
| SUBMISS | Operational condition – submarine missing, exact whereabouts uncertain | | |
| SUBSMASH | Operational condition – submarine confirmed to be in trouble | | |
| SUBSUNK | Operational condition – submarine confirmed sunk in a specific location | | |
| telegram | A message electrically transmitted over wires, normally delivered in printed form | | |
| trot | A berth for a submarine, or a group of submarines secured alongside one another | | |
| VE-Day | Victory in Europe Day, 8 May 1945 | | |
| VJ-Day | Victory in Japan Day, 2 September 1945 | | |
| VSEL | Vickers Shipbuilding and Engineering Limited (UK), currently a division of BAE Systems | | |
| WRD | Water ram discharge—part of the torpedo discharge system | | |

## RANKS AND ABBREVIATIONS

| RANK | RN, RCN | CAF | GERMAN NAVY | |
|------|---------|-----|-------------|---|
| Captain | Capt | CAP(N) | Kapitän zur See | KptzS |
| Commander | Cdr | CDR | Korvetten Kapitän | KKpt |
| Lieutenant Commander | Lt Cdr | LCDR | Kapitän Leutnant | Kplt |
| Lieutenant | Lt | LT | Oberleutnant zur See | ObltzS |
| Sub-Lieutenant | S/Lt | SLT | Leutnant zur See | LtzS |